Chloë Ivy Lily Bell is a professional journalist who has been writing since she was five years old, conjuring up stories of pirates and magical places for her family to read.

Born in south-east London, she is an avid traveller who loves to explore the world and meet new people.

After graduating from The University of West London with a broadcast journalism degree in 2016, she began jotting down her weird and wonderful stories from around the globe in the hope to one day produce a novel about tackling anxiety and getting out of your comfort zone.

For Mum, Dad and Nanny Rita. I hope you enjoy our weird and wonderful stories, thank you for supporting me in everything I do.

For Pap and Nana Cath, I wish you both could have read this with a chuckle.

Chloë Ivy Lily Bell

THE TRAVELS OF AN ANXIETY-RIDDLED MILLENNIAL

AUSTIN MACAULEY PUBLISHERS™

LONDON * CAMBRIDGE * NEW YORK * SHARJAH

A CIP catalogue record for this title is available from the British Library.

ISBN 9781398482333 (Paperback)
ISBN 9781398482340 (ePub e-book)

www.austinmacauley.com

First Published 2023
Austin Macauley Publishers Ltd®
1 Canada Square
Canary Wharf
London
E14 5AA

An extra special thanks to my mum and dad for being so supportive and always encouraging me to be myself (no matter how weird I may be). I'm lucky to have such fantastic parents and to have seen so much of the world already. Who wants boring travel trips anyway?

Special thanks to Steve Bell for the pictures.

Table of Contents

Meet Me...

I'm a typical anxiety-riddled millennial trying to find my place in life, attempting to embrace the unknown and uncertain in this weird and wonderful world.

Join me (and my frantic, frazzled brain) as I recall my favourite monumental trips. I ultimately come to realise the mayhem and mischief I've experienced abroad over the last twenty-odd years has been the best weapon in battling my weary mind.

Part One
Once Upon a Time in a Carefree Cul-De-Sac

1

Difficultly Different

Picture this, no exaggeration: fourteen-year-old me, huddled in a leaking tent, braced against the high winds, whimpering in a boggy field in deepest Kent. Freezing droplets of rain splatter down my back as I pull my sodden sleeping bag around me. My face is smeared with mud, mascara is smudged around my eyes, and my hair looks like something is nesting in it, curls sticking out at weird angles. I'm not dressed appropriately at all. Leggings with cute but impractical boots, a thin jumper and a denim jacket are what I am sitting miserably in (a choice I regretted as soon as the heavens opened during the first hour of our hike).

This was my first – and last – experience of camping: our bronze Duke of Edinburgh excursion at school.

It was 3 am, I was famished and already dreading the five-hour walk home tomorrow with no sleep. I'd been rocking backwards and forwards, silently crying in frustration, trying to calm my breathing and stop myself spiralling into a panic attack. I hit send on a text message to my dad asking him to pick me up.

'No signal' flashed back angrily on my flip phone. All I could do was wait for it to get light outside so I could go the hell home.

Valuable life lessons were learnt that night: denim stays wet, and I detest camping (or staying anywhere without access to running water, a comfy bed, somewhere to plug my hair straighteners in, and a proper toilet). Plus, it's a terrible idea to roast marshmallows on a portable cooker inside a flammable tent. Obviously.

I vowed never to put myself through anything like that again. I can't hack it. I'm not cut out for camping, backpacking or anything remotely outdoorsy. I wish I was; it would be a fantastic opportunity and such a freeing experience to amble off into the vast countryside with minimal supplies, truly taking in my surroundings and just going with the flow. But, alas, that's just not me. I've had to make my peace with the fact that I'm difficultly different.

So, this book isn't a backpacker's account of my breath-taking travels – nothing like. I'm pretty high-maintenance. I'm a worrier, a whittler, and backpacking isn't something I'd enjoy at all. This isn't the story of my self-sufficient journey across the globe, of how I 'found myself'. In fact, I still haven't found myself, not fully. I'm gradually working that out.

Travel means something different to me, and, yes, sometimes I do envy the backpackers I pass abroad: sleeping under the stars, their palpable sense of excitement evident, each day filled with the unexpected, plans made on the spot. But I have my own adventures to embark on. Slightly more planned adventures, admittedly.

Exploring the wondrous world we live in is a monumentally magical thing. You can fly here, there and everywhere, visit every inch of this planet if you choose to (I absolutely would if I had the time and unlimited funds). The earth is so much bigger than us all and there's something truly magnificent about that. The very fact that you can't possibly see every incredible thing it has to offer in your lifetime makes my brain boggle. But on the other hand, you'll never run out of amazing things to witness either. That's what I love about the notion of travel.

You can be in awe, witness breath-taking sights, see things that will change your outlook on life itself: lionesses nurturing their cubs on the Kenyan plains; New Delhi's towering India Gate, a landmark that encapsulates so much history and wonder. You can eyeball a globally acclaimed cultural masterpiece like the Mona Lisa at the Louvre in Paris or watch a sunrise on a sleepy, perfectly still beach in Cambodia, your only company the lapping waves and a lone fisherman embarking on his version of the London commute. I know if I had to trade my mind-numbingly boring stint on the Circle Line at 8 am for a leisurely bob to work, I wouldn't be complaining.

You can visit all these places, leave your home, your creature comforts, and be anywhere in a matter of hours – somewhere so different from the nine-to-five life you left behind. Travel can change you. Not to be all clichéd, but it truly can.

The smaller things are often just as special to witness. The bright green lizard we nicknamed Freddie is scuttling up to keep me company while I sipped my morning coffee as the sunlight danced across the lazy waters of the Andaman and Nicobar Islands. Waking to the chatter of birds and that muggy, stifling but not unpleasant heat in Bali. The friendly tuk-tuk drivers who have expertly mastered weaving in and out of fast-moving traffic; the constant sound of the motorbike horns echoing in your ears as you're swept along the roads; other people's colourful lives entwining with yours, even if it's only for a second.

Travelling is special because it's personal to you, to me. Everyone's experiences are so different, even if you visit the same place, see the same sights or stay in the same hotel.

And it's the very word 'travel' that's so flexible. It can mean setting off to a coastal spot an hour from where you live, or it can mean dashing off to the airport, passport in hand, and almost missing a flight because your dad was still chucking clothes in his suitcase as the taxi revved its engine outside at 4 am. That's what my brain conjures up; that's the image that springs to my mind when I think of the word 'travel'. But for others, it will be something else equally exhilarating and exciting.

My own travels are an ongoing journey of self-discovery, and although I've never set off into the big bad world completely alone, determined to prove I can cope and battle my anxieties, I have realised a lot about myself and healed a lot of worries whilst off jet-setting. I'm constantly pushing my boundaries when travelling; it's done in my own way, but I'm proud of that.

When I think about travelling, I always think of the incredible places I've been to with the people I value the most. In my view, the people you go with make the trip. But travel to me also means hilarious misadventures, missing suitcases, flights departing without us, the journey, and the funny little things I remember long after I've returned home and settled back into my normal London life.

I love taking trips with my mum and dad. When we go away, I can fully kick back and relax, even if there's always a mad mishap or ten. We have so many shared interests, shared adventures; we know what it's like to be on a Bell holiday. It's charming, chaotic and cherished.

My mum and I love to check out the best coffee shops and wander around local markets. We like to take long beach walks and meet the locals. My dad and I go on the hunt for the very best picture opportunities and often find even more astonishing sights along the way.

I get my thirst for knowledge from my dad, for sure. He's a news photojournalist and when I see the work he produces, I feel so inspired to get out there and capture mesmerising moments like him. I love taking photos too, but I capture my moments through writing about them.

This urge to write about our travels comes from my mum. She loves reading, and planning trips, and she enjoys just being in a new place, getting the feel for it and exploring at a leisurely pace. When we return from our excursions, my mum will instantly start penning her next sprawling letter to my great-auntie Joy in Australia. She details every oddity so Joy can read them like a comedy novel, giggling to herself across the world, mystified at the mischief we got ourselves into. Even the koalas are entertained.

My creative spirit is a hairbrained concoction of both my parents' personalities, smushed together like the multi-coloured plasticine people I used to make in primary school. My life as a result is vibrant but complicatedly conflicted. I'm from the last cohort of millennials, born in 1995, and it's a weird mix, an explosion of two separate worlds.

The environment of my youth was simple and serene. There was no background buzz from Instagram, Facebook or Twitter (I know, shock, horror, no filters, hashtags or trolling – nightmare), and phones were for calling rather than living life on.

My childhood played out in a bustling town on the border between south London and Kent, and I spent school holidays visiting my nan and pap, and my nana Cath, aunties, uncles and cousins up in Northampton, a smaller place with a slower pace a few hours up the M1, somewhere I'll always think of as my second home.

My cousins and I would spend hours in the garden imagining we were in Narnia, making bows and arrows out of twigs, enrolling Jacob – our family Border collie – to be Aslan the lion. I remember a life without the pressures of social media, playing outside on my Harry Potter skateboard, learning to ride my bike in the cul-de-sac, racing around at playtime with my school friends, blackberry-picking with my nan and pap, watching soaps at Nana Cath's, pretending to be a Spice Girl, the lot.

It's an odd notion now, a life without social scrolling, but I'm so grateful I experienced my earliest adventures completely, fully, before my phone was permanently glued to my hand, fingers aching to like and swipe. It's a simple collection of memories, but they make me smile. I often wish I could relive those days as my ever-present anxiety gnaws at the tassels of my brain, trying to tug the strands loose.

'Chloë, you're in your twenties, you don't have enough savings, you need to be more careful with money, why did you buy all that Lush stuff and that stupid

San Francisco sourdough bread?' my anxiety whines into my ear as I sheepishly slip the ridiculously overpriced bread out of my bag. That M&S sourdough is my weakness.

I roll my eyes as I unpack another bath bomb from my Lush order, the coloured sparkles shimmering on my fingertips, a counterpoint to my guilty mood. Yeah, maybe I shouldn't have splashed out on bath stuff again.

'You're not doing as well as everyone else,' my anxiety demon barks, more insistent by the second, 'what the hell are you going to do now?'

In the past, my answer to that would have been to sit and worry all day, frantically sipping endless cups of coffee whilst googling 'How successful should you be by <insert age here>?' and then panicking some more.

But now, I'm more clued up on how my anxiety works and what keeps its cogs turning relentlessly. Travelling has helped and so has learning about my mind, what makes it tick and what makes it spiral into a cesspit of self-doubt.

These days, I can see that my anxiety's shadow and its whispering are actually worse than the worries themselves. The shadow is always the outline of some grotesque monster when I catch sight of it in my peripheral vision; it looms threateningly, so much bigger than me or any rational thought. But when I whip around and look at it up-close, when I turn to face the anxiety head-on, it's pathetically ridiculous. It shrivels up, as scary as a tiny pug in a tutu (which, yes, I have seen before, and, yes, it was as cute as it sounds). It's like I have my own version of the Riddikulus spell from Harry Potter, when the Boggart is transformed into something laughable in a simple swish and flick.

Anxiety issues are rife in society though. In our tech-obsessed world, where everyone is in competition with each other, it's hard to feel like you're doing what you want rather than what everyone else thinks you should be doing.

Anxiety is a problem I'll always have to deal with to some extent, but I'm learning to cope with it. When I was planning this book, I knew I wanted to talk about what travelling is like for us anxious individuals, because, let me tell you, sometimes it can be incredibly maddening for us and our travel buddies.

But just because you struggle with anxiety, fear change or hate altering your routine in any way, it doesn't mean you can't travel. Travelling is truly a remedy. It's like jumping headfirst into the deep end of a bottomless pool in the best possible way; it allows you to push your boundaries, open your mind to the world.

Creeping out of my comfort zone has been something I've always struggled with, so I'm forever being pulled in separate directions: the adventurous but anxiety-ridden millennial, trying to find a place to fit in.

Part of me is chasing simplicity, my past life as a little kid, enjoying the sheer wonder of the world. Everything was amazing back then, and my imagination was the most fantastic thing. It could conjure up anything and I'd be content. I didn't care about likes and follows or how people perceived me. That mindset is what I'm chasing now; that awe.

And that awe is what I feel when I travel. I don't care about modern-day social media life. I'm back to being five-year-old Chloë, gobsmacked at the big wide world, unbothered by what anybody thinks of me, what I'm wearing or where I am in life. I'm just excited about the possibilities, my worries melting away like the sun as it sets on a tropical beach somewhere, its orange hue seeping into the dark waves, bleeding like a work of art. I long for that Zen feeling. To be at ease. Chilled.

This book is an account of the trips that made me feel that way, the special ones that will always stick in my mind, the ones that quieted the nagging anxiety.

Tribal fire dance ceremony, Borneo, Malaysia

Coral Reef, Queensland, Eastern Australia

2

The Groovy Gang

Antigua

Antigua is an ever-present sun-soaked imprint on my mind. It was my first long-haul flight, at three years old, and I refer to that trip as one of the defining moments of my life. Sure, I can't recall every minor detail, but I do remember how it felt to sprint across the soft, shifting sand and gaze up at the fierce, fiery sun.

I'm convinced Antigua instilled this need to travel in me, sculpting me into who I am.

My memories from Antigua are vague yet vivid, the trip like a shadow caught in the corner of my eye, vibrant snippets from a previous life. Sometimes I'll get this random explosion of recognition and I'll remember something, a fantastic flash of detail, and I'll think, how did I forget that?

I'll recall the beating sun and untouched beaches when sifting through old photographs. I used to make my dad play dinosaurs with me in the sand, making footprints all day long so we could follow them, searching for clues. I loved my first experience of the sea, like a warm bath sparkling beneath my fingertips. I loved that holiday; I remember that.

Antigua was my first faraway trip. Before that, I'd been to Spain and France, and I'd adored being somewhere new, somewhere exciting, setting off like an explorer, finding adventure and an abstract way to spend a day.

I remember toddling around Calais, in northern France, with my mum, dad, nan and pap. My dad took me into a sweet shop, and I was amazed at the different sweets and how the shopkeepers spoke a whole other language to the one I was still learning back home. It blew my tiny mind.

I point-blank refused to leave the apartment in Nerja, on Spain's Costa del Sol, when I went there with my mum, nan and pap one year. I crossed my arms, slumped against the sofa, my face a picture. I didn't want to go back to dreary England, sink back into normality. There's a photo my mum has framed in the living room of the very moment before I kicked off about leaving, me clad in bright yellow T-shirt and white trousers, grinning from ear to ear. I'm set for another day in the sun with my grandparents, not at all ready to be jumping on the next flight home.

So, although I'd left the UK before and been aptly amazed, I'd never witnessed the empty beaches of Antigua, the strange sea, so cautiously calm, and its swaying palm trees rustling softly in the breeze. It was one big adventure playground for me.

However, our holiday didn't start off on a great footing. Hurricane George swept through Antigua right before we arrived in September 1998. It caused widespread damage to homes, hotels and businesses, quickly developing into a Category 4 hurricane (which, if you're not familiar with hurricane talk, means pretty damn bad). It triggered a whopping seven landfalls in Antigua and Barbuda, resulting in extreme flooding and mudslides and also wreaked havoc across five other countries – St Kitts and Nevis, Haiti, the Dominican Republic, Cuba and the USA.

I can't quite believe the place I fleetingly remember – the tranquil sea, the towering palm trees and refreshingly light beach breeze – saw such destruction just days before our arrival. The hotel we booked into had its roof ripped off by the battering storm. So while they were fixing it, focussing on getting back up and running, we were placed in the only other resort with vacancies: Sandals.

If you've never heard of Sandals, it's a swanky resort with chains dotted all over the world, but its main selling point is its strict 'no kids' policy. At least, it was back when we visited.

It's a place I'd appreciate now I'm grown up. I picture myself sipping a glass of bubbly on the beach, peering out on sparkling turquoise waters as I flip through my latest thriller and top up my non-existent tan. (Seriously, I'm the palest of the pale; I'd give Dracula a run for his money.) Bliss. But at the time, I was three and very much a child.

The staff were lovely though, and I was always a weird little kid, not one for making a scene. I think I was born middle-aged. As long as I had my little Disney figures to play with, I was all set, so I was no trouble. Also, the hurricane was out of everyone's hands, so Sandals had to open its doors to a wider customer base. We enjoyed the carefree nature of the resort for a few days; the calm after the storm.

When we were welcomed back to the Rex – our original hotel – it was just as spectacular. The deep blue pool was the first thing I zoned in on, my little eyes widening at the stunning backdrop of the white sand and spanning ocean. Pure paradise.

I made firm friends with a little girl called Ashley, who was also staying at the hotel with her family. We'd chase each other around the pool, playing tag, making up dances. I was sad when her family left, but she's stuck in my head ever since. It's a memory of a more confident, less anxious Chloë. It proves to me that I can talk to people I don't know, I am capable. I just have to get over the initial freak-out. Easier said than done.

The woman running the Kids Club at the hotel was in her twenties and immensely bored – there were no other children, just me and Ashley. One day, she wandered down to the pool where my dad and I were splashing about, enjoying the sun, and point-blank asked me to come to the Kids Club. "Your dad can come too," she insisted, clearly desperate for people to hang out with. So from then on, my dad was roped into all our Kids Club activities. Picture that scene from *Only Fools and Horses* where Rodney joins the Groovy Gang to keep up the pretence he's fourteen years old so he can win the art competition. That was literally my dad at that club.

The staff were stellar at the Rex, and the pool lifeguard even invented competitions for me. I'd been given a Barbie mermaid doll for my birthday – you pressed a button and her arms would spin, propelling her through the water at speed – and the lifeguard used to race her against me and happily sit making trophies out of palm leaves if I won.

He also helped teach me to swim. I'd been having lessons back home but wasn't quite there; I'd bob around with my armbands but hadn't yet mastered the art of actually getting anywhere. I hated putting my head underwater and getting my ears blocked, and I was not a fan of chlorine stinging my eyes. But this lifeguard spent many a patient day in the pool with me, showing me different strokes until it clicked one day. I left Antigua a water baby, and ever since I've loved immersing myself in any pool, jumping in the deep end and swimming with ease.

I was never bored in Antigua and my first experience of a faraway country was one I'll never forget. It opened my eager eyes to this colossal world around us. It certainly set the bar for future trips and made me thirsty to see more, meet other fantastic people, explore this weird and wonderful world – and find even more dinosaur prints in the sand, of course.

3

Mugged by a Monkey

Bali

I miss younger me and now, in my twenties, I strive for a simpler way of life. If I could swish a magic wand and wake up as smaller Chloë – amazed by a sunset, unclouded by the chatter of social media, content with splashing around in a pool somewhere for hours – I would.

I miss the me who loved meeting other children solely in order to get to know them rather than to post on Instagram. I long to have that easiness back.

But I do remember a time when I enjoyed things completely, fully, way before I got involved in the social media game or started worrying about taxes and student loans (oh, the joys). Bali was one of those trips.

Antigua set the bar immensely high for me. I'd already seen so much – too much for my little brain to comprehend – but a few years later in 2001, we headed to Bali, and I was gobsmacked.

Asia, earth's largest continent, is probably my favourite part of this entire planet. It's where I feel most 'on holiday'. It's exotically familiar, and I can explore to my heart's content, revelling in the contrast to my frantic life back home.

I adore cities, I feel so blissfully bewildered and immersed. But everyone loves a beach, don't they? And Asia has some of the most tranquil, tropical offerings. Sublime sunshine, turquoise sea. But the towns are something special too: the bustle of markets stalls, the history and culture. I feel like I'm really pushing my limits being somewhere so completely different to London. Asia is a galaxy away from my world back home, and sometimes that's what you need to shake up your mindset.

My earliest encounter with Asian culture was beautiful, balmy Bali in 2001, when I was five years old. The first thing that hit me was the wonderful smell of that charming Indonesian island: humidity mixed with burning incense. It's a smell truly unique to Bali. It engulfs you as soon as you step off the plane, follows you through the dusty streets and blends with your soul; it's in your hair, on your clothes. Coming home and opening your suitcase gives a familiar jolt to the senses as the smell wafts from the contents. It brings a smile to my lips every time.

That's the smell I associate with travelling, a smell that cannot simply be re-created with incense or earthy perfume. It's the experiences and memories that mingle with it; that's why the smell always seems stronger when you open your suitcase at home. Well, and the fact that it's a stark contrast to your lavender diffuser from Next, isn't it?

There's just so much to see in Bali. Everything looks brighter, like someone has turned up the contrast on your vision. The trees are so much greener, the sea much bluer, the sky so clear – no blemishes, no clouds. It's so perfect, without trying.

There are a lot of traditions to learn about and lifestyle changes to acclimatise to, and there's so much nature. It's like you're on a whole other planet. It's a colourful, confounding experience. Suddenly you're seeing the world as an oil painting and realising it's always been rendered in dark, drab charcoal before. It's as if you never knew life existed until you went there, but now, you understand that there's a whole world to dive into where things seem simpler and people offer you a smile wherever you go, even if that's not the reality. That's what Bali is for me.

My mum and dad have visited Bali three times and their tales are very familiar to me even though I wasn't present for their first trip. One I could tell off by heart is the story of how my dad ended up with severe heatstroke, his skin turning scaly like a reptile. My mum laughs now but says it was terrifying at the time. She had no idea what to do, being stuck in a foreign country, not knowing where the nearest pharmacy was or how to ask for medicine in Balinese. Dad was getting worse, hallucinating, so the hotel called the local doctor. The GP tried to inject him with a sedative as he screamed and recoiled from her. Since then, Mum has instilled in me the importance of always familiarising yourself with your surroundings.

Luckily, my dad was A-OK after a couple of days spent recuperating in the darkened hotel room. But he always wears a hat and begrudgingly slaps on sun cream as soon as the sun rears its head on holidays now.

Later during the same trip, with Auntie Rani this time, they had to wade across a waterlogged paddy field. My mum and auntie refused to get their feet wet (which literally sounds like me; me and my auntie are scarily similar), so my dad carried my mum over, came back, carried my auntie across and then waded through with all the backpacks held above his head.

My auntie and dad stopped at the local bar later on and indulged in a little too much alcohol. When my mum woke up the next morning, she jumped out of her skin at the sight of a terrifying wooden Garuda statue – half bird, half man – ogling her from across the room, its widened eyes boring into hers. It turned out that Dad and Auntie Rani had made some questionable shopping choices after their bar crawl, which they greatly regretted in the cold (or humid) light of day. The Garuda went straight into my auntie's loft when she got home; even so, she always insisted it brought her bad luck, and when she finally got rid of it years later, she breathed a sigh of relief.

Also on that trip, my dad got his shoes nabbed. He'd left them by his bed in their hostel but came back to find they'd been replaced by someone else's manky, moth-eaten slippers, three sizes too small for him.

Mishaps follow us wherever we go. Maybe it's bad juju from that Garuda statue still haunting us.

Although I was quite young during both of my own visits, I remember a great deal about Bali; it's vivid in my mind's eye. One of our family's most famous photographs was taken there. It's a snap of me in a baby-pink dress with cherry print, sporting a massive white sunhat and grinning, all my irregular baby teeth on show, and with a real live iguana casually perched on my head.

The close second is a photo of me the same day, leading the way into extensive jungle undergrowth, face stern, arm out, like some sort of mini tour guide. I was fearless back then. Apart from the standard bogeyman-under-my-bed fears, anxiety hadn't clasped its claws around my impressionable mind yet. We'd ventured into the jungle on a tour and were lucky enough to see some amazing animals in their natural habitat. There's another print of my dad, looking completely chilled, with a python wrapped loosely around his neck. I didn't want to get involved with that one, no matter how fearless.

The hotel we stayed at both times, the Matahari Bungalows, consisted of several quaint, beautifully designed wooden huts set around a turquoise swimming pool with a bar in the middle. We were a stone's throw from the shops, eateries and vibrant village but six kilometres away from busy Kuta beach.

It was all about the pool bar for me – a fantastic novelty. I used to swim over to order steak sandwiches straight after breakfast every morning. The waiters let me sign for things at dinner and I felt grown up, putting meals 'on the room'. I thought it was a game; I didn't know you had to pay for all that food. My mum and dad were too embarrassed to send the sandwiches back, not wanting to offend, so we just wolfed them down whenever they rocked up. Needless to say, we were stuffed. After a few days, my parents got wise. If I appeared to be paddling over to the pool bar, my mum would expertly intercept, making sure no unwanted meals were being ordered.

Bali has a lot more to offer than tip-top steak sandwiches though. Ubud, a town situated less than an hour away from the Matahari Bungalows, is famed for its traditional rice paddies, Hindu temples, untouched rainforest and diverse dance culture. It's also home to the infamous Sacred Monkey Forest Sanctuary, which was a quirky experience to say the least.

At the entrance, we bought tiny bananas – something I will forever associate with Asia – to feed the primates with, and then, we embarked on our trek into the forest. I was ecstatically excited, eager to spy some monkeys in the undergrowth.

The monkeys, granted, were very cute. The forest is the natural habitat of the Balinese long-tailed macaque and more than a thousand of them wandered freely through it. I loved watching them swing from branch to branch, going about their daily business and interacting with each other. They dropped onto the paths, watching quizzically as we strange humans peered back. It was fantastic. You truly felt at one with nature and I'd definitely recommend the sanctuary to anyone visiting Bali.

I'd stopped to watch a family of monkeys squabbling in the towering trees and was gazing up in awe when the tiniest one suddenly hopped down and scuttled off. Oblivious, I carried on looking at the monkeys above, so when the little one crept up behind me and viciously grabbed my ankle, I screamed in shock. It happened in the blink of an eye. I dropped the bananas I was holding in a panic and stared down to see what the hell was attached to my foot.

He dug his little nails into my skin and began swinging himself around and around my leg as I squealed in panic, crying for my mum and dad. I tried to run away, but he was still stuck to me. Luckily, he let go eventually and scarpered off, probably giggling to himself in monkey language as I sniffled.

So, yes, this was traumatising, but it made a funny story when we returned home, and it's even more hilarious when I reminisce years later.

Bali is full of fond memories for me. I recall sitting with my mum by the fishpond in our hotel, waiting for our taxi to arrive and whisk us away on a day trip. I'd been absently moving my hand through the rippling water to cool down, not really paying attention, when suddenly I felt something slimy slip around my finger. I whipped my head down to see a huge golden fish attached. I immediately shot my arm backwards, but it stayed latched on, flipping this way and that. Squealing as it slid off, I rushed away to wash my hands as my mum laughed. Pretty grim.

When I wasn't attracting mischievous animals like a mini Doctor Dolittle, I was obsessed with the local amusement arcade. I'd play bowling relentlessly until my parents probably regretted taking me in the first place and collected reels of raffle tickets, eagerly queuing for my prize. The arcade was much like the UK offerings in Brighton and Broadstairs, but instead of ducking in there to escape lashings of icy English rain, we retreated into this one for respite from Bali's dusty heat.

There was also a newly opened McDonald's near the arcade and although I enjoyed sampling traditional Balinese cuisine, sometimes tinier Chloë just wanted a Happy Meal. It was nothing like McDonald's back home though; here, food was served on silver trays with proper cutlery, a five-star version of the fast-food chain.

*

When I wasn't living it up, devouring silver-plated McDonald's, I was trawling the local bazaars. Bali ignited my shopping obsession.

My dad has always filled our home with tokens from our travels. We have countless wooden figures of the Buddha dotted around and lots of hand-carved boxes and original oil paintings from all over the world. I've developed the same love of abstract things. I love to visit local shops when we're away. I don't like my home or room to look like everyone else's. I prefer everything on show to have meaning behind it; I want to catch sight of an ornament and be whisked back to the place I purchased it, a flurry of memories, smells and sights engulfing me.

Maybe that's just me. I uncovered the first glimmers of my individuality in my early teens, when I started to like different music to what my peers considered 'normal', and since then, I've developed my own sense of self. Although even now I still don't feel like I fully understand my place in this odd world we call home; I do try to live by my own style.

If you have anxiety issues, finding who you are can be hard when all you want is to blend into the background. But when I turned fourteen, I started listening to bands that would soon become my favourites. I experimented with my eyeliner, flicking it out, a trend which would eventually become my trademark make-up look. I started to buy clothes that I liked: skinny jeans, leather jackets, all different colours of my beloved Converse.

I started to understand that you can be who you want in this world, you don't have to look like everyone else your age, you don't have to like what they like or conform in any way. You might get negative comments, you might get labelled 'weird', but really that's the other person's issue, not yours. Although I still feel intimidated sharing details about myself, especially those things that I consider to be unusual; I'm getting there.

Everything unusual is what I love most. I adore anything quirky, things you can't just buy from a town centre. I love how our furniture is wonderfully odd and one of a kind, how an object can evoke a hundred memories and have its backstory woven into the material like veins.

You can have a trinket box from New Look and it means nothing, you barely remember buying it, but you have a wooden box handmade in Zanzibar with inscriptions and memories attached and it becomes special in a whole new way. I find it fascinating; you can learn a lot about a person from the items in their home.

We have a table in the front room which resembles a tree trunk; it reminds me of the trees in the Sahara. It's one of a kind, and that's exactly what I find charming about it. I like to be surrounded by memories and feel that my mind has been broadened by visiting these faraway places. Sometimes the trip is over in a flash and these mementoes are all I have to remember each detail.

So my room is full of memories, little trinkets, objects that couldn't be from anywhere but a dusty market a million miles away. My possessions are unique, and Bali is where I learnt it's okay for me to be unique too.

Cheesy, I know, but thinking of the place never fails to put a smile on my face. These objects conjure happy thoughts, like a magic spell. I like to think every trip has equipped me with a new life lesson, instilled something valuable in me.

On my first holiday to Bali, my dad met some locals selling wooden ornaments at a stall near the hotel. They learnt his name and would chat to him every day, trying to flog him their figurines. My dad loves to talk to people when we're away, to learn their names and find out their stories. Also, sometimes he's simply too nice to say 'No, thank you' if he doesn't want whatever it is they're selling; that's often his downfall. Hey, we all have flaws. Mine is my incessant urge to buy sparkly bath bombs.

This time in Bali, trying to be kind, he kept saying 'Maybe later' whenever he bumped into the men. He became so familiar to them, they'd greet him with a 'Mr Steve! Maybe later!' whilst laughing knowingly.

They were lovely locals, as was everyone we met in Bali. One morning, however, my dad wasn't feeling well at breakfast. He decided to return to the room, leaving my mum and me to finish eating. As he stood up, he whacked his head on a beam above the table. There was a deafening crunch, but he seemed okay. Rubbing the fast-appearing bump, he set off for our bungalow.

The hit on his head turned out to be worse than we'd thought. On the short stroll back, he passed out and fell sprawling onto the grass, just the other side of the shrubbery. Mum and I were oblivious to this; unable to glimpse him from our table, we just carried on enjoying our breakfast.

Dad eventually came around ten minutes later, and the first thing he saw were those same street sellers, standing over him, not calling for help but still trying to get him to buy the figurines!

"Mr Steve, good price, you wanna buy?"

He stared at them blearily, struggling to stand, unsure how long they'd been there nattering to his unconscious form.

Fast-forward to us arriving home, and, yes, we had some new additions to the family – those damn figures. But at least, they have an interesting backstory. I guess the takeaway message is that extreme pressure-selling to unconscious customers pays off.

A year later, after our second trip to Bali, I also returned to London clutching my own new favourite pals, much to my mum's dismay. On our first holiday there, we used to drop into a shop near our hotel most days to stock up on cold drinks. Second time around, we got into the same habit. Only by now, being twelve months older, I had fully cemented that love of shopping. I became obsessed with the shop's collection of brightly painted wooden cats. I played with them each time we went in and gawped at them for hours.

One day, I began whining like an annoying brat, insisting I needed these cats. My dad was just promising that he'd come back and get me one later when one of the shop assistants scurried out from the back, squealing, "Chloë!" She rushed over as I halted, mid-whinge. "I thought it was you! I remember you from last year."

Yep, this lady remembered my whining tones from a whole year before. That, ladies and gentlemen, is making an impression.

I did get the cats, if you're wondering. My mum has them kept safe, and sometimes, she gets them out to remind me my fussiness leaves such a mark that the shopkeeper remembered my moody little sun-freckled face, crazy curls and high-pitched moaning twelve months on. But hey, the cats were cute, and I loved them. They were certainly something you couldn't buy in a shop back home.

When I wasn't lining up my multi-coloured felines like some creepy cat collector, we'd go to the beach and I'd play with the children there. When I was younger, I had no issue talking to people. I played tag with those kids and they were literally the same as me, despite living across the globe. They were so happy, so content messing about each evening on the sand.

Nowadays, especially at home, we're obsessed with social media, posing perfectly and curating endless photo opportunities. It's all about looking better than someone else or creating some false narrative about your life. Just to make others feel inferior. Sometimes I wish I lived somewhere simpler, somewhere remote. If I could combine the overall feel of London with less of the social pressure, that would be my ideal place to live. I could escape from social media, the internet and the issues all of that brings.

Growing up, I loved staying at my nan and pap's in Northampton. It's such a peaceful break from the steady thrum of London traffic. Instead of double-decker buses and car horns, it's the flapping of birds' wings and the delicate tinkle of windchimes in their flower-filled garden. But it's not just that. I liked to disconnect from social media when I was there and spend quality time with my grandparents, hearing about my pap's plans for his next painting and what word puzzle my nan was doing. I'd come home with my brain decluttered, freed from the litter of Instagram likes.

Although, saying that, if I could have captured my dad's echoing screams from the Bali Slingshot on my phone, I would have. It's a story which haunts him and cracks our whole family up whenever it's mentioned.

We'd been out in the town and were sitting at quaint tables enjoying our dinner in the balmy evening air. We watched in amazement as tourists queued for a nearby catapult ride and chuckled as their excited expressions melted into pure horror when they were strapped in. They'd stumble off minutes later, faces green, staggering to grasp hold of something rooted to the ground.

You know those big catapults you get at beach piers? The ones where two people sit in a rounded contraption, get shot high into the air and come hurtling down at speed? Well, that's what this was, but to be honest, it looked less sturdy than the ones you venture onto at Brighton Pier, and I wouldn't even trust those. My mum wondered aloud why anyone would put themselves through that. It looked horrific and not one of the tourists was laughing or joking when they reached the ground again.

I'd finished my dinner and was absently doodling in my sketchbook at the table when my dad, who'd consumed a few beers, suddenly stood up and announced he was going to try it. My mum sniggered until she clocked he was serious. Deadly serious.

"Where's Dad going?" I asked as Mum watched in horror.

"On the catapult," she replied as Dad approached the now non-existent queue.

He sauntered over, spoke briefly to the guy at the booth, paid the money and was strapped in instantly. We stared, eyes like saucers, as he grinned from the catapult. Then our jaws dropped as he was suddenly flung into the air with little warning.

It all happened rather quickly. I tore off a blank page in my sketchbook and started drawing the catapult with my dad in it, screaming. We could clearly hear him yelling 'Oh bloody hell' every two seconds as he was dragged back down to the ground and flung up again, and again. It seemed to go on forever. It felt longer to my dad, no doubt. I swear the guy on the controls prolonged the ride.

My mum couldn't stop giggling. And the best part? The whole thing was filmed on a GoPro camera inside the catapult itself, so we have a live video of my dad being shot into the skies to watch whenever we please. Well, whenever we can find a video player, that is. Evolving technology, kids.

The video itself should have won an Oscar; it had everything in it: horror, humour, supporting characters. Ten out of ten people would recommend this movie – in theatres soon.

My dad didn't learn his lesson; he still loves trying anything like that. He staggered off when the catapult finally ground to a halt and made his way back to our table to the background giggles of watching tourists. We goggled at him aghast while he tucked back into his dinner as if the whole saga had never happened. The mere mention of Bali always makes me think back to that hilarious night. I probably still have my drawing somewhere. We should have framed it.

Shortly after we returned from that trip, a vicious terrorist attack killed 202 people in Kuta and injured 209 more. This became known as the 2002 Bali Bombings; there would be more attacks in 2005. Irreparable damage was caused to the vibrant district we'd loved spending time in just days before, and the local Sanglah Hospital (Bali's largest hospital) was unable to deal with the vast number of casualties. The first bomb was detonated inside the popular drinking spot Paddy's Bar, and shortly after, a car bomb was set off outside the Sari Club, causing devastation up to several blocks away. The attack was thought to have been led by a radical Islamist cleric as retaliation for support of America's war on terror and Australia's part in the liberation of East Timor.

It was awful to think of the wonderfully friendly and gentle Balinese people being subjected to something as vile as this. It was a reminder that although the world can be a fantastic place, it's full of danger too. And no matter where you are in this world, you need to exercise your choice to be kind to people.

4

But I Am Simba...

Kenya

When I first watched Disney's *The Lion King* as a little girl, I wanted to be Simba. Yes, I actually wanted to be a cartoon lion. Weirdo much. I was completely obsessed with all things Lion King.

For my third birthday, I had this wonderful handmade Lion King cake, decorated to look like Simba and was visibly upset when it was cut up so we could eat it. I watched the film over and over and collected all the lion figures from the Disney Store. I carried them everywhere. When I ate my dinner, they'd be lined up around my plate, along with my 'funny mens' – the seven dwarfs from Snow White. When I visited my nan and pap, they'd get out books to pile on top of each other, helping me make 'stairs' for the figures to walk up.

On another birthday, my mum and I went to meet my dad in London after he finished work. We were breezing through the West End after dinner and he pointed to the Lyceum Theatre, its massive yellow banner advertising the Lion King stage show jumping into my sightline. My little jaw dropped and my eyes widened.

"Do you want to see it, Chloë?" my dad asked, and I nodded vigorously. Unbeknown to me, he'd already bought the tickets several weeks prior, and to date that's one of the best surprises I've ever had. I absolutely loved the show and remember every detail. I was desperate to get up and join in and asked my parents in the interval if I could go and be Nala, Simba's best friend. We've since seen the show again on my twenty-first and it was just as fantastic.

I also went through a phase where I'd only respond if people called me 'Simba'. Yeah, I was a strange kid, but who likes normal anyway? One time, my mum and dad took 'Simba' to Greenwich Park, where I ran off down the massive hill near the observatory. That hill is extremely steep, and once I'd started my descent, my little legs couldn't stop, so my dad raced after me, calling to get me to halt before I fell over. Well, I was still in character and I assumed he was being Scar, Simba's villainous rival, so I was yelling, 'I don't know you! You're not my dad!' at him because…well, Scar isn't Simba's dad, is he?

My actual dad had to sprint past worried onlookers, assuring them, 'It's okay, I am her dad. She's playing *The Lion King*', and my mum hurried after both of us, grimacing awkwardly at the staring passers-by. It was literally like that scene from BBC's *Outnumbered*, when one of the kids, Ben, wants a toy from the petting zoo giftshop. His dad says no, but as he picks Ben up to leave, Ben starts yelling 'Stranger danger!' When his dad warns him off with a 'Stop it, Ben', he yells, 'My name's not Ben', as he's hauled out the shop. Mum, Dad and I always laugh at that episode as it's so reminiscent of me in Greenwich Park.

That park holds lots of happy memories. We'd often visit it when my cousins were down from Northampton. Once, when I was still in a pram, our family took us there with my older cousins, Oliver and Luke. Luke was only three years old, but he wanted to push my pram, so he was allowed to, under strict supervision. Suddenly, though, we reached the same steep incline, and Luke, being very short, just couldn't keep hold of the pram handles as the momentum began to pull us both down the hill. My Uncle Noel and Auntie Nicola were walking along behind, deep in conversation with my mum and dad; they all looked up in horrified unison as my Uncle Noel ran and grabbed both the pram and Luke in the nick of time. Disaster averted.

From Greenwich to Tsavo, being completely obsessed with *The Lion King* made embarking on a real-life safari in Kenya almost too much for my little mind to fathom. This was my first experience of Africa and it was everything I was expecting and more; I recall my memories with a grin. My mum always cites Kenya as her all-time favourite trip; she was in awe, seeing so many creatures up-close. And my dad's photos were incredible. He captured the serenity of the place as well as some amazing action shots of prowling lionesses and dancing antelopes. I hope to go back to Kenya and do it all again one day, refresh my brain and really remember how fantastic it was to witness those animals in the wild. Plus, I'm still a massive fan of *The Lion King*, so I'd be just as excited.

It was in Tsavo West National Park that my Lion King dreams came to life. I was ecstatic throughout the whole flight to Kenya, pressing my face against the plane window, being on an aircraft still a huge novelty. I wriggled in my seat, chewing through my bag of pretzels and imagining what the animals were doing right then as we hurtled at full speed to Africa.

We stayed in a wonderful hotel near the national park in Tsavo, Salt Lick Safari Lodge, and the staff were so welcoming. That's something that really sticks when I recall Kenya: the immense effort everyone made to make us feel welcome. There was a particular staff member who cleaned our room; he used to shuffle about humming and was such a jolly man. He was so friendly, we'd hear him making his way down the corridor, using his broom as a walking stick, constantly chuckling. I nicknamed him Rafiki in my head as he reminded me of the wise, lovable, laughing monkey from *The Lion King*.

He'd fold our fresh towels into amazing arrangements, everything from swans to intricate flowers, and he'd prop up my massive stuffed lion – the one I'd got for my birthday there – in my bed to make me giggle. Some days, the lion would be reading my mum's book with her sunglasses perched on his nose; on others, he'd be in the chair with a stack of paper and pencils like he was mustering his artistic spirit. We even came back from breakfast on my birthday morning to 'Happy Birthday' written in a flurry of flower petals on my bed.

That evening at dinner, the hotel waiters emerged with a surprise cake and sang 'Happy Birthday' to me, which was lovely. Everything about Kenya was so extra. Everyone made such a fuss, made our holiday memorable. The safari was the highlight, but the people really ensured that the whole trip was perfect.

On the day we embarked on the safari, we rose early, packed our day bags and made our way down to the rumbling old-school jeep. Rubbing my sleep-hazed eyes, I dragged my little backpack along as we joined the rest of our group. I could barely stay awake, and a yawn escaped my lips every few seconds, but weariness couldn't dampen my immense excitement at heading out on safari! I perked up after a catnap and ogled out of the window, my little eyes darting with every movement in the undergrowth.

Our safari guide warned us there was no way to predict which animals would be visible, but that didn't register in my brain. I was just happy to be on the road, which, as it turned out, was a whole experience in itself. The dirt tracks were bumpy and we were flung up, down, left and right, but that was all part of the fun.

We caught sight of zebras nibbling on the grassy plains and warthogs splashing around the watering hole. We saw hornbills and eagles, and vultures swooping over antelopes as they galloped off, so graceful and beautiful. The guide and my dad caught sight of the lone cheetah first, eagerly motioning to the rest of us, pointing as it prowled behind the trees, peeking out, its beautiful cat eyes narrowing in suspicion. It was literally like being in *The Lion King*. I was expecting Simba to jump out and start singing 'Hakuna Matata' with Timon and Pumbaa. Oh, wait, I was Simba – had I missed my cue?

Everyone in our jeep was gazing in awe at these beautiful beings, but they were also eagerly waiting to see a lion, same as me. The 'mane' event, if you will. (Excuse the pun. I can hear the groans from here.) My mum and dad had bought me a cool pair of binoculars especially for the trip, so I kept scrabbling in my seat, using them to peer into the distance, desperate to be the first to spot Mufasa, Simba's father. Other members of our group giggled as I offered my binoculars to my mum to use. Why were they chuckling, you ask? These were not your average binoculars, ladies and gentlemen. No way. This pair had a plush coating with ears and a fluffy finish, so when you put them up to your face, you resembled a puppy dog with big googly eyes.

Those doggy binoculars and my cuddly lion were my safari essentials. My mum packed all the important stuff like sun cream, water, our cameras and a drawing pad for me, but young Chloë…? A stuffed toy and goofy binoculars would suffice; that's what I deemed important. I swear, I'd be great surviving a zombie apocalypse; at least, I'd have cute binoculars to spy on the undead. (Sarcasm! I would literally be hiding out in a deserted Costa Coffee somewhere. If I'm going down, I'm going down to the familiar soothing aroma of freshly ground coffee.)

Armed with my barmy binoculars and toy lion – it was vital he came on safari to see his 'family' – I'd been drawing attention to myself as the day went on. The other guests started taking pictures of my stuffed animal in case they didn't see the real deal. As a matter of fact – spoiler alert – we did catch a glimpse of a lion, so that was the cherry on top of the perfectly sculpted cake. This trip was so magical, especially for me. It was a childhood fantasy made real.

When we hopped out of the jeep at the end of the day, exhausted from the oppressive heat beating down on our heads for hours on end, we all thought we'd caught the sun. My mum admired her new tan in the hotel room and was delighted (we're not really a tanning kind of family; we're all vampire pale, so when one of us gets a tan, it's a big deal). That lasted mere minutes though. As soon as we showered, ready to head down to dinner, we realised our tans were actually just orange dust from the dirt tracks. We were back to our Transylvanian selves in no time.

I honestly think Kenya was the best trip we've had in terms of once-in-a-lifetime sights. I'd sit on the rocks outside the hotel, mesmerised by the elephants as they gathered around the watering hole below. It was spectacular.

My mum's favourite part about the whole holiday was the tunnel you could wander down from the breakfast area in Salt Lick. We'd saunter through, heading further underground until we reached a glass panel at the end, and there we would sit for hours, watching the animals up-close and personal – stalking lions, galloping gazelles – as they went about their day, unaware that we were watching.

We'd sit for ages; it was impossible to drag me away. It was incredible to be a foot away from a lion yet feel completely safe. This wasn't anything like the zoo; these animals were completely wild, fending for themselves. I was immersed; it was unbelievable. I recall locking eyes with a lioness nuzzling the ground mere inches from my face, just the other side of the glass bubble. I could see her whiskers twitching and her eyes narrowing, and I could even hear her claws scraping the ground beneath her gigantic paws. It's something I'll never forget.

The only memory I physically cringe over occurred one evening at dinner. We'd moved on to a hotel near Mombasa and ambled down to its restaurant to enjoy a barbecue buffet. Delicious delights were everywhere we looked: pots of perfectly prepared rice, meats, curries, the lot. I like to try new things; I get my spice-orientated palate from my dad. We used to have barbecues at home most Sundays in the summer and my dad once dared me to eat a whole chilli for £1. Which I did – ever the businesswoman. It burnt my whole mouth and the tingling on my tongue didn't disappear for hours. But since then, I've lived for spice. My dad and I will add at least four chillies to most dinners, much to the dismay of my mum, who prefers her tastebuds intact.

I love to try local delights when travelling. But this dinner in Kenya was on another level. Mum took me up to the buffet, asked me what I wanted and scooped various samples onto my plate and hers. The labels on the pots weren't too clear, but the waiters were advising us to try this and that. "This one is good," they said, pointing and telling us that it was freshly caught and we'd love it. So, we headed back to our table and began to tuck in. The waiters were right. The meat was delicious; it tasted like chicken but had a steak-like texture. My mum and I finished ours just as the waiter popped over with some drinks.

"Did you enjoy the zebra?" he asked as he placed my lemonade in front of me and balanced the tray in his other hand.

Mum and I stared at him in horror.

"The…what?" My mum faltered. Then she started to chuckle; the waiter had to be joking. "Yeah, 'zebra'." She laughed. "What was it though? It was lovely."

The waiter peered at us, confused, and glanced back at the buffet, where a queue was forming. The dish was popular, that was for sure. "It was zebra," he replied with a frown.

Mum fell silent. My stomach churned and I took a gulp of lemonade. Mum gawped at him in shock. My dad though? He carried on devouring his quite happily, not even registering what the waiter had said.

So, yeah, Kenya was the trip I accidentally ate a zebra. I'd been so in awe of those magical, majestic mammals in the wild, gazing at a group of them through my binoculars, loving watching them darting around, and then the next day, I'd bloody well eaten one. Mum and I didn't feel too good about that.

Macaque monkey and infant, Bali, Indonesia

Lioness and cub, Kenya, East Africa

Wildebeest at watering hole, Tsavo, Kenya, East Africa

Lioness yawns, Tsavo, Kenya, East Africa

5

Candy the Koala

Australia

When I'm not accidentally eating them (ugh, cringe), I love learning about the multitude of animals roaming our world. The main thing I remember about Australia is gazing into the big brown eyes of a koala as he chomped eucalyptus leaves and grinned cheekily at me, showing me the green mush in his mouth as he lazily chewed.

Australia was the furthest I'd ever travelled, and to date, the longest flight I've ever been on. It was exhausting. Sure, you just sit back, relax, watch a few films absently and wait to land, but after the first ten hours, it gets old. Your head feels heavy and your eyes gritty, the recycled air of the plane becomes stifling, and outside it's just blank blackness. Other passengers are sound asleep, and you feel envious, unable to grab forty winks due to the deafening thrum of the aircraft and the intoxicating whiff of plane food. Lovely.

We travelled to Australia when I was six and I remember it with plenty of positivity, bar the flight. My dad was on best man duties for his brother's wedding in Sydney, and I was ecstatic to be a bridesmaid. We flew out for the big day and hit up Bali on the way back for a beach break (and to split up the horrendous 23-hour flight home).

Some of my Australian experiences I only remember when I look back through our flurry of photographs. My own recollections are intertwined with stories my parents have spun me about the time when they lived there. They backpacked for a year when they married, living in Perth, in Western Australia, before travelling all over Asia. I love hearing their stranger-than-strange stories. They stayed with my Great-auntie Joy (the recipient of mum's famous letters) and Great-uncle John for a few weeks and have often told me about the lovely house and how the cheeky kookaburras in the trees outside would throw pine nuts at anybody lingering on the driveway. But on this trip, we only saw Sydney, a fraction of what Australia has to offer.

Halfway into the flight, I eventually drifted into a fitful sleep, my eyes burning, the recycled air irritating them with every blink. When we landed, I was so groggy and jet-lagged, my dad had to carry me through Sydney Airport while I napped on his shoulder. That's when the real test of patience for my parents began. We still needed to source some bridesmaid's shoes to match my dress (which was cream with a massive gold bow around the waist and a matching jacket embroidered with golden swirls) as there hadn't been any I'd liked back home. It was late and inky black outside, and we could have still been in London for all I knew, but the humid air told me otherwise as I peeped around me before dozing off again.

I couldn't keep my eyes open. So, my dad had to carry me around the mall while my mum slipped different shoes on me to find the right fit. I was like a miniature sleeping Cinderella, if you will. Well, if Cinderella was six, drooled in her sleep and sported a 101 Dalmatians baseball cap. I remember zoning in and out. I'd jolt awake, startled by the glaring lights and we'd be in yet another shop, with yet another pair of shoes being eased carefully onto my feet. Eventually, some were chosen. They were a glitzy gold but beautifully delicate and I was more than happy with my 'princess shoes'. I was even more ecstatic to finally head to bed.

My Nana Cath was in Australia for the wedding, so we got to spend a lot of time with her. We visited Bondi Beach and Sydney Zoo, where we got to cuddle Candy the koala, stroke a kangaroo and hold a massive wombat that was bigger than me. The zookeeper plopped the wombat gently onto my lap and I was amazed at how heavy he was. He was so smiley though, so cute, with wide eyes and a snuffling, sniffling nose.

My all-time favourite photograph of me and Nana Cath was snapped at that zoo. She's lifting me up and we're both smiling into the camera, our faces so close together, you can see the resemblance between us. Next to us is Candy the koala, green drool dribbling down his furry chin. He's smiling too, excited to be part of this clearly iconic photo. I have the picture up in my room and it makes me grin when I look at it, as wide as Candy.

The thing I most associate with Australia though, something that really does make me erupt into a giggle, is breaking my Harry Potter glasses.

Born in 1995, I'm part of the age group who grew up living and breathing Harry Potter. It was our world and, let's be honest, still is. I still binge watch the movies and devour the books, and it's a love I share with my mum and dad, who also love the stories that helped sculpt my childhood.

My dad met JK Rowling when she was promoting the first few books. He was sent by the Daily Express to shoot some pictures of her one Saturday, and she kindly gave him the first novel to take home when he mentioned he had a young daughter. He really regrets not asking her to sign it, but at that moment, he had no idea how big the Harry Potter books would become. I don't think anyone had an inkling. My mum would read me chapters every night, thoroughly enjoying the magic herself. Then when I grew up, I read them myself. When I reached my twenties, my nan and pap would buy me the illustrated versions that started to appear in bookshops each Christmas.

When the films first came out, my dad took me to King's Cross Station, where the cast were filming, and I got to meet Daniel Radcliffe, Rupert Grint and Emma Watson. I say 'meet', but in fact, they smiled and said 'hi' to me whilst I hid behind my dad, too shy to speak.

I was obsessed. I had everything Harry Potter. If you were to rifle through my cupboards, you'd still find my old collections. I had all the figures, board games, keyrings, stuffed toys, wands, outfits, house scarves (Gryffindor only, obviously), gloves, hats, cups, bedding, ornaments, pyjamas, notebooks, pens, cards, and even a toothbrush and toothpaste set (actually, that bright red toothbrush with the plastic Harry stand is still at my nan and pap's, kept in the bathroom cupboard for when I stay). You name it: if it had Harry Potter on it, I owned it. Especially the famous glasses, they were my prized possession.

I'd acquired these plastic imitations from the Warner Bros. shop, which was my favourite part of Gatwick Airport. My lovely – and probably exasperated – parents used to take me there frequently, so I could sift through all the Harry Potter merchandise. A few weeks before we departed for Australia, my dad bought me the glasses as a treat. I wore them everywhere (apart from to school, as my mum put her foot down), and to their dismay, I also took them on holiday. In fact, they were the first thing I packed.

There I was, happily sporting my oversized glasses all around Sydney. There are various photographs of me looking pretty odd, grinning next to my family, with them all wearing humorous expressions and me doing a thumbs-up and with massive frames taking over the whole of my face.

On the day in question, we'd headed up to see the Three Sisters, a 200-million-year-old rock formation in the Blue Mountains, northwest of Sydney. According to Aboriginal Dreamtime legend, the rocks are the embodiment of three sisters, Meehni, Wimlah and Gunnedoo, from the Katoomba tribe. It's said that they fell in love with three brothers from a neighbouring tribe, and when they were forbidden to marry, the brothers took the women prisoner. The sisters were turned to stone by an elder in order to protect them during the battle to win them back.

Stocked up on history, we made our way to Bondi Beach back in Sydney and spent the afternoon there before heading up to the promenade to take in views of the Pacific. It was stunning. Crystal-clear blue waters stretched as far as the eye could see and savvy surfers caught the crashing waves, expertly dodging each other and the current. The bright sun cast a golden glow over the busy beach.

My dad was on the phone to one of his friends, telling them about the Blue Mountains, and I was being generally childlike, pretending to be Harry Potter, jumping around and zapping people with my imaginary wand. Suddenly a seagull swooped over me, dumping a massive dollop of bird poo all over my head just as I looked up to hear it squawk. I screamed, turned abruptly, and ran straight into my dad's massive Canon camera lens, which was hanging around his neck on a strap. The lens was a professional one, so it was sturdy, could probably have knocked someone out, and was the size of my tiny head. Luckily, I wasn't hurt, but that was only because the glasses took the impact and suffered the consequences. They snapped in half, and I was distraught.

My well-meaning Nana Cath, always trying to help in dire situations, insisted that she could fix them, and my mum and dad watched in horror as she bandaged them up with a plaster from her handbag. I was thrilled, and my nana was happy she'd helped. But my mum and dad had to suffer the withering looks from locals who thought they were neglecting their child by not paying for proper glasses and forcing me to walk around with bandaged frames. Harry Potter was a thing in Australia, but the movies weren't as well known, so people weren't thinking I was a film fan, wearing the broken glasses like Harry. No, they were thinking I was a problem child.

My mum drew the line at me wearing them for the wedding. I think she had an image of me prancing down the aisle, done up to the nines in my beautiful dress, hair in ringlets and finished off with a giant golden bow, and then the Harry

Potter glasses, stuck together with a peeling brown plaster. Not the angelic little bridesmaid everyone envisioned, I guess.

The service, which was held a few days later, was lovely. I'd never been to a wedding before and, to be honest, haven't been to many since. My Auntie Nobuko looked beautiful. I remember thinking she was the living embodiment of a Disney princess with her sparkling gown and tiara. It was a hot and humid day and I stood at the front as the couple made their vows, clutching my little bouquet of flowers proudly. Everyone was praising my mum, commenting on how well I was doing not making a fuss throughout the whole ceremony. My feet were hurting, and I did wonder how long I had to stay up there, but I was determined to be the best bridesmaid anyone ever had. That was my job and I dare say I delivered. (At least if this writing lark doesn't work out, I can rent myself out as a popup bridesmaid.)

I love the pre-wedding snap of me and Auntie Nobuko together. Six-year-old me is grinning, all tiny baby teeth, happy to be wearing my glamorous get-up, and she is looking incredible in her wedding dress, with immaculate make-up and shiny hair, glowing inside and out.

We returned to Bondi Beach one more time before we left Australia and spent our last afternoon there, enjoying the sea and sand. I'd been having fun splashing about in the warm water, watching the surfers, wishing I could join them. When it was time to grab dinner, I ambled up the beach with my dad, mum and Nana Cath. My feet were sandy. The grains had stuck to me as I'd emerged from the water and my mum suggested I wash them in the little shower near the changing rooms. She meant for me to wait in line behind the group of six-foot-something Australian surfers jostling to use the jets, but I'd misunderstood, thinking it was a free-for-all. So, I squeezed past the chattering crowd of guys waiting to wash their surfboards, ducked under their towering frames and essentially pushed them out the way to wash my feet. They laughed, sidestepping me as I obliviously went about my business, carefully inspecting my feet to check all the sand had washed away before zipping back through the throng.

My mum was mortified and rushed over to apologise. But hey, my feet needed washing and it was nearly dinner time. I'm sure they understood the urgency. Either that or they recognised me as the beach's resident problem child.

6

Zero Tolerance for the Stifling Heat

Dubai

I've grown to marvel at the clash of cultures during my travels. It's like momentarily stepping into someone else's shoes. You discover a lot about how others live so differently around the globe. But what I really love is that you can always find common ground. We may all be unique and have alternative ways of living, but we're similar on so many levels, despite the linguistic and cultural barriers. We all share this planet (I learnt more about sharing and waiting my turn after the Australian beach shower episode), so why not learn to understand each other more?

In 2002, we flew to Dubai, one of the seven emirates that comprise the United Arab Emirates. It's the hottest place I've been to; it was like being in a sauna every time we stepped outside. The stifling heat eclipsed everything and much of our trip involved darting into air-conditioned shops. Not to say it wasn't enjoyable, it definitely was.

We quickly learnt to always carry water, and once we'd adjusted and let the shock to our bodies subside, we began to focus and see Dubai's true beauty. Locals appeared to be immensely proud of their city. It had an extravagant air; there was a lot of money there and it showed. Everything seemed coated with gold; it had a royal vibe. But what would you expect from one of the richest places in the world?

On our short walk to the beach, we'd take shelter from the unrelenting sun in the Dubai Mall and, believe me, that shopping centre was magnificent. It showcased the richness of Dubai impeccably and was very much a retail experience from the future. These days, a lot of shopping centres have things to do in them – ice skating, cinemas, restaurants and adventure playgrounds – but back then, in 2002, this was something new, something innovative. The Dubai

Mall had roller skating and a mini theme park inside as well as an impressive array of clothes, toy and gadget stores. For seven-year-old me, it was a dream come true. A theme park in a shopping centre? My brain almost exploded with excitement as I tugged on my parents' sleeves, pointing to the wonders in front of me.

There was plenty to wonder at outside of the malls too. We hit up the infamous water park Wild Wadi, splashing about in its cool waters and enjoying the various towering slides. My mum, who hates water and rides, was persuaded onto the Lazy River. "It's just a slow one, Mum," I urged as we grabbed our brightly coloured rubber rings from the side and pushed out into the lapping water.

She dipped a toe in cautiously and glanced around at the other guests. They were all laughing, looking relaxed, enjoying the ride. It seemed harmless enough. The three of us bobbed around as we were slowly swept forwards, around the various soft twists and turns. That's when it went south. Literally. We were suddenly jolted, as though the river had embraced us in an aggressive bear hug, and propelled up an incline to reach the top in a matter of seconds. From there we could see out over the whole park, and, yes, it was high. The water splashed harshly against the rings, and we were roughly pushed towards the sheer drop ahead.

"You said it was a slow one!" Mum exclaimed as we emerged, soaking wet, hair dripping, hauling our rubber rings. Oops.

There's so much to do in Dubai, especially if you're an adventurer. You can head out to the desert to spin around on dune buggies, or take a dip and go sea snorkelling. You can even go up in a hot-air balloon or a helicopter and admire the glimmering city lights below. Whatever you want out of a trip, Dubai has something for you. I was too young for most of the activities, but I'd love to try a dune buggy if I ever return. Skidding around at an exhilarating speed, spraying sand everywhere, sounds incredible.

My dad took a work trip to Dubai with Virgin Atlantic owner Sir Richard Branson and his team a few years back, and so many activities were crammed into his time there, in between taking photographs. He got to escape to the desert, take camel rides, swerve his way around on the sand buggies and visit the swanky Burj Al Arab, the world's only seven-star hotel. He's been on a variety of different trips with Richard Branson and our family are always immensely interested to hear what they got up to on their travels.

Apart from its incredibly posh air, burning hot sand and camel rides, Dubai has one of the lowest crime rates in the world, perhaps thanks to its strict laws. Alcohol consumption is tightly regulated and although non-Muslim adults are allowed to buy alcohol, this is only in licensed venues, usually hotels. Freedom of speech is also pretty limited, and locals are forbidden from speaking negatively about their royal family, laws or culture. Being in a same-sex relationship is illegal and you're not permitted to hold hands, chew gum or point in the street; you're not even supposed to take pictures of people you don't know.

There's also zero tolerance of drugs, which actually seems like a good rule to me, given my exasperating experience with second-hand marijuana smoke.

In the summer of the first Covid lockdown, the woman who lives with her little kid two doors down from us in London moved her new boyfriend in. We've always had odd neighbours (bustling busybodies or just weird human beings in general; I swear our whole family is a crazy magnet), but this new guy was a weed-smoking menace, and in my opinion, he ruined the perfectly pleasant suburban street vibes.

I don't have an issue with people doing whatever the hell they want in their own homes, and I'm not about to head out with my megaphone and protest outside his house. Drugs aren't my thing, but hey, they might be yours. When I was at school, the teachers used to show us the horrific anti-drugs 'Talk to Frank' adverts and these have had a lasting impact on me. As a result, I've never tried any type of drugs (unless you count daily multivitamins – the really good stuff).

Unfortunately, our new neighbour liked to smoke his marijuana in his back garden, uncomfortably close to my bedroom window. The guy chain-smoked non-stop, stumbling out into the garden every twenty minutes on the dot to sit there coughing and hawking loudly. The pungent smoke wafted through my window day and night. Every morning, I'd wake up choking, my lungs burning, and with a head-splitting migraine.

I took to keeping my windows closed at night and just having my fan on instead. I was sweltering in the 31-degree heat (I know! Jeez, England, you're meant to be cold) and becoming more and more sleep deprived as his incessant smoker's cough kept me awake until 4 am. I could still smell the unpleasant earthy aroma through my firmly shut window. My asthma was getting worse, I was puffing on my Salbutamol like a junkie myself; I constantly had a pounding headache, and it was just annoying. I stopped going out into our garden to work or read (or enjoy a glass of Prosecco) because I'd get maximum ten minutes before Druggy Mc Druggerson rolled himself out of bed for another smoke.

Late every afternoon, he'd emerge from his front door dressed in a baggy, stained T-shirt, his hair stringy and greasy, and amble off to the green near the top of our road, where he'd meet other incredibly odd individuals and sell his dope to them. Had we been living in Dubai, none of this would have happened. But I guess I'd still be sweltering and sleep-deprived because of the heat, so, swings and roundabouts.

Social media is also strictly regulated in Dubai, and defaming someone on a social media platform is a punishable offence. You can be sent to prison for up to two years for claiming something untrue online. Sometimes I think it would be a great idea to combine different ideologies from around the world, incorporating all cultures and embracing our differences in an attempt to forge a more inclusive way of living. Other countries' practices often seem alien to me, in the best possible way, and no doubt, London life also seems absurd to many people. Believe me, I have found myself wishing the UK would adopt the 'don't take photos of other people' rule when some weirdo on the train steals a picture of me minding my own business for their irritating Snapchat streak. Ugh.

7

How Not to Drive a Taxi 101

Sri Lanka

Snapchat streaks aren't my thing but photographs are. One of my favourite pictures is a framed shot captured by my dad. It's of a much younger me grinning nervously at the camera, clad in a dress I used to love: bright pink cotton with gold elephants emblazoned on it. My little white baseball cap is shielding me from the beating sun and I'm feeding a hungry elephant. I'm smiling ear to ear as he chomps away, content to be spending time with his new bestie.

I love taking photos: the rush when the colour balance is just right, the subject lines up perfectly and the result encapsulates exactly what I intended. But I hate how our world has cheapened the value of a picture. I miss cameras, and when my mum and dad bought me an awesome bright pink Polaroid camera for my twenty-fourth birthday, I revelled in the 'old-school' nature of it. I prefer it to my phone camera.

Taking photos on our phones has become the norm. It's quick, easy and convenient, plus iPhones are ridiculously advanced nowadays. But social media platforms like Instagram and Snapchat seem to encourage the notion of throwaway pictures. You take more and more as you're urged to beat streak records or rack up more likes. You post incessantly until it becomes a chore rather than a pleasure.

I'm no saint in the social media rat race. I was sucked into that superficial world the same as everyone else. But the more Instagram snaps I took (of my dinner, a pretty posy or a brightly coloured cocktail), the more they lacked value, thought or reason. My holiday photographs are different. I gaze back and see real life. Rickshaw drivers zooming past an enormous elephant carrying bags of rice on its back, or a perfectly timed sunset shot, captured just as a fishing boat passed through the frame, creating a fantastic silhouette. Those photos are precious. That Instagram upload of my cheeseburger (although mouth-watering) is not.

The photo of eight-year-old me feeding an elephant was taken in Sri Lanka at the Udawalawe Elephant Transit Home rescue centre. It's estimated that in Sri Lanka three elephants a week are killed due to conflicts with humans, which unfortunately leaves a lot of vulnerable calves without parents. Since 1995, the Elephant Transit Home has cared for hundreds of orphans before releasing them into the wild when they're strong enough, and that day, I got to feed the newest member of the gang, who'd sadly lost his parents a few days before.

Every time I look at that photograph, I blink and I'm back at the sanctuary, paying close attention to the feeder as he shows me how to hold the stick and hover it in front of the little elephant's mouth so he can reach the watermelon slice with ease. He nibbled cautiously, enjoying his snack, the sun on his back and the feeling of being taken care of. Bored of munching, he pushed the stick away with his trunk, trundling off to the waterhole to play with the other elephants, who were huge in comparison. He spurted water at them, splashing away when they turned, obviously the little troublemaker.

It was amazing for me, as a child of eight, to experience something like that, to witness wonderful, worthwhile charity work happening in real life, to see how those huge-hearted locals took care of our fellow mammals, treating them with such compassion. There really was a genuine love for helping injured, orphaned elephants in need. They weren't just doing it for tourism purposes or to make money, which unfortunately is the case in a lot of 'sanctuaries'. A lot of the staff were volunteers, and their passion shone through everything they did.

Whenever I think about Sri Lanka, I think about how magnificent the locals were at looking after animals, so intent on taking care of creatures big and small. I've always had a soft spot for animals: I used to refer to our family Border collie, Jacob, as my furry big brother; I tear up when the donkey sanctuary advert flashes up on the TV; and I love to help animal charities wherever I can. The Sri Lankan elephant sanctuary was wonderful for me because I could see how inspirational that kind of work was. It mattered.

We visited the Kosgoda Turtle Conservation Centre too, swapping elephants for an altogether different kettle of fish and learning about the dangers those much littler creatures face. The volunteers there work tirelessly to rescue turtle eggs from nearby beaches, where they're vulnerable to predators. The eggs are carefully brought back to the sanctuary and tended until they hatch. Then the babies are returned to the sea to swim free. If they're not rescued, they hatch on land and have to propel themselves towards the sea, avoiding the birds of prey that loom overhead, waiting to scoop them up. The centre looks after some adult turtles too, and we watched those majestic beings loop around the aquamarine salt tanks, their fins slicing through the water as they smiled lazily at us while dancing in slow motion.

It was on this trip that I realised the importance of taking care of others. I learnt that charity work is life-changing, and that even raising money as an individual can be vital for someone. Sri Lanka instilled this deeper understanding in me. We can make a difference if we stand for something.

*

The one negative event on that trip was almost plummeting to our deaths in a taxi as our driver caught up on some Zs. It was a four-hour drive back to Colombo Airport and we'd woken early to ensure we'd be on time. The friendly taxi driver – the one who'd been so helpful, ferrying us around to sights, telling us about cool places to go to – was waiting in the hotel lobby and we hopped into the running motor, rubbing sleep from our eyes and stifling yawns. Unfortunately, he was doing the same.

The next few hours passed in a blur, for all four of us. Admittedly, it was 5 am, but the driver kept dropping off to sleep whilst steering, startling himself awake moments later. At one point, we were weaving down a winding cliff-side road, entirely in the dark, and with the rainforest to the side shrouded in inky blackness. My mum and I sat tight in the back, eyes widened, silently staring out the window at the straight drop into the abyss. The driver pulled over eventually and grabbed a coffee from a petrol station. That seemed to perk him up and we arrived at the airport unscathed.

When you're not fretting about plummeting to your end, Sri Lanka is immensely beautiful. If you don't want to take my solemn word for it, it was voted Lonely Planet's number one place to visit in 2019. But the word 'beautiful' doesn't do it justice.

I look back at the photographs, conjuring my own memories. I was swamped by the prettiness of the scenery and the friendliness of the locals, but mainly, in all honesty, I remember the tuk-tuks. Sri Lanka was my first experience of that wonderfully weird form of transport, and they've stuck with me. It's the image that instantly springs to mind when I think of travelling.

There's something oddly charming about being squashed in the back of an autorickshaw, skin sticking to leather seats in the hazy heat, taking in the whirl and collision of colours outside. You sit and enjoy the contrast as different scenes whizz by: coconut plantations, traffic jams, a bustling street market. It's hectic, quaint and everything in between. I became accustomed to hailing a tuk-tuk in Sri Lanka, jumping in with ease and enjoying the ride. They're so familiar to me now. I recall the sights and smells partnered with the exhilaration of each tuk-tuk ride, and later trips to Southeast Asia have cemented my love of them.

I'd love to redo my earliest travels; I'd love to fully immerse myself in those places and take as many photos as I do now (not to post on Instagram, just to look back on). To be able to recall as much detail about my earliest trips as my more recent ones would be fantastic, because it's those first ones that encouraged the travel bug to burrow deep inside my veins. They sculpted me as a person, taught me defining life lessons.

Antigua instilled a passion for swimming in me, and now, I'm the first one in any pool. I love heading to Thorpe Lakes in the summer for a spot of open-water swimming, and I enjoy nothing more than the touch of cool water on my skin as I dip my toes in a pool, engulfed by the smell of chlorine.

Kenya taught me about the kindness of others. That lovable hotel cleaner didn't have to go the extra mile to make my trip special, but he did; his actions made an impression. So now, whenever I'm confronted by tough people (and trust me, there are a lot of them), I remember that there are nice individuals out there. Kenya encouraged me to strive to be one of the nice people, to try to put myself in others' shoes. I give to charity as much as I can, participate in fundraisers and even took up running so I could do a 10k for Alzheimer's UK and a 25k for the British Lung Foundation. (The Chloë who used to sidle out of GCSE PE would be stunned into silence to hear that.)

Dubai taught me that people have different views and there's always a way to flip a perspective, think about a situation differently. That trip made me more aware and respectful of other religions and beliefs. (Years later, I got an A$^+$ in my Religious Education GCSE exam, so, thanks, Dubai.)

In Sri Lanka, I developed a passion for animals that has followed me through my twenties. I'd love to rescue a dog from Battersea Dogs Home one day and provide it with the life it deserves. (I've also seen an adorable Stitch doggy bed in Primark that my future dog bestie will love. Just saying.)

It's those long-ago trips that shaped me as an individual and inspired me to get out into the world and see everything. Like Pringles, once I popped, I couldn't stop. Once I hopped off that plane in Antigua and stepped out into the muggy heat, I knew I had to keep going places. Seeing things. Living life.

Those early holidays injected my life with colour; they were the base wash, and later trips added layers over the top. I wish I could rewind them, like on a video camera, and watch each scene in detail, capturing everything in my memory forever, rather than recalling only vivid snippets. But I'm grateful for the snippets too because they're special. They're snapshots of the brilliant experiences I've had, experiences that have had such an impact on my future self.

8

Nit-Picking

The Dominican Republic

Later that same year, as winter approached with steely determination, we set off to the Dominican Republic. Darkness enveloped our suburban south London cul-de-sac the night before our flight. The dark sky loomed over our cosy home, expertly stirring a cocktail of snow, ice and roaring wind in its chilling clasp.

As the streetlights flickered on like magic, so did my hyperactivity. Put bluntly, that evening I was being incredibly irritating.

I was excitedly singing and dancing. I wouldn't go to sleep, and I kept harassing my stressed parents, who were haphazardly trying to pack our suitcases ready for the taxi arriving at 4 am. I wasn't usually like this when I was younger; I don't know why that particular evening ignited hidden annoying traits. I was hyped, ready to get on that plane and go.

My mum kept folding my holiday clothes neatly and placing them inside my little carry-on bag, only for me to whip them out immediately, convinced I was being funny, sniggering behind my hands. I remember it vividly. This saga dragged on for hours as my mum flew around the house, organising everyone's passports, plane tickets and luggage. "Chloë, if you don't stop this" – she sighed as she tried to locate a pair of shoes my dad was hunting for – "you won't have any clothes to wear."

Eventually, I tired myself out and fell asleep, and my mum and dad finally finished hurling items into their own cases and set the alarm, heading to bed too.

I woke up abruptly a few hours later to an oppressive pitch blackness. The house was silent, but birds were just starting to chatter outside my window. Jumping lightly out of bed, I scuttled to the hallway to spy if it was time to get up. Catching sight of our three locked cases, all packed and ready beside my mum and dad's bedroom door, a wave of panic hit me. What if I actually didn't have any clothes in there?

Hurriedly, I came up with a hare-brained scheme and shoved a handful of clean underwear and socks into my dad's camera bag, which was also propped by the door. I'm not sure why I thought to just pack underwear and socks but no actual clothes if I was so concerned there wouldn't be anything for me to wear. As it turned out though, it was lucky I did.

I shuffled back to bed, creeping along the hallway and diving back under my covers, proud of my initiative.

The next hour was a blur. My mum woke me what felt like minutes later and we hurried to get ready. We were running late and my dad was still in the bath when the taxi arrived. I was urged out the door and we sped to the airport. We checked our bags through security and settled down at the departure gate, waiting to board. All was well…until it wasn't.

When we arrived, in the humid heat of Puerto Plata, the Dominican Republic's third largest city, me sporting my massive clumpy trainers and winter wear, my mum opened my little bag on the hotel bed and gawped in horror. She'd forgotten to repack my suitcase in the stress of organising everything else, so I had no clothes other than what I was standing in.

So, it was lucky I'd packed underwear as a backup, but I did have to walk around the tropics looking mismatched as we trundled to hunt down appropriate clothes for me. You know – summer clothes, dresses and flip-flops, things I could actually wear on the beach instead of my huge, clodhopping trainers, woolly tights and coat.

After that minor blip, we had a great trip. Plus, I got a whole new wardrobe. Result.

My dad and I would canter down the beach on horse rides. My dad had the more obedient horse and no issues following our guide. But I got landed with the asbo horse. Maybe it was karma for being a brat earlier, but this animal was a literal anarchist. She wasn't taking orders from anyone or anything.

Although she was beautiful, with a glossy white mane, she sure wanted me to know that she was the one in charge there. She'd stop every two seconds to eat, pee or just veer off, abruptly jolting and hauling me into the undergrowth with her. I panicked the third time she trundled off the track and into the thicket, our guide and my dad disappearing from view on their respective horses, heading on up the path without me. After a while, though, my anti-social friend begrudgingly got her act together and followed suit, trotting after the others. I loved spending time with the horses; they were majestic, even if mine was a little mischievous.

When we weren't hanging with the menace of a mare, we made the most of the sunshine, a welcome change from the chilly London winter weather we'd left behind. Down at the beach, I watched in awe as tourists got their hair braided. I gawped as their strands were expertly twisted and secured with beautiful beads all colours of the rainbow, and I tugged at my mum and dad's sleeves, pointing.

Ever since I was young, I've had problems with my hair. I had cradle cap when I was small, and my hair, when it did finally decide to buck up and grow, would only appear in tufts on my head, just like with little orangutans. Maybe that's why I love orangutans so much: I understand their hair-care struggles.

I dreamt of having long, sweeping hair like my Bratz dolls or my friends at school. I would rush into our local Woolworths back home and spend ages checking each doll's hair for the ultimate swish factor. I tipped them all upside down to do the hair test before deciding which one could come home with us. My mum and nan always laughed, familiar with my various oddities and my need to do these checks. The dolls had to jump through hoops to secure my approval.

I wasn't just fascinated by head hair though. Whenever someone picked me up in their arms when I was young, my little fingers would always reach straight for their eyebrows to stroke. My nan would have to take her glasses off for me to get to hers. The rest of my family thought it was cute, whereas I think it's a massively creepy (and possible future serial-killer) trait for a child to possess, but hey, we all have our quirks.

Whenever my nan and pap came down to spend the weekend with us, I had a routine of rushing into their room at 6 am on the dot, armed with various *Mr Men* books for Pap to read me. Sometimes I'd bring hair scrunchies and clips (no idea why I had these, because my own hair would not facilitate) and I'd settle behind my nan to style her strands like a top hairdresser, tying it so it stood up straight on her head like a Who from Whoville. I loved playing with people's hair.

I desperately wanted to be able to French-plait my own hair like my friends or even just have enough tresses to fashion a ponytail. I used to wear a tea towel on my head, pretending it was my long princess hair. There are various photos of me up to the age of six with towels and flannels covering my scalp. I look back and smirk at younger me, but even now, I'm envious of girls with waist-grazing strands. I doubt that's something I'll ever achieve; my hair is just uncooperative.

So, when I saw these super cool colourful beads being eased onto the braids of that group of twenty-something girls on the beach in Puerto Plata, I desperately wanted some too. I wanted my hair to look like theirs. The problem though? They had hair to begin with.

I pleaded with my mum and dad and eventually they gave in. I got my beloved braids inserted on our last afternoon. There weren't even that many of them, because I literally had hardly any hair and the lady could only work with what was there. To cut a long story short, I was ecstatic with my new style. I loved it. As the beads were heavy, I could finally swish my hair like I'd seen other girls do. And, believe me, I didn't stop bloody well swishing here, there and everywhere.

Thinking about it reminds of that episode in *Friends* when Monica has her hair braided on holiday and then gets caught in the shower curtain rails because she's swinging her head about. That was pretty much me. I'd sit at the table, swishing my (still very short) hair, loving how it actually moved now, weighed down with the braids and beads. I wasn't used to that; usually my fair curls were just there, sticking out at weird angles. They wouldn't really grow below my ears, so I never actually had that feeling of hair around my shoulders. It was a fantastic novelty.

However, the same braids I was so immensely pleased with also harboured a number of unwanted friends and were a catalyst for a super stressful few weeks. Yeah, I'm talking about the dreaded nits. Head lice. Whatever you want to call them. I ended up with bugs crawling around my scalp, laying their gross eggs and multiplying. One of my literal nightmares.

The awful thing was that we didn't even realise I was contaminated until we were boarding the plane home. My mum suddenly spotted eggs in my scalp and was horrified she hadn't spied them before. When we landed at Heathrow, she hotfooted it into Boots, having spent the entire flight identifying more of the actual bugs moving in my hair. (I want to take this opportunity to formally apologise to anyone who got nits on a flight to London from the Dominican Republic in 2003. I'm still grossed-out myself.) She bought me some treatment and began applying it as directed as soon as we got home. My braids had to be removed too, and I was upset, not really understanding what was living in my damn hair.

Thinking she'd smothered them all, Mum sent me back to school a week later. I'd been totally clear for several days and all was fine. I played with my friends and went to classes, but that's when it happened. An ominous letter sailed home at the end of that week, addressed to all parents. It notified them that there had been a particularly nasty outbreak of head lice in school. My mum was mortified as it was clearly me who'd started it. She rechecked my head and all mine had gone, but by that time, it was too late. Much too late.

The next day, my classmate, a boy called Richard, abruptly interrupted form time. He stood up, looking sheepish, and proceeded to inform the whole class that he had started the outbreak. His mum had told him that he had to stand up and take responsibility for spreading them to us all. He publicly apologised.

Me? I sat there in awe, too embarrassed to utter a word, to pipe up and say that actually it was me who'd unleashed the epidemic, not him. I slid down in my seat and didn't say anything; I let him take the blame. So, Richard, if you're reading this for whatever reason, I'm publicly apologising this time. It was me who caused the head-lice infestation. My bad.

My good friend William also got them, and I remember his mum, Karen, telling us how he got oddly attached, becoming upset when the pesky creatures were washed down the plughole. My mum also ended up catching them from me; she only realised that little surprise in the middle of getting her hair cut, so that was an immensely embarrassing situation for her. She paid, ran red-faced out of the salon with wet, half-cut hair, and phoned Karen urgently, not knowing what the hell to do.

My dad was the only one who managed to escape the horror, and he just seemed perplexed at the chaos I'd caused. But, yes, I hold myself fully responsible for the outbreak and I'm mortified that Richard took the blame. I will forever cringe at my inability to admit that, indeed, I was the phantom nit culprit. If a lesson was learnt in the Dominican Republic, it was that if you've done the crime, you've gotta do the time.

Crocodile surfaces in a billabong, Australia

Dubai, United Arab Emirates

Bathing elephants, Sri Lanka

Sleeping koala bear, Eastern Australia

9

Coke-Fuelled Chipmunks

The Seychelles

In the Seychelles, my love of animals – bar head lice – continued to grow as I marvelled at chipper chipmunks and exotically expressive elephants in their natural habitats.

The Seychelles, an island nation just off East Africa, is as blissful as it sounds. At its mention, my mind flits to those Guylian chocolates you get in a box, the ones swirled with white and milk. Seashells. And the trip essentially was like a box of chocolates (with no intention to quote Forrest Gump): there was so much variety, so much to do, it was impossible to try everything. It was brilliant. Being so young at nine years old, it was all mesmerising to me.

When I think of the Seychelles, I think of its African elephants: gorgeous, magnificent creatures, so surprisingly graceful. My mum's favourite. But I also recall a unique culture, wonderful art and really friendly people, always eager to help, always loving a chat. There's a common theme building in these tales: the people we've met on our travels have invariably been both lovely and interesting. The images from our several different trips to Africa and the many memorable encounters we had there remain imprinted on my brain like the inky stamps in my passport.

Our Seychelles hotel, aptly named The Mermaid, stood tall on its private beach surrounded by its own coconut grove, but best of all were its resident gang of cheeky chipmunks, or palm squirrels, as they're known there. They would scurry about while we lounged poolside and they were adorable to watch, their little legs peddling their stripy bodies through the blades of grass. They reminded me of those furry little Disney twins, Chip and Dale, who terrorise Mickey Mouse's dog Pluto. They made me chuckle.

My mum was reading her book outside one afternoon, while my dad and I were on the beach, and when we returned, we saw that she was completely oblivious to the saucy chipmunk who had its head deep in the glass of Coca-Cola beside her. It was upside down, its little tail twitching, tongue stretching to reach the last droplets of coke. When it clocked us staring, it scrambled out, head getting stuck momentarily before it wrestled itself free and darted off, scurrying back up the towering tree, high on sugar.

Other than the mischievous 'munks, the mosquito bites were the main thing that stayed with me long after we returned to London. In fact, almost two decades on, I still have a faint scar from a particularly nasty one on the back of my leg. The bites themselves weren't too painful, sometimes we didn't even realise we had any, and we'd spend the day out in the sunshine only to get back to the room and discover oozing, awful blisters that then evolved into great bubbles of pus. I ended up with so many dotted over my legs. I must have delicious blood or something. I remember lying on my front and my mum telling me to gaze out at the chipmunks on our balcony to distract me, while she got a warm flannel and knocked the heads off the bites in swift movements, smothering the seeping mess in antiseptic cream.

While I was in awe of the long beaches, trying to explore every inch of that beautiful place, everyone else's focus was on something else. The American rock band Guns N' Roses were staying on a private boat anchored near our hotel. They appeared at the bar one night and gave us all an impromptu tropical concert, out of the blue. Admittedly, baby-faced me had no idea what was going on or who the hell these people were, interrupting my dinner. My parents educated me about music, but I'd never heard of Guns N' Roses. I wish I'd known how big they were back then; I would have paid more attention. I literally cringe when I think about how I essentially attended a free Guns N' Roses concert without knowing. I was too busy playing Spyro on my Game Boy to notice the musical legends in my vicinity. Priorities, I guess.

We spent the next blisteringly hot afternoon on the beach, me and my mum splashing about in the sea as my dad wandered off to get his camera from the room. We absently waved as he disappeared down the winding path back to the hotel. An hour passed, then two. He still wasn't back. We stood up and peered back towards the entrance to the hotel, but he was nowhere to be seen. Suddenly, my mum turned back to the coast, having caught sight of something in the sea.

Squinting into the distance, she noticed a figure sporting my dad's trademark baseball cap and paddling a kayak against the current.

The little boat was tipping and tilting, threatening to capsize with every shaky stroke of the paddles. Behind, in the distance, we could just make out the fancy Guns N' Roses yacht. The contrast, as you can imagine, was not a flattering one. "Is that Dad?" I exclaimed as the figure lifted an arm and waved from the kayak he'd randomly rented on a whim.

When my mum describes the scene, she recalls it was like watching a budget version of *Hawaii Five-O*, witnessing him bob about, unsteadily paddling closer. The sheer oddness of the situation. It was good fun though. I swam out to him, and we raced each other. Then I had a go at paddling too; my first kayaking experience and a turning point for me. My dad is never one for being bored, so rocking up in a kayak wasn't really that weird for him. Much weirder was the sudden change in weather on the last day of our trip.

Splashing about in the coolness of the pool, enjoying having it completely to myself, I was revelling in the quiet. Suddenly, the sun disappeared behind a jet-black cloud and the sky darkened to a deep, dark grey, weighed down like a water balloon ready to pop. My mum called over to me and hurriedly gathered up our stuff from the side of the pool as the heavens opened and began chucking down buckets of water. Lightning illuminated the skies and thunder rumbled ominously. Suddenly terrified that the lightning would strike the water and electrocute me, I swam as fast as my little legs could kick and scrambled out, anxiety welling as we raced up the hotel stairs, back to our room.

Sometimes I think back to that memory, so bright in my mind's eye, and I'm reminded that life is a lot like that sudden snap in the weather. Things can change in a second, from gloriously sunny to frighteningly stormy, and we need to live for now, enjoy every bit of happiness we can.

The rain halted as soon as I hurtled into our room. I watched from the balcony as the sun peeked out from behind the clouds again, turning the surroundings a beautiful hazy orange. This too shall pass.

10

The Woman Who Cried Fish

The Maldives

The Maldives is sky high on most bucket lists, immensely popular because of its tranquillity and peaceful, pampering vibes. I see it namechecked in every 'Places You MUST Visit' article whenever I absentmindedly flip through the glossy magazines in the dentist's waiting room. I spy it all over social media as people jet off there, labelling it a 'trip of a lifetime', a 'dream come true', the 'perfect paradise'. And it is. It's not one of those hyped-up destinations that's dismally disappointing when you arrive.

The Maldives – an archipelago nation comprised of around 1,200 idyllic islands surrounded by the north-central Indian Ocean – doesn't need a filter.

I was ten years old when we stayed at Laguna Island and I've been itching to get back there ever since. I still have a framed poster of the island hanging behind my bed. My dad bought it from the giftshop when I started to get upset about the prospect of having to return home. I didn't want to leave and certainly never wanted to forget our visit. I didn't want to trade balmy beaches for my cluttered school desk back in frosty London; I wanted us to live there forever.

It's probably my all-time favourite trip, mainly because everything was so serene and simple. It was a proper deserted-beach holiday – on a deserted beach that had everything we could possibly need on it. When I flick through old photo albums, I'm struck by how utterly beautiful it was. I'm always expecting to see Wilson, the bobbing ball from the Tom Hanks movie *Cast Away*, caught in the background of one of my snaps.

Laguna was a tiny dot in the Arabian Sea, encircled by miles of calm turquoise water. It consisted only of a hotel reception, a collection of pretty beach bungalows, a generous swimming pool, three restaurants, all serving delicious delicacies, and a small activities section, complete with table tennis. The island was so small, it took a mere fifteen minutes to do a complete circuit on foot.

I know this precise fact as I worried my mum and dad sick when I went off to play one day and hid from them as a search party scoured the island. That sounds bad, but I genuinely didn't know that I'd concerned them that much, otherwise I wouldn't have retreated into the greenery, sniggering to myself as I watched the commotion through my little binoculars. Okay, that sounds even worse. But I thought it was a game, a prank. To me, I was essentially winning at hide and seek; my parents just weren't aware we were playing.

We'd been enjoying a little table tennis tournament in the activities hut. The three of us had been taking it in turns. Whoever won out of me and my dad would play my mum and then we'd switch. I'd recently been given a video camera for my birthday, so I was fiddling with it when it wasn't my turn, shakily filming everything like I was a mini extra in *The Blair Witch Project*. When the match between my mum and dad stretched on, I wandered outside to get some cool frames on my camera, bored of watching them getting increasingly competitive. It was going to be a long game.

I scurried off to the pier and leant over the side, eager to catch a glimpse of some tropical fish. I taped them for a bit, marvelling at the explosion of colour they created under the ripples and gaping as a bright yellow fish with blue stripes nipped through the dancing seaweed and flitted under the boardwalk. That was the thing about the Maldives: the water was crystal clear, so you could see all the way down to the seabed. It made the clashing patterns of the fish quite magical.

After I'd finished filming the various sea creatures, I whipped around to spot my mum and dad emerging out of the table tennis hut to come after me. Thinking on my feet, I clambered away and ducked into the bushes, ready to jump out as they ambled past, but they must have headed in the other direction to look for me, because I never saw their feet pass. I could hear them calling in the distance but thought I could catch up with them further around the island and surprise them.

Refining my master plan, I scuttled ahead, secreting myself in the undergrowth so I could pounce unseen. Granted, I took my time, stopping to video cool snippets of my little adventure, but eventually, I grew tired of not bumping into them – or anyone, for that matter; the island was pretty much deserted, apart from two other couples.

I reached the heart of the island. The restaurants and pool came into view, like a mirage, and I pushed back the overhead branches to get a closer look. The area wasn't empty of people like it usually was; there were crowds milling about. I crept out of the bushes and was caught off guard when my parents rushed over, closely followed by the other people, who turned out to be members of the hotel staff. Everyone looked relived.

"Chloë, you shouldn't run off like that!" my mum scolded. Apparently, she and my dad had panicked when they couldn't see me anywhere and had begun to worry that I'd waded out into the sea. The hotel staff had offered to help search for me, and now, they were all fixing me with the same reproachful stare. I shuffled my feet, feeling guilty and awkward; my funny joke had backfired massively.

I didn't consciously attempt any more disappearing acts after that. But there was one time when I wandered off unconsciously. Literally. One night, my dad was startled by the rattling of the front door handle of our beach bungalow. Our little home on that trip was a mere five seconds' walk from the sand and we were woken every morning by bright rays of tropical sunshine peeping through the curtains. On this occasion, however, it was 2 am and pitch black outside.

Dad sat up and realised that it was me. I was trying to get out the door. "What are you doing?" he mumbled sleepily, peering through the dark at my little form attempting to twist the handle.

"I need to get the petrol," I replied urgently.

"What petrol?"

"For the lawnmower."

"Chloë, what are you talking about?"

"The petrol for the lawnmower. I'm late!"

My mum had woken by this point and they both had a giggle before guiding me back to my bed. I was adamant about having to mow that lawn (what lawn I'm not sure, as there wasn't a lawn on Laguna Island), but my dad insisted that it was fine and I could do it in the morning. No one would mind much.

Next morning, my mum and dad took great joy in telling me about the night-time kerfuffle. They were used to me sleepwalking at home, but I never had any recollection of what had happened, not even when I'd engaged in full conversations with them. We're a pretty strange family, sleep-wise.

Filming the fish was my new daytime obsession. My dad bought me an underwater camera from the hotel shop, and from then on, I spent a lot of time diving beneath the waves, clad in my goggles and wetsuit, snapping photos of the sea world. A Japanese woman who was staying on the island was also super into snorkelling, and I used to see her bobbing about all day, every day. We didn't become buddies exactly, but we'd forged that friendly holiday bond. Each party would smile with an awkwardly polite nod whenever we bumped into each other. She and her husband couldn't speak English and we sure as hell couldn't speak Japanese, so that was about as far as communication got.

Whenever we were in the sea at the same time, the Japanese woman would motion to us eagerly and exclaim at the swarms of fish zipping around the seabed. The first couple of days this was awesome. We'd wade over and I'd slip my goggles on and head under to see. But at the end of the day, there are only so many fish you can ogle before it gets a little old.

Me and my mum were splashing around in the water one day and the Japanese woman and her husband were also kicking about idly, holding their breath, sinking down into the ripples to spy on the marine life. This went on for a good half an hour.

The woman yelled over, as she usually did, pointing enthusiastically. She kept gesturing for us to come and look. "Fish!" she hollered, grinning as she disappeared under again. We smiled and nodded, but we'd seen a lot of sea beings by this point. We'd probably even found bloody Nemo, given the sheer number of fish we'd tracked over the last week.

Mum and I carried on paddling and the woman carried on snorkelling. Her husband was a little further out but seemed to be happy as Larry, his head wobbling like a buoy on the gentle waves.

"Hey!" the woman shouted again, waving both arms this time.

"Is she ever going to get bored of those bloody fish?" my mum muttered as she turned, plastering on a smile as the woman yelled again.

"Hey!" She cupped her hands over her mouth to increase the carry of her voice and pointed energetically.

"Yeah. Hi." We nodded awkwardly, waving back politely and continuing to float placidly. We really didn't want to see any more fish. We'd been there, done that, multiple times.

Well, it turned out the woman's attention had been swerved from the fish, for good reason.

My mum and I almost jumped out of our skin as the hotel lifeguard suddenly appeared out of nowhere, splashing past us as he dived into the deep. He swam with force over to where the husband was, now barely visible in the distance. He'd apparently got leg cramp while he was snorkelling and couldn't swim back to shore; he'd ended up where the waves were choppier and panicked as he was swept further out. He shouted over to his wife and secured her attention. How, I don't know, because she was so engrossed in those fish.

The woman had actually been yelling to us for help, but because she'd been shouting in the same manner and gesturing as she had done many times before, we'd assumed she just wanted to show us more of the damn marine life. It was a real-life version of the boy who cried wolf. Or, you know, the woman who cried fish.

Yes, we felt awful. We watched in horror as the lifeguard scooped up the man with ease and hauled him back to shore. I'm happy to report that the guy was totally fine – no thanks to my mum and me.

11

The Phantom Shoe Snatcher

Borneo

Borneo was all about the orangutans for me. It was 2006, late August, and I was approaching my eleventh birthday. I remember being so excited to see these creatures. They're adorable and I was in awe of them: their tufty hair (yeah, I know the struggle; I bet they don't resort to dodgy beach braids in desperation though), their big, wide eyes, how they're so like us yet so different. I was buzzing to see them in their natural habitat. Even now, if there's a documentary on TV about orangutans, we love to watch and get immersed, like we're back in Borneo again.

My favourite stuffed animal growing up was my little orangutan, Bernie Bobs. Until I was twelve, he came on all our holidays. He's probably the most well-travelled toy on the planet. I'm amazed he never got mislaid somewhere. He's infamous in our family. He even went to Cyprus with my nan and pap on his own. I'd slipped him into my unsuspecting nan's handbag at the last minute so he could enjoy a holiday, and my nan didn't even notice. By the time she discovered the little stuffed monkey peeking out of her hand luggage, they were boarding and my mum and I were already on our way home from dropping them at the airport.

My nan texted Mum to tell her Bernie had been found as a stowaway in her bag but was safe and that she and Pap would take care of him. But they didn't just take care of him; she and Pap proceeded to take my orangutan everywhere, setting up mini photoshoots. They made me a photo album with pictures of him in banana trees, enjoying dinner, sunbathing with my nan, sitting next to my pap at the ruins and reading a book. Bernie had a fun-packed trip indeed. I love looking back at that album; I'm touched by the thoughtfulness of my grandparents. But I do chuckle as I imagine the locals in Cyprus staring in amazement as my nan and pap fished out a stuffed toy at the dinner table.

So, there's Bernie's backstory. He's been present for a lot of our trips and seen more than your average cuddly animal. When we jetted off to Borneo, he was temporarily reunited with his real-life family. But before we made our way to the jungle to meet them, we headed to the beach in Kota Kinabalu and spent a few days soaking up the sun at our hotel, the Tanjung Aru, recovering from our jetlag.

It was fantastic. I recall spending hours swimming up and down, enjoying the sunshine and the heat. My dad and I went down to the beach a few times, but the hotel staff warned us it wasn't safe at that time of year as the crocodiles liked to come up and bask on the sand. So, after a quick glance at the coastline, which was beautiful, we decided not to take a swim in the sea. My dad got some cool photographs of the fire dancers who performed on the sands at night though. Incredible to watch as they were, I was always on the lookout for a sneaky croc sloping out of the water to gobble us all up. Thankfully, that never happened.

At last, it was officially time to go and see the orangutans. We woke early that morning as we had to catch a short flight up north. Bleary-eyed, we stumbled to the taxi and made it to the airport; they upgraded us on the plane for free, so that was a plus. Mum and Dad enjoyed a coffee on the flight, and within the hour, we were landing.

The Sepilok Orangutan Rehabilitation Centre was set up in 1964 and spans forty-three square kilometres of protected Kabili Sepilok Rainforest. Its team of experts rescue injured and orphaned orangutans, many of whom have lost their families because of habitat fires or deforestation. The primates are nursed back to health at the facility's medical centre and looked after until they're ready to be released into the wild. The babies go to jungle school and learn how to forage for food and behave in a self-sufficient way. The youngest are often paired with an older orphan so that they will mimic them.

The experience of Sepilok was inspiring. It was one of the best sanctuaries I've visited. We really felt the connection between the staff and the primates; it was clear that this was a special place and the orangutans were loved and taken care of to the very highest standards. At the same time, they were encouraged to roam freely and get used to life among the trees before they were released.

Sepilok didn't seem like an attraction; it wasn't a tourist trap. As soon as we entered, it felt like we were just venturing into the jungle, and we were. We were heading into the original habitat of these orangutans; it was nothing like I expected a sanctuary to be and totally different from the tourist-orientated Monkey Forest in Bali. It was as though we were seeing them in the wild. All visitors had to stick to the designated pathways through the forest and could not handle any of the orangutans.

We walked through a massive thicket, down a meandering wooden path, with everything green and open and the trees towering sky high above us. It sounded like a rainforest, with birds squawking, water running and leaves rustling. Well, it was a rainforest. We were urged to keep our voices down; we had entered the orangutan's home, after all. I mean, I'd hardly be enthused to be chilling out in my living room, calmly going about my evening and have a group of people I didn't know amble in and stand staring at me, eyes like saucers, bringing commotion and chaos with them.

As I stood quietly gazing up at a fully grown orangutan, her baby, who was clinging on to her, turned his tufty head around to eyeball me, and I was reminded with a jolt that these were real animals. I locked eyes with the adorable little creature and smiled.

My mind was transported briefly to somewhere I used to go when I was younger: the Rainforest Café in London. If you've been, you'll know how iconic it is. If not, let me explain.

The Rainforest Café is a hidden gem situated near Piccadilly Circus. As soon as you duck in, out of the thronging London streets, you're whisked into a tropical rainforest. Your senses struggle to keep up as your eyes adjust and your brain works a million miles a minute. You've just been scurrying down Shaftesbury Avenue, swept up in the sea of busy commuters, buses roaring by, tourists chattering, cars and taxis beeping their horns, street performers singing and dancing, but then suddenly, you're here, inside this café, and it's like you blinked for a few hours rather than a second; you must have boarded a plane and set off across the world without realising.

Inside the Rainforest Café, there are craftily placed speakers playing jungle sounds on a loop: the soft patter of water dropping onto leaves, birds squawking, various animals prowling. You make your way through the shop, with its scarily realistic crocodile in the corner – when I was little, you'd throw a penny in and he'd move and snarl – beneath a ceiling decorated with hanging branches and leaves, like a real-life jungle. You descend the stone steps to the restaurant, a subterranean paradise where the tables are shaped like trees and the chairs are painted like the backsides of different animals – lions, tigers and zebras.

Imagine stepping foot in somewhere like that as a child. It was magical and I loved it. I've been back since and it was still incredible to behold.

But Borneo? It was like the Rainforest Café sprung to life. I was expecting a friendly waiter to waltz over and take our dinner order. It was like being back there. But of course, everything was real. The leaves that hung down and tickled our faces as we wove our way between the trees weren't plastic. The orangutans that observed us quietly from the undergrowth weren't mechanical.

So, we'd seen some amazing sights at Sepilok, we'd been up-close and personal with the orangutans and had thoroughly enjoyed our visit. With our jaws on the floor from all we'd witnessed that morning, it was time to return to the airport and catch our flight back. The plane wasn't leaving until late afternoon though, so we were dropped off at a nearby hotel with the other guests on our trip and encouraged to relax until our flight.

The hotel was nice. Dad and I had brought our swimwear, so we splashed about in the welcomingly cool water of the pool. They had a terrifically twisty-turny waterslide and I was very impressed. My mum read her book in the sun, and we had lunch. About half an hour before we were due to leave for the airport, the sun began to set, casting shadows over the poolside. Dad and I jumped out and went off to get dressed. I emerged from the women's changing rooms ready to go, wringing water out of my curls, the familiar, overpowering smell of chlorine mingling with the scent of my half-washed-off sun cream.

I ambled over to sit down with my mum on the sun loungers and we glanced around, wondering where Dad was. Mum peered over her sunglasses; we would miss our shuttle to the airport if he didn't hurry up.

Dad emerged from the men's changing rooms eventually, rushing over to us, looking panicked and dishevelled. "Someone's stolen my shoes," he said, desperately flipping his bag inside out, frantically checking under our sunbeds.

"But you had them. They were next to the pool." Mum pointed behind her but trailed off; the spot where Dad had so precisely placed his shoes was empty.

Now, this isn't a big thing, right? It would be a minor inconvenience for most people. But allow me to explain why someone hotfooting it away with my dad's shoes was so odd.

The morning we'd left home, the taxi had arrived at 5 am. My mum and I got in the back, having stowed our suitcases in the boot. My dad had woken up late and was still packing while we waited in the taxi, our flight time ticking closer. The driver was tapping his fingers loudly on the wheel, drowning out the low thrum of the radio. I yawned and gazed out at our quiet street. It was still dark and our usually busy road was a ghost town. Early morning mist was seeping through the trees. The only other sound was the first birds chirping, waking too early, confused by the light pollution and our taxi chugging away.

My dad emerged a few minutes later, laden down with his bags. He jumped in the front seat, full of apologies, and we screeched off, only just making our check-in deadline. It was when he went to take off his shoes to go through security at Heathrow that he audibly gasped. My mum turned to see what was happening and looked horrified. Dad had slipped his old shoes on to put the bins out that morning and had then kept them on by accident, being distracted and busy rushing around. Those shoes were what he now stood in. The airport security guard gazed down at his feet with a raised eyebrow.

Now these shoes weren't just old, no. They were what my dad kept for when he was painting the house or doing messy DIY jobs. They had holes in them, they were splattered with white paint. They looked exactly like the homeless man's shoes Simon swaps his trainers with in *The Inbetweeners* episode where the group are trying to get into the club. Actually, no, I think Dad's were worse.

So, of course, when my dad rushed over in a tizz by the pool in Borneo, insisting his shoes were gone, had been taken, we were astounded. Who on earth would steal his scruffy, paint-splattered shoes? Who the hell would want them, because even he didn't. But he needed footwear in order to board the flight, so we jumped into action.

As I mentioned earlier, this wasn't the first time my dad had had his footwear stolen. The person who nabbed the shoes before, though, back in Bali with my mum and Auntie Rani, at least left slippers for him instead. In Borneo, there was nothing left in exchange for my dad's manky shoes.

We looked everywhere. My mum went to reception and when asked to describe them was so embarrassed, she turned bright red. She felt the need to go into the whole backstory so that the hotel staff didn't think these awful things were his best shoes. We searched for ages, confused. Where the hell had they disappeared to? Our shuttle was ready to set off, and all the other guests were boarding.

"You'll have to buy some flip-flops from the giftshop," my mum advised as she bundled our stuff together.

My dad was aghast. "I'm not wearing flip-flops!" he exclaimed. He's not a flip-flop kind of person by any standards. Back in London, he's seldom seen without his trademark T-shirt, smart trousers and blazer combo. He certainly doesn't own a pair of flip-flops and the idea of purchasing some right then was out of the question. He headed off to the giftshop anyway, to find something.

Suddenly, the friendly hotel cleaner came rushing over, proudly clutching – you guessed it – the shambolic shoes. My dad was delighted, because he wouldn't now have to wear flip-flops after all. My mum was relieved we could finally get going but also exasperated – what would it take to rid ourselves of those bloody things? It turned out that the lady cleaning the pool had thought someone had left them as rubbish (obviously; I mean, if you saw the state of those things, you'd have come to the same conclusion) and whisked them away to chuck. Hearing the commotion, she'd brought them back out just in case. I'm sure she was shocked to find out that, yes, indeed, these were what the fuss was about.

So, at the end of this sob story, unlike in Bali, my dad did get his shoes back. We bundled off to the airport, made our flight in the nick of time, and returned to our original hotel in Kota Kinabalu to enjoy the rest of our holiday and hopefully stow the damn shoes under the bed, away from my mum's line of sight.

In the days that followed, we explored the expansive hotel gardens and grounds, ate delicious food and relaxed. My dad edited his orangutan photographs and proudly showed my mum and me his impressive work. He got some fantastic snaps of the mother and baby swinging through the trees; really immersive pictures. Every time I look at them, I'm transported back there to the smells and sounds of the jungle. Magical.

On my eleventh birthday, we had dinner at this great place by the sea, in the fishing village down the road from our hotel. I had a pizza twice as big as my head and texted my friends back home on my new phone, my iconic lilac LG Chocolate. Ah, remember when phones had buttons and you couldn't access a whole internet of secrets and the deep dark web in a single tap? Yeah, me neither.

The last few days of the trip passed in an excitable blur and soon it was time to go home. We did some last-minute shopping, picking up souvenirs and postcards for my nan and pap, Nana Cath and the rest of our family. I also bought a cool baseball cap for myself; it was baby pink and emblazoned with flowers, and I absolutely loved it. It had the initials 'BS' scrawled across it, but I liked the design and didn't think the letters mattered.

Well, I wore that hat everywhere and it became a staple of my holiday wardrobe on many trips from then on, until I jetted off to Spain with my cousins and aunties when I was seventeen. Drew pointed out that 'BS' likely stood for 'bullshit'.

"What?" I stared at him in confusion.

He began to laugh. "That's what it stands for, Chloë."

"But I've been wearing it everywhere since I was eleven!" I spluttered, appalled.

I think about that hat a lot and how asbo I must have looked strolling around the pool. An otherwise angelic-seeming eleven-year-old making such a bold statement (as I carried around my stuffed monkey like a mascot on my shoulder – really cool, Chloë). BS indeed.

Laguna Island, The Maldives

Newly born turtles, Seychelles, Indian Ocean

Remote palm fringed beach, Seychelles, Indian Ocean

Baby orangutan, Borneo rainforest, Malaysia

Part Two
A Mutant Anxiety Wasp

12

No Ransom Needed

Goa

Goa was a fantastically festive holiday, a welcomed escape from my terrifying first few terms at secondary school as a fresh-faced Year 7. It was my first Christmas away and an amazingly odd experience to celebrate December 25th on a beach in southern India.

For me, that time of year was all about the cold, with its snow scenes, frost and sparkling white-topped houses. All our Christmases prior had been spent in chilly London, staying cosy inside our home. We'd open presents in our jammies and enjoy a day ignoring the ghastly weather, instead focussing on turkey with all the trimmings, pigs in blankets and Yorkshire puddings swimming in gravy. We often had family to stay. My Auntie Shell would usually bring my cousin Drew down and we'd have so much fun. We'd leave out mince pies, brandy and carrots for Santa Claus and Rudolph and wake up to find piles of presents, our eyes wide as saucers with excitement.

And that was just last year. No, I'm joking, of course; we were much smaller. We were always astounded when we rushed downstairs on Christmas morning to find the brandy and mince pies gone and a bite taken out of the carrot (courtesy of my dad). Santa had officially been! He always left a scrawled note, and Rudolph would even leave a hoof print (my family are so extra at Christmas, I love it).

Most years, Nana Cath would come down and spend the festive period with us. One year, I'd been given an EyeToy webcam for my PlayStation 2. Those were the days! Ah, remember the prized PlayStation? I do. I'd been so excited when my friend at school had got one, I'd rushed to ask my mum if I could have one for Christmas. She laughed and said I'd have to see what Santa bought. I went quiet and after a few minutes piped up, "Mum, what is a PlayStation?"

Well, Drew, Nana Cath and I were playing on my new contraption in the living room. Drew was getting into the motions – I think it was boxing or something – and when my nana stood up behind him to sidestep to the kitchen he whipped around and hit her square in the face. Whack! It was an accident, of course, but he was mortified. My auntie, mum, dad and I rushed over to make sure Nana Cath was okay, but she laughed it off. That's the kind of Christmases I remember: family orientated, wintry scenes outside, staring at the frost from the warm. Maybe not the accidental assault, that wasn't the norm, but the rest was.

My nan and pap would travel down some Christmases too. We've had some truly special days with them, excitedly opening stockings on Christmas morning, enjoying snapping photos of us clad in matching Santa hats, telling bad jokes over dinner. My pap is the king of bad jokes, so Christmas crackers are right up his street. That's what the festive season is about – extended family; so, Christmas in Goa was completely different.

We arrived at our pre-booked digs in Goa a few days before the twenty-fifth, and, well, let's just say it was nothing like the photos online. A very abrupt manager greeted us as we hopped out of the taxi. He turned on his heel when he saw us struggling towards him and left us to hurry after him as he shot off into the distance to show us our room. We passed an alarming-looking pool devoid of water, with brown marks snaking up the sides and the concrete cracking. It looked like a crime scene. Hoping our room was at least okay, we ducked into the doorway the manager had disappeared through. Our faces fell in unison. There was damp on the walls, a bug was crawling across the ceiling and the bed had a red splatter on the sheet. Oh, Lord. No way.

The manager thrust a huge chain into my dad's hands and explained that we could lock ourselves in for the night. He gestured to the door, which had inhuman scratch marks down it, like it had been broken into a thousand times. This room didn't just look like it had seen better days, it looked like it had hosted a bloody séance and the demon was still lurking around, scratching at the doorframe to get out. Yeah, buddy, same.

So that, my friends, was when we got the hell out of there and left the demon to it. No way were we staying in American Horror Stories' Hotel Cortez at Christmas. No freaking way.

My mum hurriedly googled nearby hotels, but they were all fully booked, obviously, it being Christmas. "What about the hotel we stayed in before?" she said to my dad. "The Goan Heritage?" This was where mum and dad had stayed on their previous trip to Goa, twenty years earlier, well before I was born.

By now, the bug scuttling across the ceiling of our room had multiplied into two. Things were getting a little too murdery for our liking, so we booked a taxi straightaway, before we'd even checked to see if the Goan Heritage had rooms. We zipped over there at speed, and as it loomed into view, we breathed a sigh of relief. It was a truly welcome sight.

Luckily, they did have a couple of rooms left after some last-minute cancellations. My dad headed back to Murder Central to pick up our bags and cancel our reservation, and we checked into the Goan Heritage instead. It was different to how Mum and Dad remembered it. They'd loved it before, but now, it was even more beautiful. Situated in a prime location, right on Calangute Beach, it had blossomed into a really fabulous little hotel comprising bungalows prettily set around a generous pool (which, yes, actually had water in it, and no, didn't look like a grisly murder scene, shock horror). Two decades ago, there'd been nothing but the hotel, and the beach had been empty but exquisite. The beach was still immensely beautiful, but there were now plenty of restaurants and bars on it, and a lot more to do.

Now that we weren't having to grapple with the possibility that our Christmas might be spent chaining ourselves inside our room to keep out literal murderers or ending up with our faces on 'MISSING TOURISTS' posters all over town, we settled down to unpack.

The beach was visible from the rooms, and we quickly made our way down onto the sand, eager to get in the sea. Slipping my flip-flops off, I scooped them up and began to run towards the waves. The pain took a moment to register in my mind, but suddenly, I was hopping. I threw my flip-flops down and slid them back on in a flurry, but with each step, the sand still shifted to touch the skin on my feet, and it burnt. The sand was like the fiery pits of hell.

From then on, I always wore proper footwear down to the beach unless it was late in the afternoon and the sun had stopped beating down, making the sand a lava pit. Instead, I spent the afternoons lounging in one of the hanging sun seats and watching the waves lap as I read my Mary-Kate and Ashley books and enjoyed the peace.

On Christmas morning, there was no snow, no lounging in our pyjamas with the heating on. Instead, we exchanged just a few presents when we woke up, little ones that we'd been able to pack in our suitcases, then pottered about the hotel, enjoying a swim in the pool, a walk down the beach and a paddle in the sea. Christmas morning was spent immersed in the turquoise ocean with the smell of saltwater in my hair and on my skin. It didn't feel like Christmas at all, not when we were sitting on the beach, wearing sandals instead of snug socks and ogling the waves as we wrote postcards and texted our family 'Merry Christmas' back home.

When darkness enveloped the resort, tables and chairs were hauled out onto the sand for Christmas dinner. We sat around the table, enjoying the lanterns illuminating the dark, listening to the rustle of the palm trees and watching the skinniest Santa Claus I'd ever seen doing his rounds, greeting children and wishing everyone a merry Christmas. We devoured turkey with all the trimmings, roast potatoes, Brussels sprouts, the full Christmas works. My mum revelled in the fact that she hadn't had to cook it for once, but we did miss our family and our home festivities. So when we got back, we did Christmas again. Even so, experiencing such a special time of year in a different climate was exciting to say the least.

*

It was in Goa that I had my first encounter with the social anxiety bug. I returned to the room after Christmas dinner that night to get my Game Boy (Game Boys, what happened to them? They seemingly dropped off the face of the earth) and was on my way back across the sand with it when a German boy of around my age jumped out from the bushes. I jolted in surprise.

"Do you want to play tag?" he asked, his mouth full of turkey.

I felt a stab of anxiety in my stomach. I was startled at having been ambushed and this uncomfortable feeling swarmed over me like a plague of buzzing locusts. What was wrong with me? He was a harmless kid, and I'd spoken to other children before, lots of times. I smiled awkwardly, unsure how to say 'No, thank you'. He repeated himself and watched me expectantly. So, I did what any newly socially awkward kid would do: I literally ran away.

Later, I was so embarrassed at how I'd obviously come across as rude that whenever I saw him and his parents at the breakfast table or around the pool, I hid. Eventually, they checked out, but I still cringe at how weirdly I'd behaved.

Usually, I'd have been chatting to other kids I met on trips; I'd be making friends on the beach, enjoying lively new relationships. I look back and wonder what happened to my ability to natter to anyone and everyone. My social anxiety seemed to creep up gradually and then explode like a firework as I entered secondary school.

I used to make friends as quick as a flash when I was little, and although I'd still get my mum to accompany me on playdates when I was small, once I got over the initial worry, I'd be fine. I had lots of friends at primary school.

But entering secondary school just three months before Goa seemed to set off this clambering chain of events in my brain, allowing the anxiety demon to weave its way into my daily thought processes.

I began to whittle about speaking in front of my class and hated being paired with anyone I didn't know. I'd worry intensively and incessantly, feeling my stomach tighten like someone was squeezing my insides as a stress ball.

I'd obsess over class presentations weeks before the date, anxiously hoping the teacher would forget that it was my turn to speak in public.

Everything was so much bigger than me. The building was overwhelming and cold, and there wasn't any of that familiarly. Plus, I was pretty short for my age, so it felt like everything was looming over me. When I turned up on my very first day, clad in my oversized blazer and massive satchel, I felt swamped by how tall the other kids were. I was instantly less confident and retreated into my shell.

Even now, I prefer to keep my circle small and still get immensely anxious whenever I have to speak to someone I don't know. I'm filled with dread. It's like the actual world is ending. I'm getting better at it though. Ironically, I'm a journalist, so it's literally my job to talk to people.

Working at the doctor's surgery during university helped me massively. I began to grow as an individual, and interacting with people from all walks of life each day forced me out of my bubble. When I nabbed my first job as a reporter on a local paper, I pushed myself further, setting out alone to cover breaking news and interviewing people and chatting with them so I could tell their fascinating stories. Since then, I've been moving on up, becoming more capable and confident.

I'm an odd one though, and I'm the first to admit it. My personality always seems to be at war with itself. If you were a star sign fanatic, you'd say it's because I'm on the 'cusp of exposure', being both a Leo and a Virgo, polar opposites. If you're not, then I'm just a random mix of a soul who likes socialising but also needs space.

My whole personality is based on juxtapositions. I'm an introvert, but I'm super nosy and I always love to know what's going on. I'm softy spoken, but I have strong opinions on things that I'm passionate about. I hate over-sharing, but I got sucked into the social media vortex for several years. I became too eager to be the same as everyone else, posting on Instagram incessantly until I didn't know myself anymore.

I love travelling, but I also yearn to snuggle up at home with a good novel and a cup of tea. I adore getaways but revel in coming back to London, where I'm familiar with everything, where the staff at my three local branches of Costa know my order as soon as they set eyes on me. "Small vanilla latte?"

Having these contrasting traits is exhausting, and as a result, I worry about how people perceive me. I'm a creature of habit and, like many other anxiety sufferers, I truly wish I could switch the incessant rambling in my head off. I'm constantly on the alert for danger, as if I'm watching for a roaming lion about to snap its jaws and scrunch my head between its teeth. My fight or flight response is always switched up to high voltage. Ironically, when I was in close proximity to a prowling lioness in Kenya, I felt zero anxiety. But speaking to people...? Mass hysteria. Logic. Thanks, brain.

At every single parents' evening at school, teachers would invariably quip to my mum and dad:

"Chloë's doing well, but she could try speaking up in class."

"Chloë is a great little student, but she needs to contribute more."

"Chloë's work and ideas are fantastic, but she doesn't voice them to others as well as she could."

It was like they were all reading from a script, and I don't know about you, but when people are telling me I need to talk more, just for the sake of it, it makes me automatically want to speak less. Funny that.

In secondary school, I just blended into the background, my confidence from primary years all but disappeared. To make matters worse, none of the teachers seemed to notice I was struggling socially. Halfway through reading report card comments to my mum and dad during Year 8s parents' evening, a particular teacher referred to me as 'Lizzie' (my friend's name), instead of 'Chloë'. My mum was understandably annoyed at this, and it turned out that the flustered teacher had indeed got us muddled and was reading from Lizzie's notes. We often got mixed up, but other than the fact that we were around the same height, there was nothing similar about us.

That doesn't give you too much confidence in the education system, does it? After that, the feeling that I was indeed a forgettable member of the class was cemented and I found it even harder to speak up. I mean, they didn't even know who I was.

Lizzie and I joke about it now, the fact that we seemed to be interchangeable. I'm glad I ended up at that school in a way, though, because Lizzie and I had attended the last years of primary school together, and when we found ourselves at the same secondary school, our friendship lasted the years. I'm grateful to still have a wonderful coffee pal like her and to have someone who's known me all that time. We've seen each other change significantly and we've gone through a lot together, good and bad, but I can't imagine ever not being friends with her. I still keep in touch with a few of the members of our former group, so the valuable relationships I took from there were massive positives.

But it was tough to make friends when I hit secondary school, even more so as I got older. I find it incredibly anxiety-provoking even now. Plus, my classes at secondary school were nothing like my carefree days at St Mark's Primary. Back there, I talked a lot, I yapped on and on; I was happy speaking. The teachers knew me; they didn't get me confused with my friends.

My mum would be waiting outside at pick-up time and my class would always be at least five minutes late every day. Our teacher, Mrs Knapp, would usher us all out and joke to my mum, "Sorry we're late. You know how Chloë likes to put her coat and hat on before she goes anywhere." They would both chuckle knowingly and smile down at me as I peered out from under one of my various hats that matched my different dresses.

At the end of the school day, we all had to wait until everyone was ready so we could hold hands and head outside together. When the bell rang (and only then), I would go over to the coat rack and button myself up smartly, proudly slipping on my bright red school hat with the bow on the front. I'd then make sure my book bag was packed neatly. This routine was probably carried out to the dismay of my classmates, who were doubtless itching to get out. But we were all fond of each other and there was no tut-tutting, no rolling of eyes. Everyone in the class treated each other as friends.

So, this made the socially awkward encounter in Goa even more marked. It represented a massive shift for me. From then on, I would always have to make a conscious effort with my social skills. I'd always have to put up with butterflies tickling my insides, my palms getting sticky with sweat and it being impossible to sit still whenever I was faced with a speaking presentation or having to read an essay aloud in class. Secondary school was like being thrown into shark-infested waters.

The way I just ran away from that poor boy in Goa like some proper oddball makes me shake my head and chuckle now. Although it wouldn't be truthful to say it hasn't crossed my mind to behave in the exact same way since. You bump into a friend of a friend who you have on social media but low-key cannot stand? Just run away. You get to the counter, latte ordered, and your card gets declined in front of a massive queue of whispering, watching people? Just run away. Works like a charm.

I do say this with lashings of sarcasm. It's probably not the best or most normal way to deal with your problems, and to be honest, people might think you're totally bizarre. But if you're cool with that, as I am, then it's great life advice to fall back on, in my solitary opinion.

In all seriousness though, those are the things that immediately spring to mind when I think about Goa: that awkward as hell encounter, the burning hot beaches, and the murder hotel. All the same, it was a lovely Christmas break in the sun, and at least, we didn't end up on Goa's answer to Crimewatch. But with all my newfound whittling, I'm sure any potential kidnapper would have handed me back within five minutes, no ransom needed.

13

Hysterical Elephant Rides

Koh Samui

People sometimes ask if it was lonely growing up as an only child and I always answer with complete honesty that it never felt that way to me. I've always been happy with my own company, eager to either get stuck into the chapters of a thrilling novel, sit drawing for hours or make up my own stories and jot them down in notebooks. But I've also always been close to my cousins, so they're more like siblings, especially Drew, who's eight months younger than me; we were always together.

I don't feel I missed out. I enjoy spending time with my parents and grandparents, plus, although I had loads of little friends at primary school, I gravitate towards the introvert lifestyle. Having a sibling would have altered my personality hugely. Maybe I'd have been louder and more confident or maybe I'd have retreated further into my shell.

I'm more than happy with my life though, and I've never felt lonely not having a brother or sister to grow up with. It just meant my dad had to play dinosaurs with me and my mum had to line up my Snow White figures instead.

It just meant my nan had to play Hop 'N' Pop (the only board game I loved) with me for hours on end, my pap would accompany me on the carousel I sought out in the town centre and Nana Cath would write to me every month without fail. I was and still am content with my only child status.

When we flew to the Thai island of Koh Samui, I was twelve years old. I'd survived the daunting first year at secondary school and even made a few good friends there, but it was still a scary place. I'd been thrust into this mix of different children, lessons, surroundings and routines, and although I was trying really hard, it still reminded me of those horrific horror houses at funfairs. Without the fun.

Since that blip the year before in Goa, when I'd literally run away from an innocent kid wanting to play tag with me, my social anxiety had been bubbling under the surface like a witch's cauldron. Some days it was okay, and I rocked up to school, enjoyed some of my classes, giggled with my friends at lunchtime and visited their houses when the bell rang to signal the end of the day. Other days, my group was split up and I'd have no familiar faces in my lessons or there'd be a dreaded seating plan. I'd fret, my mind entangling itself in webs of worry as I counted the hours until home time.

You'd think I'd have shuffled further into the safety of my shell when we were on Koh Samui, but I didn't. I mean, if I couldn't conjure up a conversation with a schoolmate who lived in the same town and shared similar experiences to me, how on earth would I chat to a child with a vastly different life in Thailand, right? But it was easier to talk to them, and I found that my social anxieties dissipated like a puff of smoke. The witch's worry caldron merely simmered instead of threatening to explode.

To this day, I use that Thai trip as an example of how I can control my anxiety, how my anxiety can't physically stop me doing anything. That was the first time I pushed through the initial freak-out and achieved what my brain insisted I couldn't.

Speaking to the kids who lived near the beach on Koh Samui was simpler; they were upfront, non-judgemental. I remember thinking, ugh, I wish we could live here; these people are so nice, so easy to natter to. It was lovely sharing details about our contrasting lives. Also, they were pushy in the best possible way and wouldn't take no for an answer, so I kind of had to pipe up and answer their incessant questions about London fashion and weather, and the language. Sometimes I need to be gently pushed into doing things, speaking to people or having new experiences, or else my anxiety will talk me the hell out of it. Trust me.

"Chloë! Chloë!" the group of girls would shout as I loped awkwardly through the clearing in the palm trees and out onto the beach early each evening, armed with my camera. They'd wave and motion eagerly as they dashed over. In the photos of us, the backdrop of glistening sea and setting sun seems so unreal in its perfection, it's as if there was a green screen.

We talked about their school lives, they asked me what I was studying, what my favourite subjects were, and we compared our days. They were learning English and loved to practise. My Thai wasn't up to scratch; they taught me the odd word and screeched with laughter as I inevitably failed to pick up the phrases. So, we'd settle for something universal and play tag, racing up and down the beach, flip-flopped feet sliding in the sand as we giggled.

Koh Samui stands out in my mind because of the fond memories I have of those brief friendships. It also stands out for its picture-perfect views. The second largest island in Thailand and well known for its golden beaches and equally golden locals, Koh Samui is a must-see if you're going to Thailand or even Asia generally. It's a standard gap-year favourite, famed for its full-moon parties and beach bars, but even if you're not into that kind of thing or if, like I was, you're too young to do shots all night as you sway to the music and brandish multi-coloured glow sticks, there's still plenty to do and see.

Many of the beach destinations I describe in this book might sound similar, being fringed with palm trees and graced with invitingly calm water, but there's a world of difference between their cultures and landmarks, and between the lives of the people that live, say, on a beach in Thailand and on a beach in Hawaii. Koh Samui is so much more than its turquoise waters and white sands, its brimming markets and inspiring historical sites. In fact, I ended up completing a whole geography project about our trip and loved writing about my experiences there, jotting down notes about the strong Buddhist community, sticking in snaps of sparkling temples glowing gold in the sunshine.

I was especially in awe of the huge golden statue of the Buddha at Wat Phra Yai, or Big Buddha Temple, in the northeast of the island. Erected in 1972, it's one of Koh Samui's most popular attractions. The statue is a massive twelve metres high and depicts the Buddha in the 'subduing Mara' pose, which represents him resisting all temptations by meditating and keeping calm on his journey to enlightenment. I was struck by how powerful the practice of meditation seemed to be. As I stood in the muggy embrace of the day, gazing up at the Buddha towering over me, I was entranced. The sun glinted off his sturdy shoulders, and the whole statue glimmered with an otherworldly air. Despite the thrum from the gathering crowd of tourists, I felt this peacefulness wash over me. It was truly special, and I could see why this statue was so important to a lot of people. It's something I won't be forgetting in a hurry.

Since learning more about anxiety, I've come to understand why meditation and mindfulness are so effective. The art of sitting down quietly, decluttering your mind and just letting thoughts pass you by without your attaching meaning or importance to them is something I'd love to master one day. Presently, however, I can usually only last a solid thirty seconds before my mind wanders, my legs fidget and I start pondering dinner.

The rest of the trip was spent exploring the scenery and checking out the surrounding towns. Fisherman's Village, near Bophut in the north, is the oldest place on the island and was a highlight for me. There was once a vibrant fishing community there, but the fishermen moved on after the main pier collapsed. The personality of the place was still very evident, though, and many of the original sturdy wooden shophouses had been converted into quirky cafés, restaurants and clothes stores. The village backed directly onto Bophut Beach so you could enjoy the best of both worlds, whether you were a sand dweller or on the prowl for souvenirs. I weaved around, flip-flops slapping the sun-cracked concrete, taking in the bustling air, stocking up on mirrored boxes, pens, abstract photo frames and keyrings, and feeling like I was part of this whole other world.

Having said that, we did have a surprise encounter with our world back home while we were in Thailand – in the form of one of my dad's work colleagues and his wife.

In true serendipitous fashion, we'd bumped into them at Bangkok airport, where it turned out that we were both transferring onto a flight for Koh Samui. We were waiting in the transit lounge, my mum flipping through her latest novel, me engrossed with my DS, and my dad continually glancing up at the departures board as it clicked between pages, when suddenly Dad jumped up, dropped his bags to the floor and ran towards the airport toilets, hot on the heels of some poor unsuspecting man. Mum and I shrugged at each other, our eyes following Dad's retreating back, and I went back to my Nintendogs session.

Twenty minutes later, he still hadn't emerged. Heads swivelling to the board, Mum and I thought it was probably time to go through to the boarding gate. Were we going to miss the flight? But Dad had left all his bags by our feet. Maybe he'd just really needed to go to the loo.

Eventually, he reappeared. "Why did you chase that man into the toilets?" my mum began, just as the aforementioned man popped up behind us. It was my dad's colleague, off to Bophut the same as us. Small world.

When we eventually reached Koh Samui after an uneventful flight (no more loo stalking), we checked into our hotel with ease. It was pitch black and I needed a long sleep, so I dropped off almost immediately. Next morning, I woke to that 'on holiday' morning soundtrack: waves crashing in the distance, birds chirping, palm trees rusting in the gentle breeze. Sunlight filtered through the curtains next to my bed and my eyes flickered open. I was ready for the adventures to commence.

Thailand was the first holiday I really started getting into taking photographs. There was so much to capture. My dad and I would go down to the beach after breakfast and I'd watch him snap away. He taught me about colour balance and I tried taking some of my own pictures on his camera. They were mostly blurry and definitely wouldn't have won any prizes, but by now, I was fascinated. I vowed to one day learn from my dad and produce wonderful work like him (or, you know, just photos in focus).

One evening, he disappeared off and came back on a rented motorbike, which became our go-to mode of quick transportation. We made trips to Fisherman's Village for packets of Lay's crisps, with me grinning away on the back. We zoomed through the streets, alongside the twinkling fairy lights adorning the restaurant fronts, and pressed on through the throngs of evening revellers, who were surging down tiny alleyways like shoals of sardines as they went exploring.

There was a lot of laughing on that holiday. My dad and I tried our hand at off-road go-karting, eagerly revving at the start line, raring to beat each other to the finish. It must have been the pressure of having to perform for our spectators (my mum and the guy in charge of the karts) because we ultimately showed ourselves up. I totalled mine in a ditch after I panicked and swerved into the corner too soon, and my dad was so wobbly, it was amazing that he even made it around the makeshift arena once. I stood up, rubbing my grazed elbow and peering through the dusty air as he vanished into the sunset, my mum sniggering behind me, filming how utterly crap we were at staying on the dirt track.

We also visited the Samui Elephant Sanctuary, learning all about their fantastic work within the community. It reminded me of the serene sanctuary back in Sri Lanka and I marvelled yet again at these humungous but good-humoured elephants as they playfully squirted water at each other from their trunks. We were told that the locals had clubbed together to take care of these extraordinary animals and save them from poachers and the effects of deforestation. It made me more respectful of humankind. Maybe people weren't that bad, maybe they weren't that scary, I thought, mulling over this possibility.

The next day, we went on an elephant ride in the jungle, which involved trekking up an extremely steep hill. My mum sat on her elephant in tears, eyes covered, having a panic attack at the sight of the sheer drop behind us. It seems everyone conquered some anxieties that trip.

I had arrived in Thailand without any preconceptions about the country and I returned to London armed with a slew of fantastic knowledge. I knew the difference between Asian and African elephants (the African species have more rounded heads and Asian elephants have differently shaped lower lips). I learnt that Koh Samui was probably first settled around 1,500 years ago, by fishermen, and was originally known as Pulo Cornam. And I discovered that the island used to be famous for its coconut plantations and mischievous monkeys but now earned a lot of its income from tourists flocking to its breath-taking beaches. My brain felt like it had gobbled down a huge meal; it was bursting, full to the brim with facts and random titbits.

I love looking back at our photos of Koh Samui (and at my geography project, of course), although I was going through my severely awkward pre-teen phase, so I cringe whenever snaps of my geeky frame pop up. Instead of dwelling on my sweaty face, multiple pimples, frizzy hair and adult teeth that were way too big for my childish face, I prefer to remember my newfound friends and recall how much I enjoyed splashing around in the sparkling water all day, the sea like a hot bath as I gazed up at the bright blue skies.

14

Has She Got Malaria?

Zanzibar

Health anxiety reared its ugly head in Zanzibar. This was the trip where my mind spiralled into a manic meltdown. Although I remember the blissful beauty, the delicious food and sublime sunshine, I mostly recall my mum being told in hushed tones that I likely had malaria. Yep, not only was I trying to swerve social anxiety, now I had a whole other mutant monster under the bed to contend with. At least, they were keeping each other company, I guess.

When my dad arrived home one evening and announced we were going to Zanzibar, I was intrigued. Abandoning my mind-numbingly boring science homework, I scurried over to our home computer (I know, right, a life before laptops and smartphone swipes). I was fascinated by the beaches I saw flashing up, beaches so blazingly white, they became imprinted on my mind's eye. When we boarded the flight a few weeks later, I again envisaged them in my head, already feeling the soft sand beneath my feet. It was like I was blinded by the simmering sunshine despite still being seated in my aircraft window seat, facing out into the pitch black as the world below slept. I've always had a good imagination. I can picture scenes, people, and characters in books; I can build up a story in my head and see it in colour; photos are brought to life in my mind. And now, I could 'feel' Zanzibar already, as I counted the hours left until landing.

The lead-up to the trip had been hectic. My mum and I had been to see Green Day at the O2 Arena a few days before, with my cousin Harrison and Uncle Jason. It was my first ever concert apart from Live 8 in Hyde Park back in 2005 (and the Guns N' Roses gig I'd been oblivious to in the Seychelles), and I was so excited. From then on, going to gigs became one of my favourite things. I love live music, and that Green Day gig sent me down a path of constant concert-ticket booking that continues to this day.

I'd been ploughing along steadily at school. I'd established a solid group of friends and although I could still have won the National Worrier Award – if there ever was such a thing – it wasn't so bad anymore. I'd finally sailed out of my awkward phase and was slowly finding myself. I'd excitedly asked for some Converse sneakers for my fourteenth birthday; I began to don only skinny jeans, and I wore my beloved first leather jacket everywhere. Now it was all black nail polish on weekends, smoky eyeliner, and slyly adding the rock and punk magazine Kerrang! to our weekly shopping list. I was discovering me, and live music was to become a crucial part of this.

Because of the giddy, gig-fuelled lead-up, packing for Zanzibar was hurried, but anticipation bubbled and eventually our feet hit the tarmac of Abeid Amani Karume International Airport. We jumped in a taxi for the north coast and forty weary minutes later arrived at our home for the next few weeks. The Union Hotel consisted of quirky bamboo-topped beach bungalows dotted around a central lobby and restaurant. It was a stunning sight, and as I threw my suitcase onto my bed and started to unpack, I could hear the gentle lapping of the sea and the birds chirping in the palm trees. Zanzibar was exactly how I had imagined it. I couldn't wait to get onto the beach and finally see in real life what I'd been picturing since that Google Images search.

We were in the bungalow nearest the shore. We'd tumble out of bed, trundle a few small steps and be on Nungwi Beach in seconds. We were the only guests as it was October and out of season, so we essentially had an entire deserted beach to ourselves. There was a lazy, laid-back vibe to everything and it felt like a proper escape, a real holiday, a chance to really chill out. When I reread about Zanzibar while writing this book, I discovered that in 2014 Nungwi Beach was rated by CNN as one of the world's top one hundred beaches. I was ecstatic to see it gaining some recognition for its stunning shoreline.

Zanzibar was sun, sand and the most serene afternoons. We spent our first few days getting over our jetlag, exploring the beach, lazing in the rope hammocks. My mum read; I listened to Green Day's new album, *21st Century Breakdown* whilst gazing out at the brightly coloured boats bobbing offshore, and my dad snapped photos of island life and enjoyed discovering where the points of interest were. I enjoyed every second I spent out in the open air, the salty breeze ruffling my curls as I repeatedly reapplied sun lotion to my face.

Our delightful hotel manager would often come and check that we were okay. As we were his only guests until the last few days of our trip, when a pleasant French lady and another couple arrived, he had nothing much to do. He'd greet us each day with a friendly 'Jambo', which I remembered from Kenya meant 'Hello'. The island of Zanzibar belongs to Tanzania and, like Tanzania and Kenya, its principal language is Swahili. He filled us in on the history of Nungwi and how it had made its name as a fishing village. He also told us lots of stories about Zanzibar City, at the heart of the island, and gave us a long list of things to see.

One hazy, humid morning, he even kindly accompanied us to Stone Town, which is the oldest part of Zanzibar City and around an hour's drive from Nungwi. He became our tour guide for the day and taught us a great deal about the culture and history of Zanzibar. Hearing first-hand stories from such a knowledgeable local made everything so much more personal, engaging and interesting. One of the things he talked to us about was the horrific slave trade in Zanzibar. The island served as one of the main ports for the trafficking of slaves in East Africa and during the 19th century about 40,000–50,000 slaves were taken there each year. Around a third of them were expected to work on Zanzibar's coconut plantations while the rest were exported to places like Persia, Arabia and Egypt. It was a horrendous period in history and very hard to comprehend.

Stone Town was a maze of alleys lined with shops, bazaars and cafés. It felt like a familiar old antique, and yet without our jolly guide, who was continually cracking jokes and pointing out potential subjects for us to capture with our cameras, I doubt we would have found our way around. I loved scurrying down the tiny streets, listening to little titbits of information. We honestly saw an abstract side of Zanzibar that day. Our guide gave us such a broad view of its colourful culture, as diverse as the multi-coloured spices on offer at the sides of the charming dusty roads. He made the town seem like a big bag of cinema pick 'n' mix. Stone Town truly felt different, more vibrant and unusual than any town I'd ever visited. And don't just take my word for it, it's been classed as an official World Heritage site since 2000, described by UNESCO as an 'outstanding material manifestation of cultural fusion and harmonisation'.

Zanzibar was where I greatly improved my photography skills. Following my dad around like an annoying shadow, I observed his technique and began to understand how he determined what would made a good shot. My pictures were still fuzzy and out of focus (like the abysmal snaps from Koh Samui), but when

I returned from Zanzibar, I was determined to start practising so I could take better ones next trip. I became actively interested in capturing the feel of a place through a camera, thinking about the positioning and main subject instead of just haphazardly pressing buttons, hoping for the best, finger inadvertently over the lens. Admittedly, my Zanzibar photos were still crap, but it was a step up. Photography was becoming another solid interest I was picking up because of my travels – and my dad, of course.

For a year, my Facebook profile picture was an over-exposed photograph of me at a particular Zanzibar beach restaurant. It was an amazingly atmospheric place on the beach and we often went there for dinner. It was lit up with fairy lights and sat sparkling like the stars, the lights illuminating the inky sky above, the sea not visible but providing the perfect soothing soundtrack to a laid-back meal. In the photo, however, my face wasn't recognisable due to the harsh flash, my hair had tripled in size, and the background was pure blackness (although if it had been light, you would've seen the ocean, the beach and the perfectly pink flowers hanging from the tree next to me). I'd got my first Facebook account probably a month or two before we flew to Zanzibar. Everyone at school was going crazy for the perfect profile picture, so I chose that shot as mine. Oh, the things you worry about when you're fourteen. I look back on it now and wonder why on earth I thought that was a good photo. It was awful quality. If I'd shown it to my dad, he would have given me a massive lecture about over-exposure and the need to sort out a better lighting situation. Alas, I didn't, and this photo was attached to my profile for too long. I suppose I thought it was arty, but hey, we all cringe over our past selves, don't we?

Zanzibar was the most chilled-out holiday we'd been on so far. Yes, we explored, and yes, we saw different towns and tried new things, but we did enjoy just taking a break from work and school. We relaxed on the sand, taking long paddles in the sea. We devoured delicious breakfast platters of fresh fruit and coconut bread and munched mouth-watering dinners, looking out on picture-perfect paradise. Maybe we relaxed too much, because that's when it went a little downhill, and by a little downhill, I mean we nearly missed our flight home and I almost ended up in the local city hospital, panicking my parents and the general public. You know, just a normal day being me.

On our very last day, I began to feel unwell. My mum has always been one to nag (helpfully) me and my dad about wearing hats in the sun. Ever since my dad got severe heatstroke in Bali, started hallucinating and had to be sedated by the local doctor, my mum has insisted he wear a hat to protect himself. And he has.

I was rarely seen without my hats on holiday. My all-time favourite was the famed *101 Dalmatians* one, complete with floppy ears and big cartoon eyes. When I put my head down, it looked like a puppy's smiling face. I'd been wearing a baseball cap (not that one; I was fourteen by this point, might have been a bit weird) for most of our time in Zanzibar. But I spent too much time out in the fierce sun without shade or hydration. I was having a good time; water breaks would have disturbed that.

I look back and wonder how on earth I survived drinking hardly any water on a daily basis. It was seemingly a lot of effort for teenage me, and I hated how water didn't taste of anything. Nowadays, I'm scarcely seen without a water bottle (or two) in tow, but from the age of fourteen to nineteen, I hardly drank a cup of water a day, and that was only when my mum urged me to. So, I was well under the recommended eight glasses a day. I'm borderline obsessive about how much water I drink now. I get creative: I take a refillable bottle to the gym, infused with cucumbers or chopped strawberries. I know, classy as hell. But I digress. I hadn't drunk enough that day, which may or may not have contributed to the nightmare that followed.

Beginning to feel a little sick, I gulped down some Andrews Liver Salts (my dad's answer to every ailment) and stuck to plain foods, but by the evening, it had got a hell of a lot worse. I was vomiting every ten minutes, unable to keep anything down. I felt weak and feverish; I was shivering and my teeth were chattering. I couldn't stand, so I was crawling my way to the bathroom at regular intervals throughout the night to upchuck my guts.

At about 5 am, after around seven hours of this nonsense, I collapsed in the bathroom when I tried to shuffle back to my bed, welcoming the coolness of the floor against my burning face. It felt like I was on fire. But all I could think about was how annoyed my French teacher would be if I didn't hand my half-term homework in on time. Great, as if I wasn't already hopelessly bad at French, now I was going to fail my GCSE mocks too. Health anxiety clogged my mind. Was I going to die here? In the bathroom? That would be such an embarrassing way to go. Did I have something worse than heatstroke? Some unheard-of tropical disease?

My mum and dad looked after me all night, but I was still unwell the next morning. When it was time for us to leave for the airport, I couldn't even sit up in bed, let alone stand. My mum mixed up some Dioralyte and my dad hurried to the restaurant for some plain bread rolls for me to eat.

Another guest – the friendly French woman who'd arrived a couple of days before – had been chatting to us at breakfast each morning, telling us she was on a break after having been working with sick children on an aid project in different regions of Africa. The morning I was ill, she cottoned on to the fact that my dad had arrived at the restaurant alone and asked where my mum and I were. A few minutes later, she appeared at our bungalow with my dad, arms laden with an overflowing first-aid kit, Dioralyte, paracetamol and anti-sickness tablets from her personal supply. Like a health-centric superwoman.

Sufficiently dosed up and rehydrated, I made it to the waiting taxi and watched as the hotel manager waved us off, concern etched across his features. Great, I thought, he obviously knows something I don't. When the taxi driver eyed me with unease and asked if I needed to be taken to A&E, I whimpered in the back seat, worried I really was on my last legs. I was thinking about the stuff I hadn't done. All the stupid things I worried about on a daily basis seemed redundant now. I thought about how I'd never see my home, or speak to my family and friends or turn in that bloody French paper.

The poor driver had to keep stopping abruptly for me to be sick at the roadside every few minutes. My head throbbed painfully, everything was too heavy, and the same sun I'd been blissfully basking in a couple of days earlier was now too bright for my eyes. I winced and threw up again in the bush next to me. Eventually, we arrived at the airport and were ushered along by the staff. As soon as they saw me, they all adopted that same furrowed brow and worried grimace (you know, my usual expression; some people have 'resting bitch' face, I have 'resting anxiety' face). I was also attracting concerned stares from tourists, locals and officials. By now, I was convinced I wouldn't make it back to London.

I'd never felt so ill or so weak and incapable of carrying out the most basic shuffle forwards. Every time I attempted to step, my legs buckled and turned to jelly. My mum continually assured me I was going to be fine, and that kept me somewhat calmer. Having a panic attack whilst throwing up my guts all over the airport wouldn't have been a great mix. One thing at a time, please. But then, as we checked in, me propping myself up on the counter, eyes half open, willing myself not to be sick again, the man behind the counter asked if we needed the hospital.

"It looks like malaria," he said gravely, with a deadpan expression, staring at me as my mum's eyes widened in shock. "Take her to the hospital across the street. There's a specialist malaria ward there," he urged, pointing behind us.

This was the last thing any of us needed to hear. Of course, the check-in manager wasn't a medical professional, plus my mum was a hundred per cent sure I had a touch of heatstroke, but if you're stressed and trying to haul a vomiting fourteen-year-old along, it doesn't make you feel better when someone casually drops malaria into the conversation. We'd seen the hospital across the street: it had rubbish piled up outside, people were lounging on the grass and patients were smoking while attached to drips. That might have been judging a book by its cover, and I'm sure the doctors and nurses were amazing, but my mum just wanted to get back to London as soon as possible, to a familiar environment where she knew what to do and who to call.

A glass of water was thrust into my hands, appearing as if by magic, and I struggled to keep my eyes open as the airport staff rushed around like headless chickens, trying to help. At this point, exhaustion took over and I zoned out. My frazzled, anxiety-riddled brain had initially perked up at the mention of 'malaria', scanning, zoning in on something to panic about, but everything was happening in slow motion. I just didn't have the energy to entertain my anxious thoughts. I was too tired for that crap.

Finally, I stopped throwing up. Sprawled across the seats in the departure lounge, I dipped in and out of sleep and was then supported onto the plane, where I dropped off to dreamland once again, waking only when we touched down in London.

I didn't have malaria, thank God. It was heatstroke. But I'll always remember that well-meaning check-in manager, whose words filled my parents with a dread they didn't want to express in front of me, words that would have had an adverse reaction on me if I hadn't been too damn ill to register them. Great. Thanks.

15

A Midnight Kidnap

The Philippines

When we landed in Manila, wearily craving a steaming hot shower and a good night's sleep, fifteen-year-old me never thought in a million years we'd be storming the streets with the Filipino police, looking for my missing dad at 2 am. But that's how our trip to the Philippines started.

We'd landed late in Manila and checked into a Best Western city hotel, planning to move to one of the island resorts, Coco Beach, the next day. Trundling upstairs to unpack, sufficiently jetlagged, we settled in, and after mindlessly flicking through the TV stations, I asked my dad if we had any snacks. It was about 9 pm, and as the hotel bar was now shut until morning, he traipsed offsite with the equivalent of £5 and headed to the 7-Eleven at the end of the road to grab a can of lemonade and some Pringles.

Any time I see a tube of Pringles now, I'm reminded of this night. Forevermore, unfortunately.

He was gone for a while, and eventually, Mum and I drifted off to sleep, still without those vital snacks. When I woke, it was 1 am and the TV was still on, static stuttering in the background and casting an eerie glow over the room. I slipped out of bed and wandered into the living room. Dad was still nowhere to be seen. Thinking this was beyond weird, I peeped out the window. Even the city streets seemed to be sleeping soundly.

My mum, now also awake, checked the darkened bathroom and when there still was no sign of him, unlocked the front door to search the corridor, expecting to see him coming up the winding stairs. But no, it was pitch black, the hotel creepily quiet. We could have heard a pin drop.

We weren't too worried at this point, but our room was devoid of any clues. My mum grabbed the spare key and went down to reception to ask if they'd seen him. He'd left his phone and wallet behind because he'd only been popping to the local shop to buy Pringles, for goodness' sake, so where could he be?

"Hi, you haven't seen my husband, have you?" Mum asked the receptionist. "He only went to the 7-Eleven, but that was four hours ago."

The man behind the counter glanced up, a frown creasing his face, trying to recall. He remembered us from earlier, when we'd checked in, but he hadn't seen my dad. "Sorry, I haven't seen him. Four hours…?" He sounded concerned, but my mum chuckled.

"Oh, I'm not too worried. He's a journalist, so he's pretty street-smart. He knows how to get around—"

"A journalist?" the receptionist cut my mum off abruptly and gazed at her in horror.

"Yes…" My mum faltered, clocking his panicked expression.

The man quickly grabbed the reception phone and dialled impatiently. Cradling the handset in the crook of his neck, he spoke urgently to my mum as he waited for his call to be answered. "Ma'am, a week ago a group of journalists were bundled into the back of a van and held at knifepoint. It's very dangerous out there. I'm calling the hotel manager; he'll come immediately. We need to contact the police."

That's when the drama officially kicked off. Maybe my mum should have kept the 'journalist' comment to herself.

The receptionist's eyes widened as he relayed the sinister circumstances to the manager, who had presumably been slumbering peacefully at home. The manager was back at the hotel within half an hour, hair dishevelled, eyes bleary, by which time everyone was panic-stricken. All the staff were out of bed, rushing around in a tizz, eyes darting here and there. My mum and I stood in the lobby, sleep in our eyes, as all these people tried to contact the seemingly unobtainable police, using words like 'emergency' and 'kidnap'.

I started intensively worrying and, believe me, as I've stated before, I'm the world's top worrier. This unravelling situation, coupled with extreme jetlag, did not help my anxiety. I'm the self-proclaimed queen of making a big deal out of nothing, but this did seem bad. Everyone was stressed, convinced that my dad had been hauled into the back of a van somewhere.

It was 2 am now. We were in an unfamiliar place. I became hysterical, fretting about my dad's whereabouts, and burst into tears. My mum hurried off with the manager to visit a few of the local bars and ask staff if they'd seen him.

They ducked into nearby hotels, scoured the streets. Nothing. He'd disappeared into the humid evening air without a trace.

I was growing increasingly frantic by the millisecond, pacing the lobby, listening to the hotel staff whispering worriedly as they tried to come up with a plan of action. I halted to stare out of the window beside me and restlessly tapped my foot, the sound of my shoe hitting the cool marble echoing in a space that had stood dark and empty less than an hour earlier but was now packed with people. I felt like a sardine squashed inside a tin as claustrophobia crept up on me. I nibbled anxiously at my turquoise-painted fingernails.

It was proving impossible to get through to the police as the line was constantly engaged (imagine that happening if you dialled 999 in the UK), so the manager made the executive decision to march down to the nearest station, which, handily, turned out to be a five-minute walk away.

"I'm coming too," I called, hurrying after the others. I swear we looked like some sort of vigilante group, stomping down the jet-black streets. All we needed were pitchforks.

We burst into the dark, dank police station, which was just a single room and the tiniest police station I'd ever seen (not that I'd seen many), and stumbled across two sleeping officers slumped over their desks, emergency phones taken off the hook. Half-drunk cups of coffee and takeout containers were littered everywhere.

They abruptly startled awake and were quick to help, even though we'd interrupted their nap. They jumped up and listened intently as the manager explained the bizarre situation in Filipino. The police were then on the phone themselves, calling for backup, and we all moved outside to carry on searching.

But before we could split up and look for clues like in a real-life version of Scooby Doo, one of the staff members from our hotel suddenly came sprinting down the road, waving. "We've found Mr Bell!" he yelled, halting in front of the entrance to the police station.

We all turned to stare. Relief washed over me, and my mum visibly relaxed. Our makeshift search party dispersed, and we trundled back to the hotel to find my dad looking embarrassed at all the commotion. Several other guests had by now emerged from their rooms to see what on earth was going on, and Dad stood in the middle of the swarm, sheepishly peering at us as we burst through the doors.

It turned out he had gone to the 7-Eleven, but it was closed, so on the way back he wandered into a pub to see if they had Pringles. He'd only had the equivalent of £5 with him, so we questioned where he'd been all that time. Apparently, a group of Australian backpackers had struck up a conversation with him as he waited at the bar, and they then proceeded to buy him drinks all night. He lost track of time.

My mum was irritated, to say the least, but we managed to laugh about it the next morning, once the steam had stopped coming out of her ears. We were thankful that he hadn't been kidnapped after all, and we were grateful to the fantastic hotel staff, who had gone above and beyond to help locate him. Also, we now had Pringles and lemonade, although who wants either at 3 am?

Relief aside, breakfast the next morning was humiliating. We shuffled into the dining room, eyes averted, me with my sunglasses on at the table, glued to my Kerrang! magazine as I ate. My mum didn't look up at anyone either, and we excused ourselves as soon as we could to pack our stuff upstairs. Everyone was staring, eyes boring into our heads. There had been quite the racket going on throughout the night and we'd literally woken most of the hotel. What with the pacing, hysterics and staff running here, there and everywhere, it would have been amazing if anyone managed to sleep. People ogled and whispered, but my dad happily tucked into his breakfast, oblivious to the swivelling eyes.

We packed at the speed of light, checked out, scuttled off and had a good laugh about it afterwards. Throughout the following week, my dad, ever the joker, kept quipping, 'I'm just going to the toilet, don't call the police', or 'I'm just going over here to take some photos, don't get a search party out looking for me' he said sarcastically and with a roll of his eyes. But it wasn't long before he got his comeuppance.

On Coco Beach Island, we'd all been in the bar playing pool, but it had got late, so Mum and I returned to our bungalow, leaving my dad to play another game with the friendly waiter. It was like *Groundhog Day*. We fell asleep, awoke in the middle of the night and my dad was nowhere to be seen. Again.

Around half an hour later, he graced us with his presence, barging through the front door, muttering that he'd got locked in the bar toilet and it had taken all this time for someone to find him. The bar toilets were made of bamboo, so although he'd tried to bang on the door, no one could hear him, the music from the seating area drowned out his yells, and there weren't any other guests around.

He tried to climb out, but the walls were too high. Eventually, the waiter heard him calling and let him out an hour later.

The staff found this hysterical. Sulking, my dad asked why we hadn't come looking for him, and all my mum could do was smirk and say, "You did tell us not to."

Karma, ladies and gentlemen. Don't mess with it.

Apart from the potential kidnapping and my dad succumbing to his bamboo fate, the rest of our holiday was exquisite. Coco Beach Island was all swaying palms, white sand and beachfront hammocks. It fondly reminded me of Coco Island from Crash Bandicoot, a PlayStation game I loved when I was little. We spent our days relaxing, splashing around in the pool, and playing tennis on courts in the jungle behind the bungalows. We explored, drank cocktails (mocktails, in my case, as I was only fifteen) in the bar overlooking the sun-kissed beach and had a generally chilled break. I'd learnt my lesson from the year before and sported a baseball cap wherever I went, determined not to get heatstroke again.

We celebrated Halloween in style at the hotel. It was an extravagant affair like in America: they had a live band, the restaurant was decorated with carved pumpkins and fake spiderwebs, and there was even a special creepy menu consisting of eyeball curry, severed-finger biscuits and brightly coloured drinks.

The evening concluded with my mum waking up screaming, tangled in the mosquito net that hung over her and my dad's bed. If that doesn't constitute the ultimate creepy-as-hell soundtrack to a Coco Beach Halloween night, I don't know what does. Mum suffers from night terrors and often wakes in the morning at home to find she's moved ornaments or pictures during the night without realising. I've unfortunately inherited that trait too and frequently see shapes on my walls or pillow that look like spiders or bugs. I jump out of bed in surprise, but they disappear as soon as I focus on them. Creepy much.

Our holiday neighbours must have thought we were pretty odd. But hey, we left our mark on the Philippines – and it permanently branded me too. I look back on the highs and lows, the panic of my 'missing' dad, the wash of relief, the subsequent embarrassment, and the excitement of the rest of the holiday. It was a rollercoaster of a trip; we were spun left, right, up and down, but we hopped off that ride exhilarated, itching to do it again.

With hindsight, this was the first trip where I was old enough to actually experience another culture and understand its different practices. It was the first time I felt spurred on creatively to produce something that reflected the world I was seeing. I whipped out my sketchbook one day on the beach and began drawing the scenes unfolding before my eyes. I drew the curve of the island, the splash of the foamy waves and a solitary junk tied up at the pier.

I look back through photographs of Kenya, Antigua and Australia and feel so lucky, so inspired to write about, draw or paint those experiences that I can only now fully appreciate. But the Philippines was where it struck me in real time that travelling was such a special thing and I'd been taking it for granted.

On previous holidays, I'd amble along behind my mum and dad, witnessing all these fantastic things, spying temples and religious ceremonies, jumping in tuk-tuks instead of taxis, and watching all these terrific tropical animals in place of foxes snuffling for leftovers in bins back home. I'd trot along, meandering through colour-splashed markets, my nose twitching at the waft of exotic fruit mixed with the kick of spice. I'd write postcards to Nan, Pap and Nana Cath and tell them my stories but not be able to fully explain all the wonderful things I was seeing. I'd be taking it all in, storing experiences in my little brain but not really understanding the significance of these buildings and landmarks, not really getting the contrasts in every strikingly particular culture. It felt as if my mind was drinking in all this information like a runner greedily gulps down water after a marathon in 30-degree heat.

In the Philippines, I crossed the line to having more meaningful and productive trips. I took photos of local life rather than the same old beach snaps. I built on the foundations I'd laid the year before in Zanzibar and discovered more from my dad about what made an interesting picture, what made a scene so special to capture. You can see a real jump as a result; my thought processes are more apparent and the photos are a lot more interesting, more immersive.

I also kept a diary about our mishaps, recording everything we loved about the place. I was gaining vital life experience and wanted to remember every detail. On previous trips, I'd gone along for the ride, but now, I felt I was in control of what I wanted out of my travels. I wanted to learn, make memories, chase that feeling of being part of something completely different, immersed in a whole other culture. So, I recorded my adventures with pen, paper and camera.

I had a more grown-up travel experience in the Philippines. I guess having been part of an actual police search party might have helped. But I also fully appreciated the temples, the local life, the day-to-day practices and the beautiful contrast to what I was used to at home. I met so many different people who opened my mind, even if they were unaware of their impact on me.

I returned home with the start of an idea weaving its way around my brain like the fake silvery spider webs that adorned the hotel restaurant on Halloween night. I began to realise that there wasn't one 'right' way to live your life, that there were all these different paths to happiness and contentment, so many alternative ways to look at the world.

I often recall this when I'm struggling with worries about where I am in life and all the things I haven't achieved yet. There's always an alternative solution to a problem. It's the different ways we choose to live our lives that make us all so wonderfully unique.

Murmuration of birds, Zanzibar, Tanzania, East Africa

Maasai Tribe, Zanzibar, Tanzania, East Africa

Buddhist Temple, Koh Samui, Thailand

Goan woman in traditional dress, Western India

16

Just Walk Out and They Will Stop

Vietnam

Vietnam should have made my deepening anxiety a whole lot worse. Hanoi was pure chaos: an explosion of constant noise, an attack on our senses 24/7. Surprisingly, though, I embraced the dramatic change of scenery and jumped headfirst into my temporary new life. Where the Philippines had opened my mind and ushered me down a more curious path, Vietnam taught me to try and be comfortable with things that were out of my control. This would become an excellent tool to use against my developing worries in years to come.

What's the thing I remember most vividly about this extraordinary country with so much heritage, you ask? The Hanoi motorbikes, of course, and the fact that the whole trip was one massive contrast from start to finish. Ultimately, that turned out to be my favourite thing about it.

We took this trip when I was sixteen. I'd enjoyed a period of relative calm for quite a while, once I'd got used to going to secondary school and being a teenager, but as I turned sixteen, my anxiety intensified (thanks, anxiety; real smooth). General anxiety now took its unwanted cue, joining its health and social counterparts and proved to be by far the most irritating of the three. My social and health worries were limited to specific situations – like having to do a big presentation or being faced with a concerning symptom (such as possible malaria) – and they'd disappear when the situation passed. But general anxiety was there twenty-four hours a day for no particular reason. I often didn't even know why I was anxious; there wasn't a trigger, it was just there.

This was the year I noticed a huge difference in my ability to cope with the day-to-day when panic reared its ugly head. It was like that old fairground game Whac-A-Mole. Sounds fun, right? Wrong.

Before we waltzed off to Vietnam, I was having a tough time in sixth form. The large group of friends I'd steadily built up since Year 7 had dispersed to different colleges and inevitably many of us lost touch after a few months. My friends took my safety net with them, and I felt like I'd been plunged into those shark-infested waters yet again. I had just a couple of friends left. One of those was Lizzie, but we were only in one class together: RE, twice a week, a mind-numbingly boring two hours where the newly qualified, fresh-faced teacher struggled to control the class and usually ended up putting on a DVD instead.

I took English, art and history, while Lizzie was in a different English class and had opted for biology and philosophy. We'd meet at lunch, but going from being surrounded by a group of ten other girls to just one other person was hard. Yet again, I felt ignored at school. I'd sit and do the work, but no one noticed if I wasn't there. I melted into the background like I had in Year 7, though this time I eventually used that to my advantage. I'd only just found my feet in years 10 and 11, so having my confidence suddenly swiped from me was not at all enjoyable. Overwhelming dread loomed as soon as Sunday night rolled around like a black cloud.

That first sixth-form year was a pivotal point. A whole lot of factors collided to turn me into a sixteen-year-old who worried non-stop. About literally everything. (I know; it was exhausting, and, put bluntly, super annoying.)

The only class I enjoyed was history, because although I was on my own there, the teacher was great. Her teaching style was traditional, which meant less abysmally awful group work, fewer painful presentations, and more essay practice in silence. There weren't many opportunities to talk to fellow students, which suited me fine. I just got on with my work and made sure I was doing my best.

My history teacher was a real Marmite character: you either loved or hated her. She was pretty strict, but if you did your work and didn't misbehave, she was really nice. I never felt ignored in her class because she'd ask everyone questions and make sure everyone knew what they were doing. She'd scream at the badly behaved kids until the glass in the windows shattered (I mean, not literally, though she probably could have achieved that); you'd often hear her yells all the way down the corridor. But she earned a lot of respect. Not many students messed about in her classes, so I felt happier. I could carry on with my studies.

School had become an issue for me though. It was emphasised that because we were now adults, we'd have more free time, and although we had classes and homework, we were no longer legally obliged to stay in the building (this was before it was mandatory to stay on in education until the age of eighteen). This newfound freedom went on for a couple of weeks before the teachers realised that half my year weren't turning up to, well, any classes.

So, what did my school do? They turned up the full prison vibes and stopped us going out at lunchtime or when we had a free lesson. Instead, we had to go to the library if we had an hour to kill, or to the dreaded sixth-form centre. The dress code also became ridiculously strict. Instead of smart work clothes, our clobber had to adhere to various odd restrictions. I was sent home to change because my skirt was one centimetre too short. Lizzie was banished because she wore a shift dress emblazoned with polka dots, a pattern that was deemed to be 'against policy'.

The teachers started locking the doors so we couldn't get out at break-time. No other sixth form seemed to have this issue and it was beyond weird. One moment they were preparing us for the adult world, giving us more freedom, and the next, we were being imprisoned like little kids in pre-school. That school was probably my first experience of an escape room and maybe that's why I'm so fond of them now. I objected to my rights being ripped away from me and I hated the place anyway. I was just there to do my A-levels and then I would get the hell out.

I detested passing the busy sixth-form centre to get to my locker. I could hear the commotion even with the doors swung firmly shut. There was never anywhere to sit in there. The louder kids would sprawl across the sofas, laughing, shouting, screeching, throwing paper at each other and playing tinny music on their phones. It reminded me of that scene in the teen movie *Mean Girls* when home-schooled Cady is imagining the cafeteria as the African jungle, full of animals fighting each other and squawking angrily.

The first time I stepped foot inside the sixth-form centre was also the last. Expecting it to be more like the Gryffindor common room in Harry Potter was probably my big mistake; my expectations were too high. It was jam-packed full of all the kids I hadn't got on with since Year 7: the noisy kids, the chavs, the attention seekers. Sixth form seemed to have accelerated their need for that attention, the only difference being that they were now dressed up in suits, like children playing at being adults.

The library was always full with kids from the younger years, so I used to just walk the halls or hang out at my locker. (So cool; on the plus side, the inside of my locker was as organised as hell, as I spent so much time trying to look 'busy' sorting it out.) One day, though, after a twenty-minute locker-cleaning blitz, I decided to escape down the stairs to the back door that led out to the car park. I'd seen a teacher push the door; she'd been on her phone, distracted as she cradled the phone between her neck and her shoulder. The door was locked and hadn't budged, but she'd reached up, twisting the disguised lock easily. The door swung open. It was that simple to get out.

After that day, I began to sneak out in my free lessons (I say 'sneak', but I used to just twist the lock and leave, although I did have to duck behind the bushes as I scuttled to the main exit gates, to avoid being spotted from reception). I'd go home or head off into town to meet my friend who went to a different college. If she wasn't about, I'd just grab a coffee, wander around the shops and make it back for my afternoon lessons. Or not.

My social awkwardness had got the better of me, and by now, I was prepared to get into trouble for skipping class if that meant I wouldn't have to speak to the loud kids. I don't condone sneaking out – not even in sixth form, when you're meant to have a lot more leeway and aren't legally bound to be there – but it got to the point where I'd done the work, read the book, studied the play. I didn't need to have guided classes to tell me how to articulately express my thoughts on a novel or paint something conjured up by my own brain.

I'd already learnt so much about English literature from my mum, who loves the classics and my dad who is a stellar speller. It felt like overkill to have to spend an hour in a classroom with everyone taking turns reading aloud. I much preferred reading in my own time. Similarly, I got all my art education from my pap. He was an amazing painter, and over the years, he's shared many tips and tricks with me. We'd love seeing each other's work. He's taught me more about drawing than any school art teacher ever could.

I wanted to do my learning in my own way, because I knew that was how I learnt best. I didn't want to be stifled just because the way my school did things didn't suit me. In my defence, I like to say that it wasn't as if I was wasting my opportunities at sixth form. I studied in my own time, and I passed all my exams. I even got a surprising A^+ for my English Lit paper, the highest grade in my year, because I'd read the book cover to cover.

Nowadays, I prefer to view it as me deciding, arguably in an adult way, how to spend my time in the most productive fashion. It was hardly a St Trinian's-style rebellion, but it was me putting my foot down and proving that I could achieve more by doing the work on my own, undistracted by my attention-seeking, paper-throwing peers. Wasn't that what the world of work was meant to be about anyway – making decisions for yourself?

I'd been doing what I was told for so long, Vietnam taught me that sometimes you have to completely mix it up, do the opposite of your normality to see a difference. So, on this trip, I learnt to cross the road by literally walking straight out into the dense stream of motorbikes that thronged the streets day and night. We were advised of this tactic by the locals, by the way; it wasn't just some quirky, questionable idea of mine.

"Just walk out and they will stop," a passer-by laden down with bags of rice yelled at us over the beeping horns, otherwise known as the soundtrack of Vietnam. We'd been waiting for about ten minutes for a gap in the traffic – there were no pedestrian crossings. My dad peered down the street; there was no slowing-up in sight. The motorbikes stuck close behind each other like they were attached to a string that was pulling them all forward, all following some sort of weird, motorised Pied Piper.

I stared in horror at my parents. There was no way I'd be walking into incoming traffic. That would be crazy. But as we gazed around, we realised that was exactly what everyone else was doing – the locals as well as other (more assured-looking) tourists. They knew the drill.

I winced as an Australian couple, having reached the edge of the pavement, continued staring down at their map and chattering to each other as they hopped into the path of the zooming motorbikes. The bikes simply swerved around them, and the couple didn't even halt their conversation, just trundled across the road. There were no screams, no panicked expressions.

So, we tried it. And you know what? It worked. The motorbikes just flowed around us. The drivers' reactions were impeccable.

Had anyone told me a few days earlier, at home in London, that I'd soon be strolling carefree through a pack of motorbikes on a major Hanoi road, I'd have scoffed. That's just incredibly dangerous, I'd have replied; my anxiety would never allow that, no way. But it did.

On the face of things, Hanoi hardly seemed a place to relax in. It was busy and noisy as hell. That didn't mean I didn't enjoy it though. It was fantastic, and

I had to just deal with my everyday anxieties there. I had to be exposed to the noise and just 'be'. It was refreshing. Once I'd got over the motorbike thing, I felt I could do anything. I returned from that trip with an understanding that doing things out of my comfort zone was a positive act, a way to challenge my distorted thinking. And, trust me, I had a lot of distorted thinking back then.

On the way to Vietnam, we'd stopped over in Hong Kong for a one-night layover and had enjoyed our brief experience. Hong Kong was squeaky clean and had an air of sophistication. There were swanky restaurants on every street and expensive jewellery shops selling glittering gems, a magpie's dreamland. I loved strolling around, taking in local life. It was a typical city centre, similar to home. Well, similar if someone were to have airbrushed London within an inch of its life and swapped the various McDonald's and Subways for gourmet dining experiences.

Hanoi didn't possess the sleek allure of Hong Kong. Instead, it was mad in the most brilliant way possible. It reminded me of a hare-brained scientist – one with crazy tufty locks and a lab coat – mixing a hundred different potions together, hoping something would stick. That was the chaotic charm of Hanoi.

The streets were tiny, and the motorbikes were constantly weaving past you, hundreds of them whizzing by every second. There seemed to be no left or right side of the road, everyone just zoomed around wherever, through whatever little space opened up. There was a constant screeching of tyres, like nails on a chalkboard.

That scene has been imprinted on my brain forever: those motorbike memories, that noise, the sun dancing across the pavements, and the wafting smell of simmering green curry. I got accustomed after a while and found it almost soothing to fall asleep to the steady throb of traffic, my own kind of white noise.

There were oases of calm on our trip though. We discovered the beautiful and simply named Hanoi Café on the first morning. It was situated up high, overlooking a busy roundabout, and we would sit on the balcony and peer down at the craziness below, people watching. One hazy morning, as we were enjoying our lattes, we spotted an old woman balancing a pole on her shoulders, each side weighed down with bags of rice and other market buys. She was swaying to and fro, walking with intent through the commotion of the roundabout, motorbikes swarming around her. It was terrifying to watch; we were scared that she'd be run over. But her face was impassive; she was obviously completely used to it.

It was like Mario Kart, that game for the Wii console where you raced Mario characters and dodged different obstacles. I loved playing that; I didn't think I'd be in it though. Thankfully, the woman eventually reached the other side of the roundabout, and we drained our coffees. It was crazy to think that this was just normal life for the locals. For us, it was so different. I mean, London is busy, but you haven't seen chaos until you've visited Hanoi.

A lot of people immediately think of the Vietnam War when they hear about the country. The war had a massive impact, with over three million people losing their lives and vast swathes of land devastated, and it continues to affect Vietnamese culture today. It lasted from 1955 to 1975, involved North and South Vietnam, Cambodia, the USA and Laos, and was intensified by the Cold War, which was raging between the USA and the Soviet Union. You can pay your respects and learn more about the conflict at Hanoi's War Remnants Museum.

Some of the city's other big sights include the beautiful Hoan Kiem Lake, the National History Museum and the Ho Chi Ming Museum. But my favourite Hanoi attraction was the very picturesque Temple of Literature. Built in 1070 as a university for the royals and other elite members of society, it had a towering and truly magnificent red and gold archway and lots of carved and painted detail. Although it's no longer used as an educational establishment, it's a place for paying homage to learning and literature. Right up my nerdy street.

One place we didn't hit up was the glass-floored Lotte Observation Deck, which my mum would have hated. It sits sixty storeys above Hanoi, from where you can apparently see for miles. Not quite the perfect find for someone scared of heights, like my mum, but it would have been exhilarating to step onto the glass and look down on the buzzing city below.

Instead, we made do with our own version, the Rooftop Bar. As its name implied (lots of Hanoi café and restaurant names were so incredibly literal), this lovely restaurant was (relatively) high above the roads. From here, we watched the city light up at night and enjoyed brightly coloured cocktails as we sat at the window, the night air balmy and blissful. I'd never experienced anything or anywhere quite like it. I'm a city girl, but this was something else entirely and it was fantastic. I grinned, happier, feeling like I'd left some of those school worries back at home.

*

Our three-day boat trip around Vietnam's majestic Ha Long Bay was breath-taking. A World Heritage site, the bay is known around the globe for its shimmering, still waters, its tranquillity and greenery, and its enormous natural limestone islands. It looked like a film set for a tropical Hollywood adventure movie, but there was no need for editing or green screens. Even though I felt as if we'd been transported into a magical land, it was all completely real.

If you're planning to go to Vietnam, then Ha Long Bay is a real must. It's so beautiful, words hardly do it justice. It's simple to book trips there from Hanoi, with transport and your stay on a tour boat all taken care of. And so, early one morning, bleary-eyed and craving another coffee, we sidled onto a minibus in central Hanoi, ready for the long drive to the bay.

To tour the maze of islands dotted around the vast bay, we lived on a little junk for a few days. It was the perfect way to explore, allowing us to gaze up silently at the limestone islands surrounding us and fully absorb what we were looking at. Our junk wasn't just a boat, it was like an ultra-mini cruise ship. The rooms were like hotel rooms, with every amenity we could have wished for. There was a bar on deck, where we enjoyed a cocktail (or two) as we watched the sun set over the crystal-clear waters. My mum and I would order after-dinner Baileys and then stumble back to the rooms below as the boat rocked in the gentle evening breeze. That was the only downside to drinking alcohol aboard a boat, I guess. Served us right.

Our on-board tour guide was lovely, so enthusiastic, and eager to tell us all about all the things we could do on the trip, including snorkelling, island hopping, visiting Elephant Island (one thing I've noticed when out exploring in different countries is that a lot of places seem to have an 'Elephant Island' and, no, it's not the same one), and, the highlight, kayaking. There were also cooking classes. The staff taught us how to make traditional Vietnamese dishes, and their attention to detail was like nothing I'd ever seen. Every meal was garnished with elaborate onion swirls, a cucumber cut up into flowers, and even a carrot carved into a tiny bird. The decoration was truly amazing, really special.

Kayaking did turn out to be great fun, although my dad and I were always almost capsizing. We paddled the calm, turquoise waters and waved to my mum, who downright refused to come in a kayak with us. "Nope, I'll take photos," she insisted as she settled down on the deck with a coffee and her camera. Each natural looming rock formation had its own name and backstory. Teapot Island and Stone Dog were my favourites; the latter had a resemblance to a canine making his way up the side of a mountain and it was truly incredible to think that these rocks had formed that way without any assistance. But the most poignant thing I remember about Ha Long Bay was the lady with the Pringles. Yep, it's all about the Pringles, again.

It was early evening and I was sketching. I'd focussed my attention on a woman I could see out the window. She was paddling a small boat and I began to draw her and the sun setting behind her. As I got deeper into my sketch, she suddenly appeared to be nearer, waving excitedly. "Uh, guys, I think that lady is waving at us," I muttered, with the attitude only a sixteen-year-old can muster. You know, that 'everything is so weird' attitude.

My dad peered out, caught sight of her and politely waved back. When I glanced up a few seconds later, the woman was even closer. It was like the horror movie *Shutter*, when the paranormal woman in the photograph keeps appearing closer in each snap.

My eyes flicked up once again after another brief while, and this time, I did a double-take. The woman was now at the window, still waving. I nearly jumped out of my skin. "Jesus. Dad…?" I glanced over at him and motioned towards the woman with my widened eyes.

It turned out that the initial wave from her had meant "Do you want anything from my floating snack shop?" and my dad's subsequent wave back had obviously signalled 'Yes'. So here she was. She had everything aboard her tiny, dingy-sized boat: crisps, chocolate, drinks, sweets, the lot.

Feeling bad that the woman had rowed all that way due to a major misunderstanding, my dad decided he couldn't just buy some Pringles (which do seem to be a common feature in these weird and wonderful stories), so he purchased a couple of bottles of Lucozade as well. He passed the woman her money and she thanked us, by now already on her way to sell to a boat bobbing parallel to ours. A floating Tesco delivery service, if you will.

In the days that followed, I busied myself learning all about Vietnam, its history, culture and way of life. I tried food that ignited my tastebuds and would go on to become my staples for years to come: vibrant Vietnamese curries, succulent spring rolls packed with vegetables and spices, and pho, a traditional noodle and herb soup dish popular with the locals. It was so abstract to my usual lunch favourites, a tuna panini or Marmite-slathered toast.

We met loads of great people who loved to share stories about their lives, jobs and aspirations. I took even better photos – photos that showed something:

the way the mist gently rose against the backdrop of the fantastic limestone formations; someone in a traditional rice-farmer's hat bobbing about on the ripples, going about their daily life catching fish on a junk. I would eagerly show my dad my captures and then get to work sketching them.

We visited a floating pearl farm built on pontoons in the bay and learnt about how the staff there nurtured the oysters until the pearls they produced were ready to be harvested and polished to become jewellery. I loved hearing about how the pearl farmers' nine-to-five was diving down into the ocean and farming pearls, commuting by boat. I thought that was so cool, something so far removed from my world back home. Their kids played with a football on the wooden decking that surrounded the floating pearl farm and the whole place just seemed so idyllic, like someone had flipped on some spa music inside my head and was playing it on a loop.

My mum and I soon learnt to stop worrying when my dad was last back on the boat following one of our excursions. After the Philippines, we were used to him disappearing. He was always still trying to snap that last perfect photo before we departed to the next island or activity. However, a pleasant Chinese couple we sometimes sat with at dinner resorted to worrying for us, repeating what they'd heard my mum uttering the first day. Everyone but Dad would be back on the boat and the couple would exclaim, "Where's Steve? Where's Steve?" Upon which, Dad would invariably come rushing up the beach, grab hold of the rails and climb onto the boat just in time, like Capt Jack Sparrow or something.

"We were going without you," my mum would say, laughing. The Chinese couple were friendly, but due to the language barrier, our contact was mostly made up of smiles, nods and 'Hello'. But they returned home able to say 'Where's Steve?', so that was an achievement, I suppose.

For me, though, the pivotal part of our Vietnam trip was something I carry with me to this day, a metaphorical souvenir that will last longer than any postcard, keyring or fridge magnet. It's an image I use in my most anxious moments.

Sometimes, if I'm fretting about something, trying to push through and embrace the unknown, I just visualise crossing a busy Hanoi road. I'm taking that brave step out into oncoming traffic, knowing that the bikes will stop or swerve, because they always do. Taking that initial risk will be worth it; it always is. It's the same with anxiety. I've learnt that if I make the decision to sit with the anxiety for enough time, it will eventually disappear. Not reacting will always be worth it in the end.

17

I'm Worth How Many Camels?

Morocco

Morocco was a crazy clash of cultures. I was used to people being friendly while we were out exploring, but the locals in Marrakesh, although happy to talk, made me feel a little uncomfortable. We travelled to Morocco when I was seventeen, and I distinctly remember the markets of Marrakesh, the windy beaches of Casablanca, and the mint tea that I loved but my dad detested. But mostly, I remember middle-aged men trying to buy me with camels. They'd haggle with my parents in the street, offering goats, donkeys, entire bloody zoos in exchange for me.

It was an odd experience, and at first, I assumed they were joking. But after a few days of the incessant shouting and leering from across every street we walked down, I got seriously creeped out. Plus, as my irritation bubbled beneath the surface, I found myself wanting to snap back, "I'm worth sixteen camels – is that it?"

I guess every culture is wildly different, and that's the beauty of our world. I'm totally open to discovering new things; that's the coolest thing about travelling. I wholeheartedly believe my previous experiences with other practices helped me not get mad and yell at these men. I open my mind when I'm travelling; I try to appreciate every aspect of the country I'm in. I mean, some things we do back in the UK would certainly be considered odd to Moroccans. The way we Londoners are always running to catch some mode of transport, how we love to ignore each other on the tube and moan about the weather. We endure sexism, racism, discrimination, and biased opinions in the UK too, of course; these are ongoing issues right around the globe.

I've endured many a sexist remark out in the world. I've been discriminated against due to my height (I'm five foot and proud) and talked down to countless times. Such behaviour is a universal problem and not something that only certain Moroccan men are guilty of. But I started to feel awkward when we were out in Marrakesh. I was only seventeen, still at school and not even a proper adult yet (whatever that is; if anyone figures it out, let me know). I felt lucky my dad was with my mum and me, and I was thankful I wasn't there on my own with a female friend. I know I shouldn't have had to feel that way; it's appalling that in some places it's not safe enough for women to go out on their own or with other females.

My general anxiety had been building throughout the year (no surprises there), steadily increasing month by month as I attended sixth form less and less. I withdrew and was by now spending most of my time at home, so I was excited to get away somewhere. I didn't want to think about my final exams for a while, and I longed to be far away from my loud fellow students and patronising teachers, but Morocco was scary at night, and I felt the familiar claw of anxiety grip my shoulder. This time, it seemed different though. This time, it seemed more of a problem.

As I blended into the background at school like a withering wallflower, I'd found ways to momentarily decrease the anxiety that was now a depressingly daily occurrence. I'd been learning so much, especially during more recent travels, processing valuable life lessons – how to appreciate different ways of living in the Philippines, how to embrace the unknown in Vietnam – but I hadn't yet worked out how to apply this knowledge to my own anxiety. The main quick fix for my worries was carrying out specific routines and rituals, and this marked my mad two-year tumble down the rabbit hole of OCD. (Fab, now I didn't just have worrywart traits but a full-blown anxiety disorder. The fun never stopped.) In my own barmy brain, if I did these rituals right, nothing bad would happen to my family; I'd pass that exam; I wouldn't have to read in class; I'd be all right. It was flawed thinking to the max, but I wasn't aware this behaviour was making me more anxious in the long run. Seriously, who created the complexity of brains? I want a refund.

I had started to develop these routines a few months before we went to Morocco. For example, I found that tapping something – a tabletop, desk or chair, for example – in a certain rhythm helped banish my worries temporarily. But as our trip to Marrakesh approached, a sense of dread began to build. I worried that when we were abroad, I wouldn't be able to perform the rituals I'd normally carry out at home. So, when we actually arrived and found that not everyone was lovely, I wasn't necessarily in the best frame of mind to deal with that.

I don't know if it was the unsavoury expectations I'd drafted based on daytime interactions with a few leering locals, but everyone seemed more threatening when the sun set, more sinister. It was like they put on these scary masks at night. Or maybe the real masks were what they wore in the day.

It's naive to expect everywhere to be safe, and I don't. I know the world can be a poisonous place, but I wasn't used to this vibe, especially when on holiday. In Marrakesh, even my dad was targeted. He bought a beautiful oil painting one evening, an original piece from a market seller. My mum and I were already back at the hotel, getting ready for dinner, and he returned in a fluster. He'd been mugged on his way back, pushed over, the painting snatched away. Luckily, he wasn't badly hurt, but it was terrifying to say the least, and after that, we preferred to go out as a three.

When you're travelling, you have to be aware. My mum got her bag slashed in Vietnam in an opportunist attack; they didn't manage to nab anything, but it was still unsettling. In London, we're inundated with pickpockets in Leicester Square, Piccadilly Circus and Oxford Street. That's where they all hang out, and you have to keep your eyes on your bag at all times. And in Morocco, certain men creeped me out massively. It's not somewhere I'll ever head back to on my own.

Luckily, our Marrakesh hotel was an immensely peaceful haven, and we all loved spending time there. It was nestled in a maze of tiny, winding cobbled streets lined with brightly painted buildings accessed by doors heavy with amazing designs of swirls and gold spirals. You couldn't drive to it, you had to walk the last bit. On our first day, the taxi driver from the airport stopped the car abruptly and hauled our suitcase out without a word. Then he led the way down a series of narrow alleys, and we followed, expecting to see the hotel pop up soon. In fact, we were walking for about fifteen minutes. The sunlight was dimming and casting a golden light over everything, which made for a serene scene; it truly looked like a prized painting. It reminded me of Indiana Jones in the first film, *Raiders of the Lost Ark*, where he races through these little streets, trying to lose the bad guys chasing him.

The street markets and bazaars we passed were mesmerising. Snake charmers crafted their tunes to a backdrop of multi-coloured spices as the snakes danced from woven baskets, fixing us with icy stares. A man in traditional dress was running after his escaped monkey, which was dressed in a mini fez and cheekily darting away through the chaos. It was hard for our senses to process everything, and as we stumbled around another corner, my mum and I wondered how on earth anyone remembered their way. It was like a rabbit warren but much more wondrous – although I've admittedly never been down a rabbit warren; it could be like the Ritz down there.

Eventually, we reached our hotel, the Riyad El Cadi, and it was truly fantastic, a real hideaway from the mania outside. We entered through a wooden door in the wall on one of the cobbled streets, a door so tiny and insignificant that we expected it to lead to a similarly tiny interior. But no! When we stepped across the threshold, we were amazed – speechless, in fact. The inside was huge, like a palace, and there was white marble everywhere, adorned with gold trim. It was obvious the owners took pride in their business; they'd made such an effort with the rooms and clearly loved the finer things in life.

Our rooms were upstairs and comprised a little apartment of two bedrooms, two bathrooms and a living area. There was a small restaurant downstairs, where breakfast was served each morning, and there was also a roof garden, where we loved to sit on sun loungers under the deep red canopy. It was like being royal. We could see for miles as we relaxed there, spying on the hectic hum below. The tiny streets and haziness of the air made the whole scene look magical. We listened for the calls to prayer and watched as the locals made their way to the mosques.

It was such a juxtaposition. Inside the hotel, everything was still, silent and serene; I always got a great night's sleep in my room. Up on the roof though, that typical bustling city soundtrack resumed, and our ears were filled with a thousand different noises at once. It was like someone pressed play, and boom, the volume was up high again.

Up on the roof, under the canopies, enjoying the setting sun one afternoon, we ordered mint tea, a Moroccan specialty. This order also became our go-to when stopping for lunch while we were out and about. But at the hotel, they went all out. Fresh tea would arrive in a pretty silver pot, and we drank it out of tiny glasses. My dad, who'd just finished taking pictures from the roof, sat down and we convinced him to try some. He doesn't like tea; he's on Team Coffee, no question. But this tea was different. It wasn't like the Twinings mint offering I was used to at home; it was sweet, strong but delicious, and fantastically fresh.

Dad tried it, and the series of photographs Mum snapped of him on her camera are legendary. She took about twenty frames, and you can flip through them like one of those little moving picture books and marvel as my dad's face turns from apprehensive as he's sipping, to confusion as he swallows, and then pure disgust. Eventually, his face scrunches up as the pungent tea hits his tastebuds. It was hilarious to watch. Whenever I need cheering up, I look back on that face in those pictures. I'd include them in this chapter, but I don't think it would go down too well with my dad.

*

From Marrakesh, we took a two-hour flight to Casablanca, Morocco's largest city, to spend a few days on Ain Diab beach. Its distinct lack of chaos soothed my frazzled mind. The only issue was that it was October, not the warmest of months. It wasn't cold by our standards, but when out, we were certainly sporting light jackets. That was fine with us though, as we wanted to explore the sights. This wasn't a beach break as such, it was more about capturing the rich beauty of everything around us. So, our beach walks were primarily to see the area rather than enjoy sunbathing.

After a walk around town one evening, we found somewhere for dinner, and my parents attempted to explain the plot of the movie Casablanca to me. At seventeen, I'd never heard of it. Back at the hotel, my dad stayed to have a beer on the terrace, and my mum and I headed upstairs to our apartment to read our books. Now, this hotel was nice, very nice, but we had left the windows open to get some fresh air while at dinner. When we got back there was a little friend waiting for us. We both caught sight of it instantly as the heavy wooden door swung closed. It was my worst nightmare. I swear they stalk me; I'm like the original roach master.

My mum yelled in surprise, and I screamed and jumped on the bed. Yes, we overreacted. I hate bugs at the best of times, but cockroaches are on a different level.

We shrieked at it for a bit. This was in no way constructive, but we didn't know what else to do. We were both now hopping on one of the beds, eyes peeled for more. When the roach started moving, we really freaked out. We needed to get my dad, but we couldn't get out because the roach was on the back of the door like a creepy-crawly guard. Every time we inched towards it, it scuttled into action.

We Rock-Paper-Scissored to determine who was going to run out to get dad and who'd stay on watch. We were as bad as each other, weighing up the pros and cons of being the one who stayed. On the plus side, you wouldn't have to go past it, and you could watch to make sure it didn't disappear and then pop back up in the middle of the damn night. On the other hand, you'd be in the room alone with it, and if it scuttled, what exactly would you do? Plus, what if *more* emerged?

In the end, I opted to get my dad. Also, I lost at Rock Paper Scissors.

My mum slowly made her way to the door and carefully creaked it open, hurtling back to the bed as I ran for it, taking the stairs two at a time. I finally reached the bar outside, a gibbering wreck, my dad's peace and quiet now shattered. I mean, that's what having kids is about, right? Hurriedly, I explained the situation, and he hauled himself upstairs to catch the bug. This took him the best part of an hour. Every time he hovered over it, waiting to encase it in a wad of tissue paper, it would scurry off, out of reach. I refused to jump down from my safe space on the bed until he nabbed it.

Dad did finally catch the roach, but even that didn't make my mum and me feel any better. There could certainly be more. That night was the worst sleep I'd ever had. I clasped my hands over my ears, pulled my sheet over my head until the early hours, and jolted every time the material shifted or touched my leg. I'd heard that roaches could crawl into your ear holes, so that's why I had my hands glued to my head. Awful things. I'll never see the point of them. I adore animals, but if I could get rid of one species, it would be cockroaches. The mere mention of them makes me squirm. I'd happily see them extinct.

It got bad, this aversion to those pesky creatures. I distinctly remember fifteen-year-old me adding music to my bright pink iPod Nano. I'd been discovering some good bands and downloaded metal group Papa Roach's first album eagerly. For anyone who isn't familiar with their music, this particular album cover is a close-up of a cockroach on a white background. Well, every single time the album cover appeared on my shuffle screen, I'd cringe. I ended up having to download a generic picture of the band from Google Images, which I swapped with the original album art. It was way too much for me. I wanted to vomit every time I caught sight of the horrible little thing. So, yeah, great band, love them but awful name and awful first album cover in my personal, cockroach-hating opinion.

The morning after that fitful night's sleep, spent dreaming of pattering insects, I was up and awake as early as possible. We headed out on a walk, covering more ground than on previous days, and stumbled across a new beach. And wow, was this beach different from the picturesque one we'd been strolling on each morning prior. Those had been littered with coffee shops and cafés overlooking the choppy waters. These new sands were littered all right but not with quaint, quiet places to grab a latte. No, we nicknamed this sweep 'Stig of the Dump Beach' because, bluntly, it was a dump.

Discarded needles and tissues lay buried in the sand, food wrappers flew through the air and we had to dodge animal poo (at least, I hoped it was animal poo) and old clothes with every cautious step. Rubbish was strewn everywhere, and we had to bypass the odd shoe and an array of cigarette butts. The sand itself was barely visible. We left swiftly, backtracking to our familiar beach and sinking into the safe embrace of our regular coffee shop.

Morocco was a clash of contrasts indeed. Casablanca was chilly but chilled (bar the cockroach incident) and, apart from Stig of the Dump Beach, it was a calming place to wander at our own pace, enjoying things and seeing the sights at leisure. Casablanca was self-assured. Marrakesh was a different kettle of fish. It was hard to not get swept up in its vibrant day-to-day life. It was loud and lively; it wanted attention all the time. We always felt we had to rush everywhere, but it was great, and I'm glad I sampled both those Moroccan destinations. It was particularly fantastic to experience them side by side. It made me really ponder how different cultures can be even within the same country.

18

The Wonky Donkey

Nerja

Nerja will always be special to me. This radiant little resort town on the south coast of Spain is a third home (after London and Northampton) and holds a prized place in my thoughts. It's been familiar to my family ever since I was small. Some of my fondest, earliest travel memories were spent in Spain with my nan, pap and mum, clambering over rocks, gazing out to sea, watching ice-cream cones melt in the humid heat, hearing the squawks of seagulls as they danced daringly just above the waves. My dad was working so didn't make it to Nerja when we went, but he enjoyed looking at my blurry photos and listening to me gabble on about my adventures when I returned home.

We had such a great time. The bustling Balcon de Europa in the centre of town was my stage. This massive 'balcony' – actually a circular viewing platform atop a rocky outcrop – overlooks the Mediterranean and is packed with local cafés and restaurants selling Spanish delicacies. For me, though, it was my personal performance space. I'd belt out Spice Girl songs there, performing to my audience – namely the poor people just trying to eat their meals in peace – hopping around like a right little weirdo as my nan and pap clapped from a nearby table.

I loved it in Nerja. We'd go to the beach to relax during the day and I'd enjoy the February sun, an odd sensation when you'd come from the freezing temperatures and winter snowstorms of the UK. On one visit, three-year-old me climbed up onto a massive rock overlooking the sparkling sea, playing – you guessed it – *The Lion King*, but then, I couldn't get down again. I was essentially stranded, so my pap had to clamber up and rescue me. That moment was immortalised in a photo showing Pap lifting me down. It's one of lots of lovely photos in a beautiful 'Grandparents' keepsake book that my nan presented me with on my eighteenth birthday. Mum had bought the book for my nan when I was born and my nan had filled it over the years, sticking in photographs, writing about her life and mine. When she gave it to me on my birthday, I instantly spotted that photo of me on the massive rock, and I grinned, chuckling to myself.

Nerja is a little family hotspot. It's somewhere we all instantly know and natter about fondly. The first time I went, I refused to leave. I'd revelled in the sunshine, the beach trips and the exploring; it was my first experience of Spain and I wasn't ready to return home to chillier weather, school life and a distinct lack of sun-sprinkled afternoons.

The following year, I went there with my mum, Auntie Shell and Drew. Drew and I were so excitable and gobbled up the change of scenery like we did the mouth-wateringly bright ice creams we queued for every afternoon. It had to be lemon sorbet for me. No question. As soon as we'd finished our dinners, Drew and I would rush up onto the stage at the Balcon and sing and dance like we were born to perform (or born to be massive attention seekers; you decide).

My third trip to Nerja was in 2013, when I was seventeen and at the very peak of my anxiety, immersed in my (unhelpful) OCD rituals. (Cue dramatic music with ominous underlying tones.) By this time, the anxiety and coping mechanisms I'd been clinging to over the last year (tapping surfaces or neatly lining up some item or other) had morphed into full-blown OCD, and, believe me, it wasn't fun.

Despite having to constantly disappear off to carry out the various rituals my brain was insistent on me doing, I enjoyed myself the majority of the time. But worries still buzzed in the background. I was due to start university the following month and was feeling the nerves creep up, mingling with my normal preoccupations (oh, you know, existential dread, the usual everyday stuff). When I look back now, I feel sad I was that anxious, permanently on high alert. It makes me annoyed I let that mindset take over my life for so long, but at the time, I didn't really know how bad it was getting.

I'm hardly a carefree, relaxed individual now, but I am much more in control of how I deal with my worries. I take whatever my anxiety whines at me with a pinch of salt and a roll of my eyes. I've gained the ability to poke fun at myself and tut at the incessant gibberish my mind produces. Yeah, it's still there, but it doesn't take over my whole life now; it's just a small part of me, an annoying wasp that needs to be swatted away. Now it's a normal-sized wasp, but when I was seventeen, it was a 'mutant' wasp with big, bulging eyes that occupied my entire line of sight and blocked my path whenever I tried to dodge past it. Ugh, mutant wasps, what an awful thought. They sound almost as bad as cockroaches.

My uncle's parents owned an apartment in Nerja, in a private complex nestled in the picturesque countryside, and that's where we all used to gravitate to. The caretaker there was a questionable guy and over the years he'd developed an intense hatred of my cousin Drew, for no apparent reason. He'd watch Drew beadily, waiting for him to bring a drink near the pool, start up a ball game in the water or just do anything he deemed 'unsuitable'. He'd pop up when you least expected and follow Drew practically everywhere like a shadow, muttering angrily in Spanish, giving everyone the evil eye. We spent most of our time dodging this mad caretaker.

One overcast afternoon, I was flipping through my latest novel on the balcony of the apartment, zoning out, lost in the story, when I was abruptly startled by the distinctive sound of a lawnmower firing up. I glanced up, over the top of my sunglasses, and saw that this same caretaker was aggressively mowing the lawn around the small crowd of sleeping sunbathers, coming dangerously close to a shocked woman's hair. The guests started jumping up, snatching their towels away in the nick of time, just before they were turned to ribboned shreds by the manic mowing. I motioned to Drew and we both watched the scene unfold from above, flabbergasted.

We always got weird vibes from the caretaker. We'd be chilling by the pool and suddenly our other cousins, Harrison and Adam, would start humming the *Jaws* theme tune. Drew and I would look up and there he'd be, peeking from behind a tree, holding a rake menacingly, eyeballing us with this unfounded hatred. Weird guy.

Creepy caretakers aside, there were many other events that stuck in my mind from that trip. Including how my almost nightly sleep visions would cause Auntie Shell to wake up in a panic, as I jumped out of my bed in a tizz, screaming about spiders and weird-looking patterns on the walls, before settling back to sleep almost immediately. It's safe to say, no one particularly liked sharing a room with me.

I also got incredibly sunburned on that trip and had to watch the rest of my family top up their terrific tans while I ended up resembling some vampire/lobster crossover fail. Because of that, I decided to lounge by the pool while everyone else did the Nerja River Walk. This sounded spectacular and exciting, like an Indiana Jones adventure – a sixteen-kilometre circular hike up through the natural park and along the course of the Chillar River, a perfect way to cool down as the water lapped at your ankles – but I was feeling sorry for myself, sporting my ridiculous-looking sunburn, so I opted to stay behind.

I ended up wishing I had gone with them, because when Harrison, Adam and Drew returned, they smugly insisted I'd missed out big time. "We saw the best thing, Chloë! There were these two pugs in lifejackets." Drew laughed as my face fell. I'd have loved to have seen that. I adore pugs: their squishy little faces, the way they waddle about.

My boyfriend Brandon and I went to a socially distanced pug book-signing back in the summer of Covid. It was a factual story about a disabled pug called Bertie and his owner Anushka, who set up a place called the Pug Café in the hope of finding Bertie more friends. The cafés have since become a huge success, and there are now events for other breeds too.

The book-signing was so cute. People brought their pugs to the local Waterstones and, honestly, it was like living in my dreamworld. I purchased a copy of the book and queued nervously to get it signed, feeling a little odd that I didn't have a dog and was attending like some sort of weird pug fanatic. But Anushka was really lovely and chatted for a while about Bertie, who was adorably sitting upright in his special stroller, looking done, like he just wanted to head home. He'd been the centre of attention for hours and his social meter had clearly run out. I know the feeling.

But, yes, I adore pugs and wished I'd joined the river walk to witness this super-cute-sounding scene. Although I probably would have nabbed one of them and returned home with a furry head poking out of my suitcase.

From pugs to donkeys. The infamous Wonky Donkey incident is a story I'll never live down. One balmy evening we all went to a local pub after dinner. I ordered a Bacardi and lemonade, not realising that Spanish measures are by no means stingy. I was tipsy after one and laughing at everything. Oh, to be seventeen again. Living life.

On the way back to the apartments, I started running up this hill, the same steep incline I'd spent the past few days complaining about walking up. The alcohol had made me feel like I could run anywhere. I reached the top of the hill and was squinting through the darkness in search of my family when I spotted this clothes shop named The Wonky Donkey. It was lit up like a beacon in the street and was pretty much the only thing I could see. Well, I laughed and laughed, almost toppling over. Then I skipped back to my cousins, unable to even talk as I pointed back up to the shop and wheezed out my words. They looked confused. I found it hilarious.

"Guys!" I spluttered, as they shot glances at each other. "Guys, that shop is called The Wonky Donkey!" I collapsed into fresh peals of laughter and everyone else started giggling too, but you know, at me rather than the shop I'd deemed side-splitting. It's a long-standing joke between us all now and clearly an example of how easily amused I am.

Alcohol makes me even more easily amused, but it also makes me even hungrier than usual. I'm one of those people that needs feeding at regular intervals, and when I say feeding, I mean a substantial meal. If not, my blood-sugar levels drop and I get super cranky, fast. I realise that makes me sound like some sort of sad, overgrown baby, but I get very irritable and emotional if I don't eat properly.

One night, we were deep into a tapas crawl with some friends of my auntie and uncle's. We had sampled a lot of delicious delights, but as the evening went on, I found the tiny portions didn't sustain my energy. I love tapas as much as the next person, but for dinner…? Not really. The thing about tapas is there just isn't enough of it. I'm always craving a burger afterwards. I'd also had a few drinks and my mind plummeted into darkness as my stomach rumbled noisily.

It got to 10 pm and everything caught up with me. I was tired; I was hungry; I was stressed at having to start university in less than a week, and I was also a little homesick. Plus, my sunburn stung. Suddenly, the pleasantly muggy evening felt stifling and oppressive. I burst into tears at the table, feeling overwhelmed, and poor Drew had to look after me, taking me on a walk around the block, telling me jokes and making me laugh until I was sufficiently embarrassed at my bizarre outburst to return to the others.

He's always been good at managing my strange personality. As we've grown up, we've developed our individualities, me with my mad anxiety and emo taste in music, him with his easy-going attitude and ability to talk to literally anyone, but we've remained close. I love heading up to Northampton and spending an evening sipping Prosecco and playing Mario Party with Drew and his fiancée Nikita, Harrison and his fiancé Siana, and Brandon and Ads.

I look back on that night in Nerja as the most extreme example of what happens when I drink alcohol and don't eat much along with it. Although I felt instantly better once I'd nibbled something, whenever I see a tapas restaurant, I'm reminded of that time. But now, I can look back on it and snigger to myself.

I think my anxiety, my lack of food, the hefty Spanish alcohol measures (seriously, a single out there is like a triple in an English pub) and my looming dread at starting the next chapter of my life all collided to create the perfect mess. Something flipped that evening, though, and I realised that, yes, my university start date was inching closer, and, yes, I'd have to accept that life was changing and everything was going to be different now. I'd left school, and I was pleased to be away from sixth form, don't get me wrong, but the next stage of life seemed pretty scary. I'd have to learn how to 'adult'. I mean, where was the human manual? Did a helpful sidekick ever pop up out of the blue and let you know how to get past each level like in the Xbox games I'd spent my childhood playing with my cousins? It didn't appear so.

I left Spain feeling apprehensive about the future but ready for it at the same time. We'd survived a creepy caretaker, after all, so I could take on anything.

When I look back on that trip, it's tinged with a bittersweet filter reminiscent of the Haribo Tangfastics I used to adore (and still do). I have so many amazing memories from that sun-soaked holiday, and they're the sweet part. But there was an underlying sourness as I battled to keep my anxiety at bay and hide my OCD, and that's the unexpected tangy aftertaste.

I realise now that that entire summer, and its finale, that holiday in Nerja, was the initial crucial turning point for me. It was when I first understood that something was wrong with the way I handled anxiety. Jetting off to Nerja was the first steppingstone towards reclaiming my life. I just didn't know it yet. God, don't I sound like a self-help book.

Having been unable to carry out my more specific OCD rituals while I was in Nerja, I returned from that pivotal trip and found that nothing had happened back at home. No one had crashed their car in a fiery inferno, no one had gone missing, and the house hadn't burnt down. My life back in England was exactly how I'd left it.

Those rituals literally made no difference and I'd unknowingly proved my anxiety wrong for the first time. I didn't arrive home to a scene from a Final Destination movie in which people had perished in the most absurd ways. Everything was normal. Or as normal as you can get in this weird and wonderful world of ours.

The OCD had become this personified monster, entangled unhelpfully with my general anxiety. (I'm a bundle of laughs, honest.) Now I began to read about the disorder itself, facing up to the fact that there was a name for the way I was reacting to stress. I learnt that there were two parts to the disorder: the obsessions (the scary thoughts) and the compulsions (the rituals a person carried out to neutralise these thoughts and feel 'safer').

I opted not to visit my GP. I wasn't ready for that step, but I was ready to educate myself a little more. In my own weird way, I felt like it should be me alone who handled the fight against it. I would defeat it once and for all when I was ready.

There's still a stigma around anxiety and OCD, and almost everyone you meet will proclaim that they're 'a little OCD' if they like things to be ordered. What I've grown to notice is that a lot of the time these people don't realise they're being insensitive to sufferers of a genuinely crippling anxiety disorder, and that's because most people don't know enough about it. I believe that needs to change. Not only that, but doctors and therapists need to be more aware of the symptoms and they need to emphasise that there is help out there and that OCD can be overcome.

I'm not perfect, and my anxious nature is just an annoying part of me but learning to deal with it in more helpful ways has given me my life back. And Spain was the very start of that. I returned to London with a more hopeful frame of mind packed away inside my suitcase. I had evidence I was tackling my anxiety in a negative way, but I'd had a good time so I could still do everything I wanted to do in spite of it.

Feeling like I was on the edge of something – I didn't know what, just that I would definitely be heading in a different direction from then on – I knew I was ready to take on life, no matter what it brought. When I returned home, I asked my pap, a brilliantly talented painter and always on the hunt for his next artistic project, if he could paint one of the photos I'd taken of the sea view from the Balcon.

He got to work and produced a wonderful painting, which I've chosen to use for the cover of this book. I have the original proudly hanging in my room, alongside some of his other works. These include a sketch of some practising ballerinas he drew for me when I was little; a lovely one of me and him playing in the dollhouse he made for me in real life and another he painted to celebrate my first job as a reporter. That one shows me flying a Spitfire with the words 'Chloë Bell – Ace Reporter, First to the News' etched along the bottom. One of the very first jobs I covered as an official journalist was the Biggin Hill Air Show and I got the chance to take to the air, so that's why I'm in a Spitfire.

The painting of Nerja is my favourite though. It depicts a place that's very special to me, part of my earliest travel memories, and somewhere that always reminds me of wonderful times spent with my family, and my nan and pap in particular. But most of all, it represents my very first attempts to battle my anxieties head-on.

My pap was the perfect person to create the work of art that marked that initial shift in my mindset. He was always able to laugh at himself. He'd chuckle and call himself a 'silly old sod' when he located the piece of his jigsaw puzzle he'd been searching for all day. As I look at the painting, I can smell the saltwater mingled with the aroma of freshly cooked paella on the Balcon. I hear the distant rush of waves as they hit the rocks beneath and I breathe a sigh of happiness. Above all, when I gaze at that painting, I'm reminded to giggle at myself and not take life too seriously. Thanks, Pap.

19

Hati-Hati!

Java

We set off for the Indonesian island of Java just after I turned nineteen, dreaming of hot climes, mouth-watering coffee, dense jungles and expansive white beaches. Granted, we experienced all the above, but our trip was peppered with many a mishap: an intolerable anxiety disorder, my dad stepping on an actual volcano, and the Bug Mobile – which still haunts me to this day.

Whereas I remember Cambodia and the Andaman Islands as looking like oil paintings – all bold, bright colours – being in Java was like finding ourselves immersed in someone's watercolour sketch. Everything was softer, subtly beautiful rather than exploding with crazy charm. We stayed in Pelabuhan Ratu, West Java, in a homely hotel made up of little bungalows set high in the hills overlooking the sloping forest, with glimpses of the beach in the distance. There was plenty to do, and our holiday had more adventure vibes than our previous few trips. We visited temples, marvelled at waterfalls, went hiking and paddled in the sea. And the mountain views were truly something.

Java was overcast, but that didn't mean it wasn't hot. The humid air wasn't uncomfortable, in fact, it was the kind of heat that always reminds me of being 'away'. Sometimes, back home in London, I slip out into our garden in the summer and catch a fleeting sense of that feeling, that smell. Our garden, like our home, is full of reminders of our travels. We have a beautiful Buddha water feature, and it's so lovely to sit out there in the summer, enjoying the sound of trickling water. The rest of our space is filled with greenery, towering pampas grasses, and exotic, brightly coloured flowers. It always makes me feel like I'm holiday when the plants start blossoming in the warmer months.

But it's that smell, that certain scent, that reminds me of being away even when I'm not. Sometimes I'll be walking somewhere (probably to Costa, let's be honest), and it'll be overcast but hot, the warm breeze ruffling my hair, and that smell will suddenly seep into my nostrils for a second or two: humid heat mixed with the anticipation of imminent rain. I'll be engulfed by a wave of nostalgia as I recall my travels and imagine gazing out over the sea somewhere tropical, enjoying the freedom.

This scent was ever present in Pelabuhan Ratu. Although we rarely saw blue skies, it hardly ever rained. My favourite place to sit was at the breakfast table. We were the only guests, and as I drank my coffee, I would watch the waves crashing onto the distant empty sands. We were surrounded by vivid green jungle, and I'd look out of my window each morning and spy all different species of birds swooping through the balmy air. It was a fantastic way to start my day.

In Java, I was shrouded in my ever-present anxiety cape. OCD was there in the background of everything I did. Since Nerja, I'd been researching the disorder, but I wasn't ready to quit all my rituals yet, so they built up. It was the end of my first year at university, so now I whittled about my course rather than sixth form and seemed to be having an existential crisis daily. Fun.

I'd relax in my beautiful Javanese surroundings for a minute or so, but then, my (stupid) over-active brain would nag, forcing me to do another ritual and spoil my newfound Zen state. Relaxing did work at times, but that trip was dominated by more OCD rituals than I could count. I'd be constantly disappearing off to check locks or participate in ways to ease my anxiety. Me and my brain were the ultimate frenemies.

I'd started to struggle with rigid thought patterns in Morocco, and these had become magnified by the time I went to Nerja, but when I arrived in Java, I was sick of it all. I was sick of the constant anxiety, sick of the stupid rituals that didn't even lessen my worries anymore, and sick of my infuriating brain ruining yet another trip. I loved travelling. I wanted to jump in and embrace the captivating culture, the cuisine. But it was hard to do that when my mind was constantly flitting, looking for danger everywhere.

I was bored of anxiety, and that was a weird feeling. Boredom mixed with a dollop of worry and a sprinkle of annoyance at the whole ridiculous scenario. Don't go ordering that ice cream combo, it's *not good*. Lemon ice is better.

In Java, I was away from my routine and physically couldn't carry out some of the usual, everyday rituals I'd become so reliant on. I was forced to cope with the anxiety head-on and just deal with it.

The last two years had been my very worst period. I'd got into the practice of waking up an hour earlier than necessary for uni in order to complete my steadily growing stream of tasks. On a bad day, it would take multiple efforts to dress, do my make-up or even leave the room; everything had to feel sufficiently 'right' for me to move on or else something catastrophic would happen to my family. Ironically, though, I was never late for anything, which was impressive, if I do say so myself.

Flipping light switches on and off, touching surfaces in multiples of four, repeating 'safe' phrases in my head or redoing various activities over and over made the odd occasion I woke up late impossible to tolerate. I would head down the winding stairs of our cottage, terrified that stepping on the last step with the 'wrong' foot would cause bad luck to befall my loved ones, so I'd run back up the stairs just to come down again. And again. And again. Until I was satisfied I'd ensured no harm could occur.

It was exhausting, and deep down, I knew I was being utterly ridiculous. But for a few seconds, my panic would ease, so I craved that small window of freedom, however fleeting.

I'd throw away items that I deemed to be bad luck. I'd bought these cool burgundy jeans on impulse (they were swaggy to the max) – I loved them as soon as I spied them in New Look, hanging from the rack, beckoning to me. I'd excitedly worn them once, but then, an anxious thought passed through my head while I was admiring them in the mirror, and all hell broke loose. What if these jeans were bad luck? My flawed thinking pattern was working at record speed to find an issue and I let that strange thought become a fixed idea. Crazy, I know. They were just jeans. But my mind was not my friend.

A cold sweat enveloped me, and I tore them off and changed into another outfit entirely. I hurried downstairs to the bin and hurled the burgundy bundle into it, slamming the lid shut in a tizz.

"You just bought those, Chloë." My mum glanced up from making coffee and looked over at me with a confused frown.

"They don't fit. I can't be bothered to take them back," I lied, before rushing back upstairs to engage in various rituals to counteract the demonic jeans. I know. Madness.

I hid my erratic behaviour well, but inevitably, my family started to question why I kept disappearing every few minutes. My mood dropped. I was snappy, low, frazzled and just plain sick of life being so hard.

I was never not anxious, and it became increasingly impossible to hide my secret life from everyone. I turned up to university lectures but couldn't focus because my mind was elsewhere. I stopped making an effort socially and withdrew from my friends. It was too awkward to explain and I was concerned they'd think I was weird.

Those two years were lost to panicked flurries over situations that weren't even real or remotely possible. I'm amazed I graduated university and held down my part-time job.

Java showed me something special. I was forced out of my tightly planned routine, the one I'd built so carefully, and made to realise life didn't have to be so hard.

The spectacular sights all around me were a distraction, and a few days in, my mind learnt to calm itself, even if just for a handful of minutes per day. I was overwhelmed with new views, scenes, amazing things. I'm not saying heading off on holiday will ultimately fix every mental health problem, but, personally, it helped me make those next steps in my recovery.

I began to enjoy myself completely. I was reminded, albeit temporarily, what life had been like before the crippling anxiety and disfigured thinking latched itself onto me. I wanted my previous adventure-seeking nature back and this trip was pivotal to securing that.

Sitting on the balcony one evening as the heat of the day cooled, I watched bats dancing across the darkening scene. A brilliant burst of orange and red was illuminating the sky like a multi-coloured fireworks display as the sun set on another day. As expected, feeling somewhat calm for once, my brain scanned for danger and leapt into action.

"You need to…" it muttered but then faltered.

"I need to *what*? I can't do any of my normal rituals. I'm not at home, so any safety behaviours I do here won't be the same. I may as well just enjoy this evening." A more logical part of my mind had found its voice. And, believe me, I hadn't heard from logical Chloë for a while.

"Well, you'll need to do your rituals perfectly when you get home to make up for this," the anxiety spat back venomously.

And then, I did something involuntary. I shrugged it off.

"Yeah, maybe, but right now, I don't need to do anything at all," I decided, as I continued to watch the swooping shapes in the striking sky.

Sometimes travelling – the act of simply going somewhere and opening your eyes to a different scene – can put things into perspective. Even if it only alters your thinking a tiny bit, that's still progress. That's why I am firmly of the opinion that travelling is good for you. I know I'm incredibly fortunate to have seen so much of the world already, and I'll always be grateful for that.

Anxiety works in wondrous ways. Even though a structured routine helps alleviate symptoms in many cases, sometimes you need to flip it and try a completely different approach, an absence of routine. Sometimes you need to mix it up and try ditching everything you assumed would work. You need to see somewhere else or go somewhere different. Even if you just hop in the car and drive to the beach an hour from home, you're essentially kickstarting your brain into coping with stress directly.

So, I mixed it up. And although I still whittled internally, I threw myself into an array of activities in Java.

Despite Pelabuhan Ratu Beach appearing close enough to our hotel that we could almost feel the sea spray at the breakfast table, the walk down to it from the hotel took ten minutes, and it was an eventful walk each time. A pleasant little path led us down through the trees and the undergrowth and emerged in a tiny village, where locals were building houses and selling fruit. Eventually, we stumbled through the dense forest and out onto the white sands at the bottom. It was like an adventure movie, and we were the starring actors. Hiking back up though? That took a lot longer. The hill was never-ending. I often grabbed hold of the camera bag slung across my dad's back and he dragged me up. Yes, it was that steep, I promise. But, granted, I am kind of lazy.

The trip had all the elements of a relaxing beach break until it didn't. We swam in the deserted pool, enjoyed delicious dinners in the empty restaurant, explored the mountains, shopped in the nearby markets, and met the locals, who loved to recommend food we should eat and places we should see.

We hired a car so we could head out further and check out the hot springs the hotel staff had told us about. We wanted to do things under our own steam and be able to stumble across cool things to do rather than always know where we wanted to end up. So, we hired a car. Simple, right? We nabbed the last one at the hire place, which was lucky. We all clambered in, our bags filled with sun cream and water bottles, our cameras at the ready. It was a sweet ride, spanking new with a shiny exterior, plus the seats were immensely comfortable. It was no means an old banger, which made what occurred next even more horrifying.

It was all fine and dandy until fifteen minutes later we stopped at some local shops. My mum needed a cold drink and my dad wanted to take photos. I opted to stay in the car as they weren't going to be long. So, I did, happily swiping through my iPod, jamming to my music.

I was staring around, gazing out the windows at the people selling cold drinks on the roadside, watching the leaves of the overhanging palms swaying in the mild breeze, just generally zoning out, when I caught sight of a cockroach scurrying along by my feet.

If you've been reading so far, you'll know I can't stand those things.

I screamed out loud, leapt up, unfastened my seatbelt in a flurry and pulled my legs up hastily. I crouched on the seat, my eyes darting all over as it disappeared from view. My mum and dad arrived back a few moments later, swinging open the door, eyebrows raised, faces questioning the screeches coming from my mouth.

After I'd explained, my dad, resident bug catcher, sought out the roach and flicked it outside with ease. But I couldn't get the damn thing out of my head. If there's anything worse than your standard run-of-the-mill bug, it's a cockroach. I can't even stand to type the word; I get this mental image and feel like they're scuttling over me.

I've detested them ever since I watched *Men in Black* when I was little. The alien that smashes them on the tabletop with his hands makes me shudder. My dad and I used to drop in at the local Blockbuster's on our way home from the weekly shop and I'd pick *Men in Black* to rent most times. I'd watch it religiously, but that part I still can't stomach to this day.

Eventually, I settled down again in the back seat of the Javanese car. My dad had got rid of the bug; everything was fine. I relaxed a bit, and we continued our journey. I was still a little jumpy, convinced one was on me every time my bag strap touched my leg or a strand of my hair brushed against my shoulder, but my parents just laughed. "It's gone, Chloë," my dad said chuckling as he rounded the bend.

But when we next stopped, to have lunch, we returned to the car to find that there were now five roaches scooting about. An unsavoury welcome back, for sure. After our third stop, we opened the car doors to find that there were now fifteen of the critters. They only came out when the engine stopped running, which was why they were never visible until we parked up. After our fourth stop, I'd had enough. This time, the roaches were everywhere. It was like a horror scene. I point-blank refused to get back in. I stood at the side of the street in the blistering heat, shaking my head like a five-year-old having a tantrum. I was jumping out of my skin every few seconds and brushing myself off, convinced they were on me.

"No. No. NO." I crossed my arms and turned my head away from the Bug Mobile.

"We have to, Chloë." My mum peered into the car herself and jumped back as three roaches zoomed towards her. She slammed the door hastily. "We have no other way of getting back," she added, sounding less sure now.

My dad didn't mind too much. He got back in and started the engine, which sent the bugs into a frenzy as they hurried to their hiding spot. "They've retreated to where they came from," he insisted, "and they won't come out again while the engine is running."

I stood aghast for a good twenty minutes, refusing to even touch the passenger door. Eventually, I had to get in though. My mum was right, it was too far to walk, plus we couldn't just leave the car there. My dad was correct too. When the engine was running, we didn't see any. But the thought of them still freaked me out; the sheer number of them. Jesus.

I plugged in my earphones and sat hunched on the seat, on my heels. I was watching, my eyes flickering, letting out yelps every now and again, setting my mum off too. My dad must have been happy to get back to our hotel, his eardrums probably damaged from the shrieking. As soon as we turned the corner and I set eyes on the hotel, I unclipped my seatbelt and jumped out, practically before the car stopped. Mum and I didn't get into the car of horrors again, not to go for dinner, nor to go exploring the next day. I was starting to see why it had been the last vehicle available for hire. We nicknamed it the Bug Mobile, and my poor dad had to drive it back in the dark with God knows how many roaches crawling around his feet. Yuck.

I didn't sleep that night. I was sure there were bugs everywhere and I kept jerking awake and flicking on my light to check. My dad had to do a cursory sweep of the whole bungalow, looking for any unwanted visitors.

The next afternoon, he suggested hiring a car again as we wanted to go to the hot springs in Cisolok. My mum and I spluttered in indignation.

"It might not be the same one." He shrugged.

"No way," I replied, scooping up my day bag.

My mum backed me up. It was fine, we'd find another way to get to the springs.

So, a tuk-tuk it was. Tuk-tuks are my all-time favourite way of seeing a new place. They always feel less constricting, more open; you can see, smell and hear more. In a tuk-tuk, I feel like I'm getting the whole experience as we whip through a town. You're getting the collision of smells: spices, fruit, humid heat. And you're getting the sounds: market sellers, laughing children on their way to school, the beeping of other drivers greeting each other. In a car, the windows silence the outside world and you're trapped in your air-conditioned constraints. You miss out on this whole other exhilarating experience, the jolt to all of your senses at once. You miss out on the feel of the hot wind in your hair and the general freeness of a tuk-tuk ride.

The springs in Cisolok were very picturesque. The whole place had an enchanting feel to it. Everywhere you glanced, there were beautiful rock formations, geysers spewing out reels of steam, and inviting bodies of water to take a dip in. We wandered around, taking in the different pools and checking out the baths. It was tranquil, despite the floods of tourists inhabiting every available space, and impressive to see something so naturally awe-inspiring; the best kind of readymade spa.

The springs reminded me of a lost magical kingdom, and when a heavy mist descended, it was aptly atmospheric. I stopped to snap some pictures of the biggest spring, the main attraction, and my mum sat down on one of the nearby rocks to sort her bag out. My dad disappeared off to get a close-up of the springs.

There were stone steps down to a lower level. The water down there was ankle deep and several visitors were milling around in it. I watched them as they took selfies, just wading about, exploring. Steam rose from the waters and every now and again a huge gust of hot spray would burst out from the rocks. It was hot underfoot, and everyone was wearing shoes.

I made my way down, glancing back to see my dad following. I walked slowly, careful not to slip on the smooth rock beneath the shallow water. The hot mist was thicker now, and it was difficult to see in front of me. It was quite spectacular, like stepping into a really hot footbath. I mean, I love a steaming bubble bath, but this water around my feet was scorching, even by my standards. It was a volcanic spring, after all. There was probably molten magma somewhere deep beneath those burning rocks.

Along with everyone else, I was gazing in wonder at the springs when suddenly I heard an exclamation.

"Ow. Ow! OW!"

I spun around, and at first, I thought my dad was dancing. He was shifting from foot to foot, slipping and sliding. His arms flailed and I stared at him aghast. I couldn't work out what was happening.

"What are you doing…?" I laughed as his arms shot forward and his left foot slipped back.

Everyone, and I mean every single person in the vicinity, no exaggeration, was staring as he hopped and yelled. Eventually, he made it back to the steps, howling. When I reached him, wading over as fast as I could whilst still being careful not to slip and land face first in the boiling water, he was clinging onto the side with one hand. In the other hand were his shoes.

He hauled himself up the stone steps and I followed him out, shaking my head in disbelief. My mum stuck her head over the side and peered down, a confused expression on her face.

We both made it out and my dad slumped on a nearby rock, feeling faint, his head in his hands. His feet were burnt badly. They were a vivid red and peeling already.

"What happened?" my mum asked incredulously, passing him some water. "I looked up and you'd both gone."

"He took his shoes off to go down there," I replied.

My mum stared at him, astonished. "I didn't know it would burn my feet! It doesn't say to wear shoes," my dad protested.

My mum and I both raised our eyebrows, turning to look pointedly at the massive sign next to the steps. It wasn't written in English, admittedly, but the words 'HATI-HATI!' jumped out at us in bright red lettering. If that wasn't enough to make you realise it would be hot, then there was truly no hope. ('Hati-hati!' means 'Watch out!' in Indonesian, I discovered later.) Also, every single person venturing down had shoes on. Plus, it was a volcanic spring. You could see the steam rising and there were eruptions of burning spray every now and again. That in itself screamed 'Do not step onto this volcano without shoes on.' No? Maybe it was just me getting those vibes.

My dad was whimpering as he held a warm bottle of water against his head. "I didn't know it would be that hot," he reiterated.

"Dad, it's literally a volcano!" I said, my eyes wide.

"And what did you think 'Hati-hati!' meant?" my mum added as she rooted through her bag for some wet wipes to cool his feet with.

"Would you get him some Lucozade or something sugary from that shop?" she asked me, jokingly rolling her eyes as my dad groaned and repeated that he felt faint.

I set off for the little shop we'd passed a few minutes back. Well, I say shop, but it was actually a tiny wooden shack selling lukewarm drinks and crisps. It was on the other side of the springs, accessed by a questionable-looking rope-and-wood ladder bridge.

"Oh God, this is like Indiana Jones," I muttered to myself as I hesitantly placed a foot on the first rung and gripped the sides, cautiously testing my weight on the bridge. The whole thing swung, and I grasped the fraying ropes to either side desperately, glancing down at the bubbling waters below.

The bridge spanned the hot springs and was set high above them. Far below me, the volcanic steam curled upwards, making it impossible to see any further than a foot (ironic really) in front. The ropes were worn and the wood beneath my feet creaked with every baby step. I had to work my way around rotting holes in the structure, shuffling slowly, keeping my eyes on the hut in front of me. It didn't seem to be getting any closer though.

I'm not scared of heights, but this bridge was high, and very unsafe. The wood whimpered with every step I took, but I pulled myself across and eventually reached the other side, thankful to be on solid ground again. I purchased a dusty bottle of Lucozade and a packet of Lay's for my dad, thinking he might need something to eat.

I scooped up my items, never having wished to see a Tesco Express so much in my life and then was on my way, hauling myself slowly but surely back across the death-trap bridge. But this time, I had only one hand, the other being full of snacks. I didn't make the mistake of looking down on the way back; my gaze was averted, eyes trained forwards.

When I reached the safety of the other side, my dad was still sprawled on the rock and my mum was tending to him with an expression that was half worried, half exasperated. He gulped his Lucozade in one go, needing the sugar hit, and ate his snacks, then felt a little better as the colour returned to his cheeks.

His feet were badly burnt, one of them more so than the other, but after a day or two, he was laughing about his stupidity too, rolling his eyes whenever we mentioned it. If he thought the trolling would end when the trip did, he was wrong. This saga remains the maddest Bell mishap that's ever occurred, so our whole family never lets him forget it.

Lessons were learnt. Don't stand barefoot on a volcano was the main one, but I realised something helpful too.

When I came home from this trip, I realised that I'd called BS (maybe that's why the hat is such a memorable item in my life) on my anxious thinking twice now: first in Nerja and then two years later in Java. So, feeling like it was time to make that jump into the deep end, I began to read up about OCD treatments in London. I was finally able to consider the next step.

I researched ways in which I might heal my frazzled brain and focussed on success stories, finding them incredibly inspiring. I became an OCD expert, if you will. I knew everything about this irritating little gremlin in my mind, and I found it fascinating to discover how the disorder develops and how I had unwittingly been allowing it to thrive.

OCD is essentially a flawed way of coping with anxiety, but the disorder can be triggered by lots of things: a massive life change, high levels of general anxiety, genetics, a chemical imbalance, or a lack of serotonin (the brain's feel-good hormone). There's even been extensive research into how streptococcal infections can trigger OCD behaviour in children. The disorder can pop up at any time in a person's life, causing widespread havoc and leaving in its wake an unhealthy way of coping. Fun times.

I gulped down this knowledge like my favourite vanilla latte, becoming familiar with treatment options. CBT (Cognitive Behavioural Therapy) and ERP therapy (Exposure and Response Prevention Therapy) became my besties for life. Although these abbreviations sound downright daunting, CBT is literally talking therapy that helps reframe your thinking and establish healthier ways of looking at situations. ERP means exposing yourself to irrational fears and allowing your mind to feel the full throttle of anxiety without using any coping mechanisms to neutralise negative feelings. ERP is the leading, gold-standard treatment for OCD patients, with a success rate of eighty-five per cent if done right.

But at the end of the day, to overcome OCD, the rituals have to go. Yes, all of them.

They're fuelling the anxiety, reinforcing the idea that there is danger and that you are controlling the impacts with these behaviours. Which is false. Believe me, if that was the case, I'd wish myself a bright red Porsche, a pug, and massive mansions for all my family and friends, stat.

When you've reduced the number of negative behaviours you're participating in, you can work on the scary thoughts and negative thinking pattern. But to recover, the rituals need to be banished. Like a demon. Think of ERP as a hi-tech exorcism.

I'm not saying you should stock up on holy water, adorn your walls with crosses and start yelling 'the power of Christ compels you' at yourself in the mirror. Neither am I suggesting people with OCD are in any way possessed (we're not abnormal; we just worry enough for everyone on the planet). It just used to be a helpful analogy for me. The OCD was separate to me as a person, something that could be sent away into the sunset. But I digress. The rituals have got to go.

Think of them as a toxic friend always talking about you behind your back. You know they're bad for you, they add nothing to your life, and they make you more stressed in the long run. You initially used these rituals as a crutch and, before you know it, one turns into a hundred and you're opening and closing bathroom doors at 3 am like some manic insomniac, trying not to wake your whole household. (Totally didn't ever happen in my house…ahem.) But at the end of the day, that's what's great about a qualified CBT therapist; they know how to wean you off behaviours in a slow and steady manner.

I annoyingly don't practise what I preach though, and I gave up my rituals all at once one day, after a particularly stressful couple of weeks where none of them went right anyway. I didn't seek help from my GP or a therapist because I was worried they'd dismiss me or think I was odd. I now know this to be far from the truth, they're literally there to help you, it's their job and they would have been far more qualified than me.

Instead, I embarked on a strange but wholly worthwhile experience. It was a gruelling, gradual road and an overwhelming uphill climb. My anxiety spiked to unmanageable levels when I first stopped the rituals. After all, I believed they were what had been keeping everyone I cared about safe. But although it was beyond awful to sit through the terror every day, as the weeks turned into months, I started to reclaim my life.

When I look back, I'm proud of how far I've come. Opting to give up my rituals by going cold turkey was the best decision I've ever made – apart from trying a Costa vanilla latte for the first time, obviously.

I'm a pessimist and an extreme perfectionist (what a joyful mix), so you don't usually catch me clapping myself on the back and praising anything I've done, no matter how much my family hype me up (which is a lot; they're like my own personal cheerleading squad). But, you know, I'm proud of having realised there was a better way to deal with stress.

I think of all the things I let slip past me because I was too wrapped up in this negative cycle. Looking back, I understand that my journey to feeling better would have run a hell of a lot smoother with medical support. But hey, I never like to do things easily. It's another one of my annoying character flaws. So off I went with crazy plans, deciding I'd fix it myself. In my head, it was my battle to win.

My mindset in Java changed things and I unknowingly hopped onto the next step in the winding staircase to OCD freedom. That's what I mean about travelling; it's medicine for the mind – not to sound incredibly clichéd and cringey. It forced me to cope with an abrupt change of routine and showed me that not doing those rituals wasn't going to make something catastrophic happen. I started to realise I didn't have to live that way. My brain didn't have to be that insolent; I could work with it.

I was seventeen, my fresh face dotted with freckles, when I headed off to Morocco and Spain at the start of my battle with the OCD monster. I was nineteen when I sat on that balcony in Java with my unruly curls expanding from the humidity and understood that these rituals had no place in reality and that maybe I didn't have to do them. I was twenty when I realised that the progress I'd made with my recovery meant I was now having more good days than bad, and I was twenty-three and finally embarking on a career in journalism and carving out my future before I could look back and make light of my past situation, finding the funny side of the things I used to do.

Plus, my brain really showed itself up. For someone constantly scanning their surroundings for danger, I did a pretty abysmal job of preventing the 'Hati-hati!' disaster. Maybe that's what finally tipped me over the edge and encouraged me to bin my unhelpful behaviours. Thanks, hot springs.

Vietnamese fishing village, Ha Long Bay, Vietnam

Volcanic hot springs, West Java, Indonesia

Moroccan spices, Marrakesh, North Africa

Part Three
Sometimes You Have to Flip It

20

Meet Lobster Man and Baby Boy

Cambodia

People make a trip. I wholeheartedly believe that, and Cambodia was no exception. The locals had this glow about them, this friendly aura, as though they were fictional characters I'd invented in my mind. I could have created a whole world centred around Lobster Guy and his trusty sidekick Baby Boy as they dodged the corrupt Cambodian police.

Visually, Cambodia was as magnificent as I'd imagined, and after a short stay amid the blinding lights of the capital, Phnom Penh, we travelled to the coast (Sihanoukville, to be precise), where Otres Beach II boasted stunning views. We enjoyed exhilarating boat trips and snorkelled to our hearts' content in sea that was filled with tropical fish, then headed out afterwards to different towns, taking in the many markets.

It was a fantastic, colourful experience. Everywhere we went, it was like walking through a rainbow. The multitude of market spices attacked our eyes (in the best way) as we browsed the indoor stalls. Handmade wooden ornaments were beautifully painted and decorated with little mirrors which glistened and cast dancing shapes across the ceiling. It was magical.

I threw myself into the bustle. The social part of my anxiety seems to melt away on a sun-soaked trip. Maybe it's because I'm unlikely to see these people again, so if I make myself look stupid, it won't matter. But I don't think it's that, not really. It's as if I get a confidence boost on holiday along with some much-needed vitamin D. I'm a more adventurous version of myself, less fearful, even though my routine is shifted and I'm nowhere near the safety of my home.

We visited Sihanoukville in southwest Cambodia back in 2016, when I was twenty-one. I'd been working hard at progressing my OCD recovery and was feeling better. I still had social and health anxiety, but it was manageable. I'd been given my life back and was determined to live it to the fullest. I was finding my voice a little more, taking on more responsibilities at my job at the local GP's surgery. Even so, I still found it anxiety-provoking to speak to people I didn't know. I'd break out in a cold sweat and start stammering and stuttering. Cambodia helped me see that people are just people and that there's always common ground to yap about. You just need to find it.

My dad will speak to anyone. It's part of his job, and although he's quite reserved and studious, like me, he loves to find interesting stories. In Sihanoukville, he adopted a beach seafood seller as a new best friend. The guy would wait eagerly on the sand for us. He was so incredibly friendly, and, yes, I know he was selling something, but he was genuinely interested in my dad and our differing lives.

Dad would buy ready-to-eat lobster from him most afternoons and that was it, we'd welcomed an addition to the family. He'd sit and tell my dad all about his loved ones, how long he'd been selling seafood, where he got it, the best delicacies to try. They were lovely, wholesome conversations and it was interesting to hear about his life.

He lived locally with his wife, five children and wife's parents and was always chuckling, slapping his hand on his thigh, wheezing from laughing so much. He couldn't say my mum's name, 'Jacqui', so he fondly pronounced it as 'Sharkie', which is why my dad and I still call her that, years on. When she got a new car, we nicknamed it the Sharkie Mobile, which she hates but we think is hilarious. He pronounced my own name as 'Curry'.

"Mr Steve, Sharkie, Curry!" Lobster Guy would yell every morning when we emerged onto the beach. He'd wave eagerly and dash over, watching in wonder as my dad took photographs with his camera (his professional ones are quite the sight and put my handheld Samsung to shame). Inevitably, we'd then end up buying seafood from him later. It was good food though, and what could be better than devouring freshly caught lobster as you sit there with the sand between your toes and saltwater glistening on your skin? Nothing, I say.

My dad hired a motorbike a few times and would zip around on it. He used to have one when he was younger and has always had a soft spot for a good bike. Me, not so much. The idea of owning a motorbike back home isn't something I can get my head around. I'd rather slip into my warm car when it's pelting down outside, turn up my music and drive in the dry than get drenched on a bike. Also, a helmet would ruin my curls and smudge my expertly applied eyeliner.

On holiday, it's different though. I have no qualms about jumping on the back of a bike, mostly because of the blissful weather, a different vibe from London. Also, my hair is usually beyond help in the humidity, so helmet head isn't an issue. When I'm away, I actually enjoy the warm air ripping through my strands and the exhilaration of speeding down dusty dirt paths, beneath tropical palms shielding me from the sun overhead. I love nipping past street sellers and the array of fruit stalls, enjoying the hustle and bustle. Back home though? No way in hell am I hopping on a motorbike.

My dad happily set off to explore with the bike, taking his camera and returning with fantastic snaps and a list all the sights we could visit. Inevitably, though, he ran into a spot of bother. A police officer in Sihanoukville town took a petty dislike to him and got into the habit of blowing his whistle at Dad, waving him over for no apparent reason and aggressively demanding bribes. This is a notorious practice in Cambodia, as we found out from locals, so just something to be mindful of if you're visiting.

The officer was always very vague about why he'd pulled my dad over. The last time, near the end of our trip, I was riding pillion and my dad had given me the lone helmet to wear. This innocent move got us hauled into the tiny roadside police station, the officer yelling in Khmer, spittle landing on my cheek as his eyes bulged and hands gestured wildly.

The helmet was yanked right off my head and chucked at my dad with a clatter. We assumed he meant the driver had to wear the helmet rather than the passenger, but we'll never know. Feeling like disobedient school kids, we were finally let go, his whistle echoing in our ears as we sped off.

So, from ducking and diving the fuzz to sunnier stories. I adopted a new friend, a different beach seller who used to always wear this bright pink baseball cap with the words 'Baby Boy' emblazoned on the front. He insisted on waiting for us every morning and accompanying my mum and me on our daily walks down the beach. He's in most of our snaps, grinning, thumbs up, just happy to be enjoying the beautiful beach and the wonderful weather.

"Chloë! And MUM!" he'd exclaim, jumping up from his waiting position on the sand, ready to get his steps in. The people (apart from the dodgy-as-hell police) were friendly, and not because they were trying to sell us something; everyone we came across was just…nice. Baby Boy in particular. He was a sunny, smiley person. It was refreshing to swap my chaotic commute to uni, with its soundtrack of grumbling trains and Twitter notifications, for a new routine of leisurely ambles in the company of a happy local who just wanted a natter. Back home, I was used to everyone avoiding each other.

Cambodia is a popular destination on gap-year trips. I think that's how I first heard about it (also, that song by the Dead Kennedys: *Holiday in Cambodia*). I'm not the backpacking kind, as I mentioned, although I'd love to be, especially given the beauty of that country. Cambodia would be the perfect place to jet off to and do some writing. It would be blissful to relax by day with my laptop, tapping away as I gazed out at the steadily bobbing fishing boats, taking inspiration from the bright sun casting blinding rays over the rippling turquoise sea.

In Cambodia, you can enjoy yourself no matter what your preferences are. We stayed on the aptly nicknamed 'quiet beach', which suited us greatly. The neighbouring beach was nicknamed the 'party beach' and was packed with students enjoying the freedom of living under the stars in little bamboo huts. Want to party all night, go to raves in the moonlight, live out of your rucksack and be woken every morning by spectacular sunrises? Cambodia can give you that. Or maybe you're more drawn to relaxing in plush hotel rooms, having breakfast at quaint bamboo tables on private sands and taking dips in the icy pool to escape the heat; in which case, Cambodia can give you that too.

As lovely as the hotel rooms were at St Mary's Beach Resort, I spent a little more time in them than I'd have preferred. I wasn't feeling myself at the start of the trip. I was so excited to be relocating to sunny climes, but, as usual, my brain had other ideas. I hadn't quite got over a health anxiety blip I'd had in the lead-up to the holiday.

The OCD rituals had been banished to another realm. I hadn't participated in any for a good two years by this point, but I was still having to resist flawed thinking on a daily basis. Although it got easier month by month, adopting better ways to deal with concerns was my new routine. I was actively seeking out healthier ways to cope with the uncharted waters of anxiety but still hadn't got the knack of telling it to shut the hell up. Not fully anyway. So, I was a little on edge (although nothing like previous trips). Then I got a minor but still annoying as hell touch of heatstroke a few days into the holiday and was throwing up everywhere for two days straight. (Sigh; why didn't I learn from my Zanzibar experience?) A few room-service deliveries and a couple of Dioralytes later, I was up and about, enjoying the surroundings, making the most of that beautiful place.

But you know what made it all the better? I could finally properly relax for the first time in years. I could feel my brain decluttering itself: no rituals, no need to do anything but explore and enjoy.

The light in Cambodia was blindingly bright. This wasn't the first time I'd experienced that – the brightness of the tropics had struck me on a lot of our trips – but it still amazed me. Until you've been woken up by sunlight streaming through the window somewhere tropical, you don't realise just how dark England is. I love London for a whole slew of reasons – I could give you a very long list of its countless charms – but its weather is not one of them.

Tropical sunlight is different, exotic, otherworldly. It comes with that glowing heat and beaming rays upon your face. Tropical sunlight is indeed a sensation I forget as soon as I return home but remember again the instant I arrive somewhere new, like an old friend that hasn't changed. It's that first moment you step out of the aircraft, the humid heat hitting you in the face, as familiar as a warm hug.

Speaking of my face, I got very sunburnt towards the end of our Cambodia trip. I'd been wearing my sunglasses and had slapped on my usual moisturiser, assuming it had SPF in it. Note, it did not. There's a top travel tip: don't forget about sun protection for your face, even if you're wearing sunglasses or moisturiser. You don't want to end up looking like me.

When I took my glasses off at the end of the day, I strongly resembled a panda. My face was a ghastly, painful red, bar two rings around my eyes, which remained ghostly pale. I'd been swimming underwater, so my mascara had smudged its way down my face, collecting under my eyes unattractively. Classic Chloë. Who wears make-up to swim?

Most of the snaps we have of me enjoying the pool on holidays, from age fourteen onwards, are ruined by make-up smears. You'd think I'd have skipped the mascara or at least invested in a waterproof alternative. But no. I never learn.

On another day (wearing enough SPF this time), my mum and I were swimming in the sea, enjoying the way the ripples reflected the light of the beating sun. Dad was chatting with Lobster Guy on the beach. Mum and I were quite a way out, up to our necks in water. Suddenly, I scrambled away, splashing about, catching sight of a jellyfish ominously floating through the transparent water. I yelled.

"Jellyfish!"

My mum rolled her eyes and laughed, thinking I was joking, until she caught sight of it dancing along the seabed.

We'd never moved so quick. We sprang into action to get to shore, but the more we struggled against the current, then more we got nowhere. If you haven't attempted it, trying to run through water is beyond hard. Add a humongous, looming jellyfish to the mix and it's even more horrifically comical. It kept inching closer as we were swept backwards.

Eventually, we made it to the sand and collapsed on the sunbeds. My dad, as usual oblivious to the commotion, looked up vaguely before continuing his in-depth conversation with Lobster Guy. Typical.

If you're visiting Cambodia, Angkor Wat is a must. Formerly the capital of the Khmer Empire, it offers breath-taking views of ransacked ruins nestled deep in the forest like a real lost kingdom. We didn't make it there as it was a nine-hour drive from the coast, but it's somewhere my dad and I desperately want to visit. The photographs would be out of this world.

So someday, we hope to visit Cambodia again, see the wonders of Angkor and catch up with Lobster Guy and Baby Boy. Maybe not the pesky police officer though.

21
Illegal Jungle Raves and the Cannibals Next Door

The Andaman and Nicobar Islands

When you're researching a decadent desert island to travel to, a vital piece of advice is: make sure the locals aren't cannibals. I think that's self-explanatory.

I'd never heard of the Andaman and Nicobar Islands until we headed there in 2017. Neither had most people. When my friends asked me the standard 'Going anywhere nice on holiday this year then?' question, my answer was met with puzzled expressions and the raising of an eyebrow. "Where?" my colleagues at the GP's surgery asked, peering over their monitors. We'd been talking about upcoming holidays, passing the time in between booking appointments.

"It's an Indian island in the Bay of Bengal," I read off my screen (thanks, Google – making people look smarter since 1998).

They gathered around to take a peek and we marvelled at the images that flickered up: white, soft-sand beaches, cloudless skies, a tropical paradise for the senses. And the islands didn't disappoint in real life; they were just as exotic as they appeared in the photographs, if not more so.

My dad has great taste in destinations and often comes home with flights to places I've never heard of. He loves to stray from the norm, explore properly and see unfamiliar things. That's the fun of it, and as a result, the sublime shores we get to lounge on are usually empty and we're frequently the only guests at our hotel.

Dad often travels for his job, and I've always said he should write a book about his assignments. When he worked as a photographer for the Daily Express, he'd get sent on business trips with Sir Richard Branson. After the press calls, it was one big party, and some of his stories were wild. He's been present at so many momentous events. He was in Kansas to witness the celebrated adventurer and businessman Steve Fossett setting off on his record-making non-stop solo flight around the world. Fossett famously disappeared on his next expedition, so the photos my dad got are even more moving. Dad also bumped into Amy Winehouse not long before she died; that was at a bar in St Lucia before she went on stage to perform what turned out to be one of her last shows.

He's done charity work with Christian Aid in Africa, visiting villages to give out pens, pencils and paper to children and help with campaigns. One day, the jeep he and the team were in broke down in the middle of the Masai Mara; they were stranded with a flat tyre as a group of lionesses emerged to watch from the undergrowth. He worked on photography campaigns with the late Dame Daphne Sheldrick, a conservationist famous for setting up her own elephant sanctuary in Nairobi. I remember doing my Year 9 geography project on her – or, rather, my mum did it. She got so engrossed in researching the elephants. We used my dad's original photos, and I got an A, more than happy to take the undeserved credit.

In Canada, he got up-close and personal (maybe a bit too close) with a big black grizzly bear who was yawning away in the greenery at the side of the road, its razor-sharp teeth on full display, glinting with saliva. The picture is fantastic; I have a copy of it on my photo noticeboard.

Because of all the amazing places he's visited and the adventures he's had, he's a pretty good judge of places. The Andaman and Nicobar Islands were no exception.

Twenty-two-year-old me spent the weeks leading up to our flight cocooned in the swiping, scrolling life of an Instagram fanatic whilst simultaneously trawling the shops for summer clothes. As we often go away in October or November, trying to pick up a new swimming costume or some colourful beach dresses is always a tough but not impossible task. I was full of excitement. I bought a travel journal, vowing to write every single day and include as many photos, boarding passes and tickets as I could. It was that holiday, spent jotting, that initially inspired me to write this book. I wanted to remember my travels and collect my thoughts about each one in detail. When I got home, I purchased an even bigger journal and began to document all our trips. I became eager to collate our adventures in a different format, make something bigger, more creative. However, it would be another two years before I'd stop being so lazy and kick myself into writing chapters.

We departed on our adventure to the Andaman and Nicobar Islands on a chilly winter's morning and arrived in blissful, blistering heat. Just the way I liked it. That's what I love about heading somewhere hot when it's freezing cold at home; you truly feel like you're utterly removed from life back in England. If it was thirty-six degrees in the UK, one of those freakishly un-London August days, I'd feel cheated. The only downside to travelling in the cold is you set off bundled in your cosiest winter warmers and exit the same plane sweltering, gasping for air, peeling off your layers.

The island we stayed on, Havelock, was truly something. We had so many amazing days there, but as this was one of my lost years spent caving to the pressures of Instagram, I could have enjoyed myself so much more if I hadn't been worrying, anxious about posting to keep up with everyone else. Ugh. Hindsight is immensely irritating, isn't it?

I'd become one of those people; the kind I didn't want to be. I was posting five times a day: snaps of the beach, my afternoon coffee with a backdrop of beautiful sunsets. My photos were lovely (if I do say so myself), but now, I wish I'd just put them in an album for myself, not shared them with people I didn't know on the internet. I wish I'd enjoyed those moments fully, keeping them private. They're more special that way.

There's nothing wrong with being on social media. I don't want to seem 'anti-Gram'; I'm not. I'm just observing how it affected me personally. If you like using the app, then that's cool. It's when you feel you have to post rather than want to, that's when the whole thing becomes a dilemma. That's where I was at this point.

I'd secured a grip on my OCD rituals, but now, my brain was panicking, needing something to fill the hours I'd freed up. It needed a new obsession to grasp onto. Enter Instagram.

I should have come back from that trip so relaxed, but I hadn't had that break. I was always looking for the damn wi-fi. I wish I could go back and snatch that bloody phone away from my Insta-swiping fingers. I'd throw it in the sea and be done with it. But, alas, I can't. So now I'm older and a little wiser, I'll just roll my eyes at myself instead and cringe.

When I wasn't glued to my phone, my dad and I rented pushbikes and went cycling around the island, stopping for fresh coconut milk by the roadside. We hopped onto motorbikes to speed to the local village, my mum and I sunbathed and I got as much of a tan as I can get (where I still look like a vampire, but a slightly healthier one), and we took long walks down endless stretches of white, sandy beach. Paradise. However, this trip had its hitches. The first of which was the jewelled-pants-baby incident.

'What?' you're thinking. 'What the hell are you on about? What on earth is a jewelled-pants baby?' Well, it's exactly as it sounds. A baby in jewelled pants. Allow me to explain the saga in full.

Our hotel, the Pellicon, was a series of beautiful bungalows on (originally named) Number 5 Beach. We only had to walk about a minute and we'd reach the sand, sea, and welcoming waves. I frequently strolled to near where hammocks were fastened to the swaying palm trees and would sit there after my morning coffee, taking in the scenery, listening to *All Time Low* on my iPod (I had to keep up those alternative vibes; emos like the beach too, you know) and either reading or just enjoying the sunshine. I'd been carrying out this morning ritual for a week, loving that I could get some amazing photographs so close to our hotel, and appreciating the peacefulness of the breaking day, the empty beach, the perfect weather.

One particular morning, while my parents were still on our balcony, finishing their breakfast, I'd trundled onto the beach and taken up my usual spot. I lay back on the sand, feeling the sun on my face, earphones in. Bliss.

Suddenly, over the top of my loudest song came a bloodcurdling screech (like, seriously, this echoed over the screamiest Motionless in White track). I jolted, sat up in surprise, pulled an earphone out and glanced around quizzically. My eyes narrowed in the blinding sunlight as I searched for the source of the noise, and that's when I saw him.

A little boy emerged from the trees a short way up the beach and charged onto the sand, wearing nothing but a pair of ridiculous jewelled pants, a malicious expression and a full head of dark curly hair. Disregarding the minor interruption and rolling my eyes at his parents' choice of swimwear, I shoved my earphone back in and settled back into relaxation mode.

A few minutes later, some grit hit my sunglasses with a crunch. As I brushed it off, I caught sight of that same little kid, now a foot in front of me and staring chillingly, sand in hand, ready to pelt me again. I tut-tutted at him and checked my sunglasses for damage, annoyed now. I turned up my music and focussed on tapping at my iPod, hoping he'd go away if I ignored him. Such a British reaction.

Alas, he did not move. More sand hit my glasses. This time, I muttered angrily to myself and stood up. I made to walk hastily away down the beach as he threw yet another fistful of sand at my retreating back. "What the actual hell?" I stomped off, eager to go and whine to my parents about the audacity of this random child assaulting me on the beach.

Good plan, right? Not quite. That, ladies and gentlemen, was when I felt a solid object hitting my leg – hard. I spun around in horror to see the little kid eyeing me demonically, not blinking, clutching the coconut he'd just lobbed, the one that had just bounced off my leg and rolled back to him like a severed head. He held it above his little form aggressively, getting ready to hurl it again with full force.

I stalked off, a little faster now, shaking my head at this weird kid, wondering where on earth the parents were and why I was being picked on. Also, who had dressed him in that ridiculous getup?

I made it a few metres before I heard more commotion. Turning again, I clocked the child running after me, like a crazed miniature gladiator. His little legs were struggling to keep him upright as he held the coconut over his head, the weight of it almost toppling him over.

My fight-or-flight response kicked in and I panicked and started running too, but in the opposite direction, away from him. This seemed only to spur him on, and he now staggered towards me at speed.

"What the hell?" I muttered again as I shot a glance behind me. How on earth was a little child holding a coconut bigger than him almost catching up to me? I needed to get to the gym more if I couldn't outrun a toddler.

This kid was some sort of Chucky-like being, no exaggeration. You know the horror film, the one about the crazy ginger doll in the dungarees? He becomes real and starts bumping people off left, right and centre. That was all I could think of as I circled back and headed towards the water, away from him and back towards the hotel entrance. I was being bullied by a three-year-old kid. How did that happen? I thought incredulously.

That's when he threw the coconut again. It missed my head by inches and smashed against a rock as I darted between palm trees, up the path and into the safety of the hotel.

Just to reiterate, I ran away from a three-year-old child in ridiculous jewelled pants who was intent on throwing coconuts at me for no apparent reason. He was out to kill that day, I'm certain. Note, I didn't upload that onto Instagram.

Obviously, the stress response that had come into action in Goa all those years ago, when I'd run away from that kid wanting to play tag, was still alive and kicking. I still thought scarpering was the best option.

I raced back to our balcony, where my parents looked up, eyebrows raised at my rattled expression. "What happened to you?" My mum laughed, sipping her coffee as I caught my breath.

"I just got attacked by a baby wearing jewelled pants," I muttered, shading my eyes from the sun and tilting my head cautiously towards the beach.

My mum and dad were in hysterics. They didn't believe me and thought I was exaggerating. There was no way that had happened. "What are you talking about, Chloë?" My dad sniggered as they both peered around me towards the sea and sand, seeing nothing. No demon baby in sight.

I slumped down on our balcony to recover from my brush with death. Or at least concussion. I felt myself relax as I watched our adorable new friend – a neon-green gecko who visited our bungalow every morning – dipping into my abandoned mug. You couldn't leave your coffee cup unattended without coming back to see his tiny bright form disappearing inside to lick the remnants. He had big, unblinking eyes and a swift little tail that twitched left and right. My mum would be reading on the balcony before we went to dinner most nights and he'd scurry back to keep her company. He'd scuttle over when I was enjoying my coffee or my dad was flicking through his pictures. Mum jokingly called him Freddie, and the name stuck. He was a cute little thing and I wonder who he's keeping company now.

A little later, after Freddie had departed, we all traipsed back down to the beach. That's when we saw him again. The real-life Chucky.

My mum and I were side by side, reading, when we heard a small group pass us, chattering away. I looked up absentmindedly and caught sight of two local women; the one on the left was carrying the demon baby.

"Mum!" I stage-whispered, nudging her. "That's him!"

She glanced up, peering over the top of her sunglasses and snorted. "Really? That little boy?" she began in disbelief. But as the two women trudged past us through the sand, he turned his head and stared at me with pure hatred, his beady eyes narrowing as he was carried down the beach. He reminded me of an owl, the way his head twisted right around. Or that head-swivel scene from *The Exorcist*. Both fitted.

From then on, my mum and dad did believe me. They'd witnessed the stony expression of the jewelled-pants baby themselves, his creepy eyes boring right into my soul. It was unnerving, to say the least. For the remainder of the holiday, I watched over my shoulder, on my guard in case the demon child struck again.

*

Havelock Island was small and had many different hotels, all with their own restaurants and bars. The food was delicious and the spicy aromas would catch in our nostrils as our mouths watered at the sight of our dinner being carried towards the table. My favourite place we ate at was an impromptu beach barbecue arranged by one of the neighbouring hotels. They offered fresh seafood and it was incredible. My dad had lobster and I sampled a little and have loved it ever since, although it's expensive at home.

Several years later, when my boyfriend Brandon and I went to a nice restaurant, local to where we live, to celebrate his birthday back when Covid restrictions lifted, I remembered eating lobster on that Havelock beach and how much I'd loved it. I eyed up the lobster ravioli on the menu, excited for our first dinner out since God alone knew how long.

"Would you like the lobster ravioli as a starter or a main?" the friendly waitress asked, jotting down our orders.

"As a main, please." I grinned as my stomach rumbled. I was starving; there was no way I was just ordering a starter.

They brought our food, set it down on the table with a flourish, and my face fell. I literally had five pieces of ravioli. Five measly scraps.

Brandon had ordered spaghetti bolognaise, so his bowl was full to the brim with meatballs and pasta. He tucked in and I ate mine sullenly in the space of two minutes. It was delicious, but I wished I'd known there'd only be a tiny amount to savour. Those are the only two times I've ever tasted lobster.

The Havelock Island beach barbecue was the epitome of al fresco dining. It was so chilled to sit at our tables on the sand, enjoying the sound of crashing waves, seemingly more prominent because we were in darkness and couldn't see much. The stars shone like torch beams, reflected in the inky waters. The food was indeed amazing. The drinks? Not so much.

For some unknown reason, most of the hotel bars had just had their alcohol licences revoked the week before we arrived. Some were still serving, but you had to really hunt, and even then, they acted a little suss about it. I researched this oddity when we returned home, but there wasn't much information about the abrupt revocation. All I could discover was that there was a limited availability of imported alcohol. I mean, yeah, we knew that.

Honestly, whenever we ordered a glass of wine with dinner, the waiters would shut down, eyes glazing over as they stared blankly at us. It was like we'd asked for some coke. And no, not the cola kind. In fact, I'm pretty damn sure it would have been easier to get drugs on that island than a cocktail.

The lack of alcohol wasn't a problem as such, although I would have loved a pina colada. Relaxing on the beach with something terrifically tropical while gazing at the stars would have rounded the evenings off perfectly. But halfway through the holiday, it was my dad's birthday, so we searched everywhere to get him a celebration beer. Eventually, we discovered a hotel that insisted they had a bar on the premises and were still allowed to serve alcoholic beverages. We went back there later, after dinner, and that's when it got a little weird.

We were directed through the hotel quickly, ushered through the gardens and instructed to follow the winding path up to the top. The staff member leading us walked fast and glanced around every few seconds like he was on the run. After a few minutes, he came to a sudden halt. The pavement had ceased to exist and all we could see was a dirt track that wound between the towering trees. He pointed ahead of us, into the jungle, and we squinted through the dimming light to where a small group was hiking ahead of us.

We traced their steps, trundling further into the forest and walking for a good ten minutes, batting away stray branches and ducking under low-hanging palm leaves, before finally emerging into a small clearing. A few tables and chairs had been set up under a bamboo gazebo, and there was a small bar at the front with a mini fridge selling lukewarm beers and Bacardi Breezers (I hadn't seen Bacardi Breezers in supermarkets for years, so this was a novelty). There was a makeshift dance floor, booming music, strobe lighting, the works – like a jungle rave. It was louder than our normal tastes, but this was the only place on the island you could get a beer.

We ended up visiting that secret club in the forest a few more times over the coming days, sipping on blackberry-flavoured Bacardi Breezers, blinded by the flickering lights. There were strong illegal vibes though. The hotel we passed through to get there was pretty hush-hush, and the range of drinks was limited. There were no cocktails or spirits; it was beer, Breezers or get out.

Word must have got out about this jungle bar as it was busier each time. On the final night, as we braved the strobe lights and out-of-tune singing from drunken guests one last time, there was a particular woman dancing to literally every single song. She kept trying to pull in any passer-by to join her and us three were terrified of heading off to the toilet in case she grabbed us en route. Eventually, having got more and more intoxicated by the hour, she was escorted out (of the jungle, yes), swaying unsteadily and still singing at the top of her lungs. We took that as our cue to go too.

The remainder of the holiday was spent taking in the surroundings, snapping beautiful pictures and soaking up the sunshine. I was constantly on the lookout for the jewelled-pants baby, but luck was on my side, he didn't care to reappear. The only thing we wanted to do but didn't was travel up to Elephant Beach, which would have involved a lot of trekking. The beach is home to a huge herd of retired elephants. They're looked after and can live in peace there, enjoying each other's company, and, if you're lucky, you might get to see them lumbering into the sea to cool off. We would have loved to have witnessed that, but the weather was incredibly hot and we didn't fancy making a long car journey and a tough hike through the jungle with no guarantee of seeing any elephants at the end of it. We'd already had enough of trekking through the jungle to get a Bacardi Breezer. We opted to just chill out for once instead.

One day towards the end of our trip, I'd been enjoying my book while my mum and dad had wandered off to paddle in the sea. I'd been engrossed in the pages, but as I glanced up, I caught sight of them peering down at something in the shallow water. They were quite a way out. The tide had stripped itself back, exposing the seabed, and crabs and other scuttling creatures were going about their day just as we were going about ours.

I could just make out my parents' expressions if I lifted my sunglasses and peered into the dazzling light. They continued staring down for a minute before almost simultaneously leaping away, splashing through the water back to the beach. It was like someone had snapped their fingers. They sped off in unison.

Apparently, they'd seen a crocodile. They'd been staring at this great gathering of wet sand, wondering what the hell it was, when suddenly it shifted. My mum yelped and they both took off. I'd never seen them move so quick (apart from during the jellyfish incident in Cambodia). I don't know if it was a crocodile. We had been warned by locals that it was the time of year when crocodiles came out to bask and that they tended to bury themselves under the sand when it was too hot. We'd been advised to be cautious and to not go swimming in the sea, so maybe it *was* one. I'm dubious.

I don't like crocodiles. The thought of how fast they move puts me off considerably. I know they're still animals and should be protected, but they give me the creeps. I hate it if I can't see the seabed beneath me. *Anything* could be under there, lurking, waiting to snap its jaws around my leg.

But would you rather be eaten by a crocodile, pelted by Chucky wearing jewelled pants or devoured by real-life cannibals? Because those were all options right there on the Andaman and Nicobar Islands. It was like the horror movie *Saw*, with all these different methods. Choose one or time's up.

Oh, did I not mention the cannibals? My bad. Neither did anyone else until after we'd arrived.

An American missionary had paid a local fisherman to take him across to North Sentinel Island on a small boat a few months prior. Despite the locals warning him against it, he departed anyway, keen to find out how the Sentinelese lived. North Sentinel Island, which is approximately 94.7 km away from the safety of Havelock, is still reportedly inhabited by cannibals. I'm not sure if he was aware of that massively important fact before he set off, but he was shot with an arrow and hauled away as soon as he set foot on the shore. So maybe spying a possible crocodile napping under the sand was the less dangerous sight. I mean, I've seen Eli Roth's *The Green Inferno,* and it made me feel queasy for weeks. (Never again.) I wouldn't fancy being in a live re-enactment of it.

The Sentinelese are one of the few tribes that refuse to have any interactions with the outside world. It's estimated that between fifty and two hundred individuals live on the island, and they're extremely hostile to outsiders. And by extremely, I mean that whenever anyone manages to land on North Sentinel, they're immediately attacked and killed. When the Indian Government had previously flown a helicopter over to see if they were okay, the tribe shot arrows at it.

The last Indian visit to the island was back in 1997, and to this day, the Sentinelese are a protected tribe. They've been established for over sixty thousand years and the Indian Government advises that they should remain uncontacted for several reasons. One, because as a visitor you'll get dismembered as soon as you hop out of your boat, and two, because the tribespeople would be very vulnerable to any diseases brought in from the outside world.

The coastguards and Indian Army are usually patrolling the area, to stop people reaching the island, for the safety of both parties. But this missionary bypassed them and met his grisly end. Hearing about the death of this American so close to Havelock sent a chill down my spine. Thank God, we managed to get to the right island; imagine a mix-up like *that*.

22

The Tuk-Tuk Ambulance

Port Blair and New Delhi

The sea was choppy on our return journey from Havelock Island to Port Blair, the biggest town on the Andaman and Nicobar Islands, located on the large South Andaman Island, but we didn't think much of it. Well, those choppy waters turned out to be the beginnings of a full-blown cyclone, and when we finally did dock at Port Blair – feeling sufficiently seasick – it was pelting down. Heavy, streaming, unforgiving rain was lashing down from the heavens. We seemed to have unsuspectingly arrived in the eye of the storm.

We sought refuge in our hotel, whereupon all the lights fused, plunging us into darkness. The entire area's electricity supply was compromised and although it eventually came back on, the whole affair was how I imagined an apocalyptic movie would play out – the first inklings of the end of the world. We watched anxiously as lightning zigzagged across the moody sky, deadly flashes of colour exploding in front of our eyes. It was monumentally creepy.

I'm usually up for the weird and wonderful, the spine-chilling suspense of a thriller movie, but this time, I was immersed in a real-life version. There seemed to be danger everywhere; there'd been crocodiles in Havelock and cannibals on the next island, and now, a cyclone was stalking the region, like a black panther under the cover of inky darkness, ready to pounce.

We couldn't see the cyclone, but we sure saw the poolside sun loungers being whisked up into the air and then smashing back down again. Needless to say, we didn't hit up the pool during our short stay. Instead, we watched *The Hills Have Eyes 2* (how apt to choose a horror film in the middle of an apocalypse) and ordered room service, not wanting to venture out, the angry tapping of the rain evident through the night.

It cleared up the next morning, though. The sky brightened enough for people to start repairing damaged properties, and the power returned. The rain was ushered away and the clouds thinned, revealing the sun we'd been missing, but by then, it was almost time for us to continue on to New Delhi. We thought that was more than enough drama. I mean, a cyclone? Come on.

Somewhere back on Havelock Island, my dad had stubbed his toe on a rock. He hadn't thought much about it, expecting it to heal over the next few days. Well, it didn't, and when we were in Port Blair, he started hobbling everywhere.

"What happened to *you*?" my mum asked as we turned around to look for him and he hopped towards us.

We'd been browsing the fruit markets, doing some exploring before our flight to New Delhi the next day. The air was humid and the ground saturated, but the skies were now blue instead of an overbearing grey. We'd been checking out the town before we left, a crazy, colourful treat for the eye.

"I think my toe is infected," my dad said, examining his foot as though he was a doctor and knew exactly what he was on about. Maybe he should retrain, though, because he was absolutely right. By the next day, his whole foot had ballooned, turning angry, red and painful. He could put hardly any pressure on it, and my mum was concerned, so we googled the nearest urgent-care hospital, researching how to get there.

We got our stuff together and located the only form of transport in sight. Yes, you guessed it – a tuk-tuk. Asking the driver to drop us at the hospital elicited a response we weren't expecting. He put his foot down hard (even more forcefully than tuk-tuk drivers generally did) and we were soon hurtling towards Port Blair's A&E at what felt like a hundred miles an hour, arriving there in record time.

The sight of us all jumping in a mad panic into the nearest tuk-tuk and it speeding around corners and grinding to a screeching halt outside the hospital was probably an odd one. I imagined the tuk-tuk having its own blue light on top like a proper ambulance. Good side hustle. If I was a tuk-tuk driver, I would a hundred per cent try that.

My dad hobbled into the hospital with us trailing behind. I slipped through the double doors and my eyes widened in surprise. It was nothing like the hospitals at home. It was chaotic. There were so many people milling around, jostling each other. There were crowds gathered outside each side room, which I guessed were where the doctors were. There was so much noise, hundreds of voices all having separate conversations, the sounds echoing around the massive building.

As we wandered around, looking for someone to ask for guidance, I caught sight of a prominent sign (I say 'sign', but it was just a note scrawled in marker pen on a piece of scrap paper and stuck haphazardly on the wall) advising 'Leprosy Patients Please Queue Here'.

It was hot inside and there were people pushing past, huddling everywhere, throngs of patients jostling for access every time a door opened anywhere in my eyeline. It was stifling and surreal. Panic began to swell inside me.

Not only do I suffer with anxiety generally, I also have a bad case of health anxiety dolloped on for good measure. I know, I sound like a barrel of laughs, right? Doctors' surgeries and hospitals make me anxious, which makes it odd that I managed to enjoy working at a GP's office for five years during and after university.

My eyes flicked around as my brain flipped through my thoughts like an encyclopaedia. Did I know the symptoms of leprosy? Did I have it? Did my mum or dad have it? Didn't we learn about it once back in science at school?

I told myself this thought process was ridiculous; I was only thinking about leprosy because I'd seen the sign. If I hadn't glanced up and read it, I wouldn't even be contemplating this illness. I followed my mum and dad, wrapping my arms around myself and breathing slowly, feeling lightheaded.

We eventually found a staff member who showed us where to queue, so we stood at the back of the crowd outside this consultant's room. As soon as the door opened, the doctor – a stern-looking guy in a white coat and glasses – would appear, ask for the next in line, and then retreat as the mass of people waiting surged forwards, with one lucky patient able to duck or squeeze in first. It was a literal take on first come, first served. We stood back and waited our turn.

"Next!" the doctor boomed as he poked his head out again a few minutes later. A guy who was near the back of the line with us dashed forwards, barrelling under other people's arms and pushing through non-existent gaps until he reached the door. The woman who'd been just about to enter after the consultant was taken by surprise as this ninja slipped past her and made it into the room a millisecond before. The door slammed shut and we began the waiting game again.

A few of our fellow queue buddies kept glancing at us, and then, the second time the door opened, the crowd, who were mostly locals, all turned to my dad and gestured him through. "You first, please." They pointed to the door, where the doctor was beckoning to us.

"Oh, no, we only just got here. You're all first," my dad said, but they just stepped back and propelled him forwards, despite his assurances that he didn't mind waiting.

"Thank you!" My mum and I smiled gratefully as we passed by. The friendliness of those people was overwhelming. We were fine waiting in the line. I mean, we're from England, that's what we do.

My dad is a massive wuss when it comes to hospitals, so my mum motioned for me to go in with him. (Yeah, I know, send the other wuss in too.) The consultant was incredibly efficient, and he got to the issue straightaway, diagnosing cellulitis, an infection of the skin, brought on by the cut on my dad's toe. The cut he probably got racing away from the 'crocodile'. He prescribed antibiotics and sent us on our way within minutes.

Drama averted, we enjoyed the last days of our trip, visiting the infamous Cellular Jail and admiring the historic Gandhi statue.

The Cellular Jail, or Kālā Pānī, was haunting to wander around and taught us more about Port Blair and the many bad things that had happened there. The jail was used by the British to hold political prisoners during India's fight for independence. The Andaman Islands had been a place of exile for freedom fighters since 1857 and many executions were carried out there during the struggles. It was uncomfortable hearing about that episode in British history.

After we left the jail, we took a trip around the local area, walking very slowly – because my dad still couldn't manage anything but a shuffle – around the various entrancing markets. It was a reassuringly quiet last afternoon.

*

New Delhi was the last leg (ha) of our trip. Aiming to make the most of our one-day stay in India's crazy capital, my dad and I hailed a tuk-tuk and sped off to India Gate, the city's famous war memorial designed by Edwin Lutyens and based on the Arc de Triomphe in Paris. Now, I've been in many a tuk-tuk, but this one was a whole different experience, even crazier than the makeshift ambulance back in Port Blair.

It started pouring with rain again, and the sound of the droplets hitting the tuk-tuk's metal roof was deafening, like bullets bouncing and ricocheting. I couldn't see through the shield of water, and we gripped the seats as the driver wove in and out of the gridlocked New Delhi traffic, taking corners at speed, beeping to tell other drivers to get the hell out the way. It felt like we were in a go-kart but had no control.

It was rush hour and the trip took us about an hour (for a less speedy driver it would have taken double that), and by the time we hopped out, our legs were jelly and we felt queasy. But the tuk-tuk driver had got us there, that was the main point. Sometimes I wonder what it would be like to drive in India. I get overly annoyed if someone cuts me up in London traffic, but imagine having to nip around millions of other road users in those little contraptions. It was another example of organised chaos, but everyone in India seemed so at ease with the zooming tuk-tuks, the soundtrack of beeps, the clusters of milling people. I know that I can't possibly base my opinions of New Delhi on a few measly hours, but I love the impression it made on me. And that's fantastic, I think; really refreshing. It made me want to embrace my chaos, like I did in Vietnam, rather than just mope about back home.

There are a lot of things I love about our English culture, of course. Our punk scene, our literature, our famous royal family, Beefeaters, and landmarks. Our prim-and-proper attitudes. Oh, and don't forget the tea. But there's the godawful moaning too, and that gets tedious, especially when I find myself engulfed in a whinge multiple times a day (as I sip my PG Tips and nibble on my scone).

I don't know how the rest of the world perceives us British folk, but I always get an image of the White Rabbit from *Alice in Wonderland* when I think of our culture. You know, the one with the little waistcoat and pocket watch who proclaims he's late every two seconds. He's the embodiment of London life, in my opinion.

But we're not the friendliest bunch, are we? The Indians we encountered seemed to always be eager to help. As I made my way through the gathering at India Gate, people smiled, waved or said 'Hello'. You'd never get that in London.

At home, I melt into the background with ease, but on trips, people are so friendly, so forward. They want to talk; they want to hear about our culture the same way I like to hear about theirs. Usually, I'm totally up for chatting with people and hearing their stories; I'm a journalist, after all. But pushing through the never-ending New Delhi crowds around India Gate, with groups turning to gawp at me, was making me self-conscious.

I hid behind my dad as we made our way around the monument to find the best view. The rain had eased, giving us a tiny slither of a window in which to admire the gate properly (an hour later, the heavens opened again, and it was impossible to see your hand in front of your face). Dad got an amazing photo of the sun setting behind the towering white marble gate and we stared in amazement for a bit, taking in the colours, the pink and orange skyline looking like an explosion, a cornucopia of different hues streaking together.

The monument stood proud, silhouetted against its striking background. I forgot where I was for a minute and just stared, lost in *being* there, thinking about the meaning of the gate and the fallen soldiers it honoured from the First World War and other conflicts between 1914 and 1921.

Then this group of teenagers in school uniform appeared and one tapped me on the shoulder. "Can we have a picture with you?" he asked. The other five peered around their ringleader as I smiled.

"Yeah, no problem."

I reached for their phone, thinking they meant for me to take one of them. I hate that pressure at home. We all know how to use a phone, but when I'm out and suddenly a couple approach, asking me to take a quick photo of them, this mad pressure instantly swarms my brain.

"Noooo, a picture with *you*!" The guy laughed.

"Oh…I guess." Embarrassment flooded my face. Did they think I was someone else? Was I being pranked? I grinned for the snap, then ducked out to find my dad in the ever-growing sea of people.

I got asked to be in two more photos as I navigated the crowds, and I'm not going to lie, I felt like a little celebrity. No, I'm just kidding. I felt uncomfortable but didn't want to be rude. So, I probably appeared on three different Insta accounts, smiling awkwardly into the camera, tagged as someone else. Or maybe (a more likely scenario) I had some food smeared on my face and it was some sort of joke.

After I'd finished posing, and signing autographs in my head, we jumped in our tuk-tuk and zipped back to the hotel. I pondered how I might pick up a nifty little tuk-tuk back at home; it would surely be easier to parallel park. The rain had started up again, but it was still only a drizzle, so we were back showing my mum our photos within forty minutes. Another record tuk-tuk journey time. I'm convinced we should have put the driver forward as an up-and-coming expert racer, the way he was taking those corners, slaloming this way and that. He could be the next Stig for *Top Gear* or something. Or maybe he was the Stig with his helmet off. We'll never know.

23

The Hotel from Hell

Glasgow

My boyfriend Brandon and I are avid Twenty-One Pilot fans and were eagerly waiting to book tickets as soon as a slew of dates were announced. Well, we waited, fingers poised, the morning they got released. We logged on and joined the online queue the second the pre-sale went live, but the London dates sold out in the blink of an eye. We panicked, disappointment taking over, but then suddenly, after I refreshed the tab, an option appeared on my screen for two tickets. I clicked immediately, assuming someone had decided not to complete their transaction and snapped them up with a swipe. Grinning, I tapped on my emails to read the confirmation, but then…

"Oh my God. Oops." I bit my lip, staring at my phone, willing the words to be wrong.

"What?" Brandon asked, glancing over my shoulder, studying the email text.

"I've booked the tickets for bloody Glasgow." I winced, showing him my phone screen fully. This was just typical of me. I'm always too keen to purchase things. It's a weird impulse I have; I'm a marketing team's dream. As soon as there's a hint something might sell out or go out of stock, my brain jumps into action and I buy without thinking. And that includes cars.

My beloved Suzuki Alto got written off when a DPD van smashed into the back of me (I know, zero points for their driving skills). I loved that Alto. It was my first car; my dad kindly bought it when I passed my test aged nineteen. I was devoted to Suze. Her bright red exterior was home for me; she was my trusty companion for many years, and, yes, I know it's silly to get attached to material objects, but Suze had been through everything with me. She'd seen me transform from a jittery road user to a confident one who didn't bat an eyelid cruising down the motorway or jumping in for a journey on a whim.

183

She'd been there when I was too anxious to drive around the block on my own. She'd endured hours of my mum re-teaching me how to parallel park and my dad encouraging me that yes, I *could* drive. She was driven to many a deserted car park as my parents patiently helped me get my confidence back.

Suze was there when I started driving to my first job at the GP's surgery, and she was there when I left to join the local paper as a fresh-faced journalist. She ferried me to all my interviews, attending the stories I covered around Kent. It was just me, her and my trusty satnav. And maybe an occasional panicked phone call to my dad asked where the hell 'Caterham' was.

She was there to big me up when I stomped on my fears and drove on the M25 for the first time. She went everywhere: up to Northampton, all around London, to the coast. She was present for many a joyful ride with my family and for chilled-out drives with my friends. She gave countless lifts, held thousands of Costa cups in her holders, was my makeshift office and lunch spot. She was present for all the laughter, the panic attacks, the stresses, the lockdown job interviews, the speeding when I was late and the dawdling when I was enjoying my music. Suze was a special kind of car.

I was so stressed about getting a replacement, I went into a blind panic after Suze was deemed 'undriveable'. I scoured the internet, finding a car I liked, a sporty little red Vauxhall Adam with a black roof. It was a cute car and a good deal too. Fretting that it might get sold, I paid the deposit in a flurry and arranged for it to be delivered from Yorkshire.

Well, I hadn't actually been paid by the insurance company for Suze yet, so it was a shock when I woke a few mornings later to a text notifying me that my new Vauxhall was ready to collect from a nearby garage. "Oh crap, nooo!" I jumped out of bed and hurtled downstairs, hair sticking up at all angles, eyes bleary, only half adjusted to the morning light. My dad was pouring coffee into our mugs and my mum was in the front room, finishing hers.

"My car is here, and I don't know I'm going to give them their money!" I wailed unhappily.

My dad looked up, exasperated. He'd told me in no uncertain terms not to make any commitments until the insurance company had finalised everything. Luckily, it worked out and they paid that very day, but you can see how my impulsive nature often gets me into pickles. Pesky pickles that could easily be avoided. I'm not sure where this panic streak comes from, the weird nature that spikes sometimes and causes me to make rash decisions. But it's annoying to me and anyone else involved.

So, when purchasing these gold-dust Twenty-One Pilots tickets in haste, I stupidly didn't double-check the venue. Brandon and I stared in horror at each other, weighing up just how much we wanted to see this band. But then, we decided it might be cool to go to a gig in a whole other city. It was 'Glasgow, here we come'.

I love concerts, and this one was a gem. I fell in love with the atmosphere at live music events when I was fourteen – the waves of people all singing out the same lyrics, all united and together – and that's been with me ever since.

Rock music is another thing that's always eased my mind, made me feel like I belong and am not weird. Concerts feel comfortable. I can turn up in skinny jeans, Converse and a band T-shirt and not stress that people are staring with raised eyebrows. You'd think that a room filled to the brim would be an anxious person's nightmare, but it's exhilarating for me. I forget my worries at a concert like I forget them when travelling. I love that sweaty room of strangers. They always seem like my kind of people.

So, having decided that we were indeed going to Glasgow, we booked the hotel and flights. Swept up in the pleasures of planning, we opted to stay a few extra days and see the sights. It was a nice trip in the end and a great opportunity to explore a city I hadn't thought about visiting before, but we did miss out quite a lot. We weren't there for long enough and the primary point of our stay was to attend that bloody concert. Now I look back, there's so much more I'd like to have done. I never even tried haggis or a deep-fried Mars Bar, although we did head to a local doughnut shop and purchased sugary rings bigger than our heads. Best doughnuts ever.

Scotland is special to me as Nana Cath was born there. Although she only lived near Hamilton with her family for five years, she never lost the accent and I'll always remember her softly spoken voice and Scottish air. I got really into researching the Bell clan when I got home. I loved finding out what our crest colours were. Our tartan pattern is pretty: a shade of light blue with a yellow stripe running through it. I find Scottish heritage so interesting. Also, the crests and the clan colours remind me of Hogwarts houses. (I promise I'll stop rabbiting on about *Harry Potter* one of these days. Probably.)

We arrived in an overcast Scotland after the shortest flight and waited for the shuttle bus with our suitcases. Scotland is immensely pretty, but the weather, not so much. The Glasgow downpour seemed to be worse than the torrential rain we'd left back in London. After a short ride to the centre, we headed outside into the biting cold with gritted teeth and hauled our cases around Glasgow in the wet, getting lost in the maze of streets. We were thankful when we finally arrived at the hotel lobby. Eager to have a shower and change my clothes, I ran my fingers through my sopping curls, feeling sufficiently saturated.

The hotel interior was cool, all 1920s style, with art deco vibes. There was an extravagant red carpet running all the way up the stairs to the rooms and I breathed a sigh of relief. It looked nice, a city hotel with a twist.

However, when we checked into our room, it became evident there was a second twist lurking, and this was far more terrifying than the quirky decor. Admittedly, my expectations may have been too high. I felt mildly irritated that I'd been lulled into a false sense of security by the nice hallway.

When I say our room was bad, I mean it was abysmally awful. As Brandon and I unlocked the door – you had to really jiggle the key; it was a struggle to gain entry – my face fell and my anxiety spiked. How on earth was I going to stay in there? It was dirty, there was dust everywhere, and when I pushed open the door to the bathroom, which, granted, was twice as big as the bedroom, for some weird reason, the floor sloped at an angle. It was like a creepy circus fun house.

Dance music thumped under our feet and in the room next door we heard something smash as shouts tore through the paper-thin walls. A devastatingly vile smell rose to meet our noses and I grimaced. Sometimes I recall that smell in my deepest, darkest nightmares.

Like I said, I'm not a backpacker and can be a bit high-maintenance when it comes to accommodation. This room probably wasn't even that bad, but I'd built it up in my mind. I'd been so glad at the prospect of finally getting out of the rain and into a hot shower, and I was looking forward to unpacking before braving the cold again. Maybe that's why this room seemed worse than it was. Because I was disappointed.

Some people insist that pickiness doesn't make you a proper traveller, that it's not being authentic. Proper travelling is all about winging it, after all. I love getting out there and exploring, pushing myself, daring my anxiety to question my choices, but I also like having a comfortable place to come back to, somewhere to relax in afterwards. That's my compromise, my own way of stretching what I'm capable of whilst also not going too far that I'll end up in a panic.

Maybe if I'd approached this room with a clear head and hadn't been dripping rainwater onto the carpet, I'd have felt differently. As if to dispute this claim, however, another loud shriek echoed from under our feet and mad, hysterical laughter followed. The godawful music was turned up another few notches and boomed louder, making the lamps either side of the bed shake.

It was 3 pm. Who has a rave at 3 pm?

Brandon glanced around happily, threw his bag on the bed and went over to look out the window. It boasted no views whatsoever; we were facing a literal brick wall. I sat down gingerly and eyed the dirty marks on the bedding. This had to be what prison was like, I thought dramatically.

I started unpacking, feeling disheartened but not wanting to say, because I didn't want to look like a diva. It was bad though. Spying a mutant spider, I watched it beadily as it scuttled under the bed. I took a deep breath and held it for a few seconds before releasing it loudly. I stared around, dreading the prospect of returning later and having to crawl into a bed that looked anything but clean, a bed that clearly housed bugs underneath it.

I'd flicked briefly through the online pictures of the hotel and it had been fine, totally unlike this unclean lair I found myself in. It was my own fault; I should have read the reviews thoroughly. My mum always does that for our family trips, so it had slipped my mind. I'd been too trusting, that was for sure. Nowadays, I don't book anywhere without reading everything first.

I attempted to pull myself together and scooped up a change of clothes along with my washbag. Maybe I'd feel more positive after a shower. But, alas, the taps in the bathroom spurted noisily, dark liquid oozed out, and when the pressure fought back, the water was freezing cold. I snatched my hand back and groaned. This was literally like *The Grudge*.

"The shower is freezing," I moaned as I shuffled out of the bathroom, gripping the wall as my feet navigated the severely sloping floor.

Brandon went to try the shower and came out looking sheepish, finally admitting it was dire in there. He shrugged, nonplussed. Nothing ever bothers him. "I'll ask if they can do anything at reception."

I winced as someone in the next room drunkenly shouted and something smashed against the wall again. Jesus. "I'll come too," I muttered, slipping my shoes on, clasping my handbag to my chest.

So, off we went. I scurried after him down the dark hall, and we descended the winding stairs to reception to politely ask if someone could possibly look at the shower.

You had to ping one of those old-fashioned bells to alert the receptionist. I was feeling increasingly like I was an unwitting extra in a low-budget slasher movie. The manager popped up from behind the curtain with the air of someone running a haunted hotel. I was half expecting him to creep through a secret door behind a bookcase and make us jump with a creepy 'Yeeeeeees? Can I help you?' You know, eyeing us with suspicion as he wiped blood from his mouth, like a vampire. Or at the very least be tossing a severed limb to the side as he addressed us.

But he was normal, not a blood splatter in sight, and he apologised profusely. He decided to move us to a new room as the shower wouldn't be a quick fix. "The only room we have left is over the other side of the hotel," he explained apologetically as he fished out another set of keys.

Oh God, I thought, is this going to be a worse room? Surely not. Why does he look so worried? Am I about to be murdered? Jesus Christ. I do not want to make the national news like this. That's what I get for being too impulsive. We could have seen Twenty-One Pilots back in London next year. The safety of the O2 Arena seemed like a massive great bear hug in comparison.

"It's newly refurbished, but it's the quiet section," he continued.

My train of thought snapped back as he held out the keys, dangling the escape from our rave room in front of my eyes.

'Quiet section?' Well, that sounded right up my street. I tried not to look too ecstatic, but I couldn't help it.

He caught my eye, shooting me a quizzical look. He was probably thinking that, being youngsters in our twenties, we were hardly the sort to go to bed at 10 pm with a cup of tea and a good novel, not the type of guests to enjoy the 'quiet section' of the hotel. Oh, how little he knew me. Because that's exactly what I live for.

My ideal evening consists of running a bubble bath, slapping on a Lush fresh facemask and emerging feeling brand-new. Jammies are on early, a cup of hot lemon water is on the go, and I'll settle down to watch a creepy film or enjoy a few chapters of my next read, typically a psychological thriller. That's my night sorted.

"Great," I piped up, my little ears listening eagerly as he ran through the rules: no loud music, no gatherings or parties, and everyone to keep their voices low after 10 pm. Oh damn, I thought sarcastically, no more midday raves then.

I nodded. "That sounds great. Thank you."

We hurried back to the original room, and I threw all my stuff into my suitcase as quick as lightning before the guy could change his mind. I zipped it up and bumped it along after Brandon and the hotel manager, keen to see this mystical, magical 'quiet zone'.

Well, the new room was fantastic. I felt happier knowing there was a working shower, hot water, no weird sloping bathroom floor and no dust in sight. The horrendous smell had disappeared completely and there was no irritating thumping music or screaming rows bouncing off the walls.

No, this room was silent, apart from when you opened the double-glazed windows. Then you could hear the bustling Glasgow street outside and spy various restaurants opposite. It was an improved view compared to the brick wall. It was clean and, to be honest, that's all I want in a hotel room. A place to lay my head after a long day of exploring; somewhere I'm not going to catch lice.

More than happy now, we headed off to a Japanese restaurant for dinner (I know, how authentically Scottish), where I tried blossoming flower tea, shamefully uploading a million photos to Instagram like a social media slave. A bulb literally unfolded as it was heated by the hot water in my glass, and after I'd finished snapping my pictures, I stared in awe at the unfolding white petals.

I secured another few pictures for my group chat (the one consisting of me and my mum and dad, which is mostly just me and mum sending each other endless Bitmojis as my dad rolls his eyes at the number of notifications) and emailed a few to my nan and pap.

Sufficiently mesmerised by the delicate, fascinating flower tea, we then continued to nearby rock club the Cat House, which was so my scene. I absolutely loved it; it was like they'd plugged my iPod into the speakers. I danced all night, enjoying a few too many shots and vodka cranberries.

There'd been jelly shots advertised on the door, and I was so intent on getting some, I went on about them every two minutes. But they never materialised, much to my disappointment. "Are the jelly shots out yet?" I asked Brandon for the umpteenth time over the boom of the *Bring Me the Horizon* track blasting out at top volume.

He laughed and shrugged, but, alas, they didn't come. Other than that, ten out of ten people would recommend the Cat House if you like rock and metal music. If you don't, then I absolutely would not recommend it. If you were hoping for a normal club and wandered in obliviously, expecting chart music, you'd be terrified, I'd imagine. Metal is an acquired taste and not suited to everyone's eardrums. Me though? I love the guitar riffs, heavy drumbeats and songs that send me back to my teenage emo days with my sweeping side fringe and heavily lined under-eyes.

It was only when we got back to the hotel that I realised I should have called it quits on the non-jelly shots a bit earlier. All that travelling, along with not having had much to eat during the day, was a risky situation into which to introduce alcohol. I puked up in the bathroom, bright pink sick seeping down the plughole (yeah, you could tell I'd been on the cranberry juice) and felt pretty sorry for myself for the remainder of the night. It wasn't my finest moment. It was the grossest thing I'd seen in a while, and I haven't been able to handle shots since. At twenty-three, my youth was over, clearly.

The next morning, after a much-needed McDonald's breakfast, I was as fresh as a daisy, more than ready to get out and see Glasgow. Over the next couple of days, Brandon and I visited some cool sights, even though the weather continued to play nasty. One of these was the Botanic Gardens, although wandering around looking at plants on a rainy day probably wasn't the best idea. We spied the art gallery and a few famous historical sites, including the famed Duke of Wellington statue, the one that always has a traffic cone stuck on his head.

I bought a book all about the Bell clan and loved flicking through that. It turns out our Bell family motto is 'I Bier the Bel', which to me sounds very ominous, as if we'll sweep down a dimly lit Scottish cobbled street in a dark cloak like some sort of weird Jack the Ripper copycat and pillage your goods. (Watch out for your Lush bath bombs and Costa cups, people.) Also, our crest is a hand holding a dagger, so that kind of emphasises my point, right?

We hit up the doughnut shop a couple more times, enjoying the delicious sugar rush whilst watching fellow Twenty-One Pilot fans queue up to meet the band outside the local HMV. They were all dressed in camouflage jackets and had neon-yellow strips wrapped around their arms, like in the band's latest music video.

We encountered a very talkative taxi driver who recommended reels of places to eat in between shouting out of the window at passers-by, telling jokes, and laughing at the punchline before anyone had a chance to answer. My pap, self-proclaimed king of bad jokes, would have been proud.

I had an allergic reaction at a local Chinese buffet, where I must have digested something cooked in peanut oil, but, overall, it was a cool trip. I snapped a tiny part of Glasgow and got a glimpse into the culture.

We rocked up to Glasgow's answer to the Natural History Museum and got lost around there, appreciating the heritage. Also, yes, we made it to see Twenty-One Pilots, and, yes, I can confirm, they were worth heading to another country for.

Since Glasgow, which was back in March 2019, Brandon and I have been on a few more successful (and not accidental) trips, although, due to the pandemic, we've been a little restricted. That's given me a chance to see more of the UK and experience a different kind of travelling. It's allowed me to appreciate brilliantly beautiful spots in England and realise that learning about my own culture is important too. I've been neglecting that a bit, itching to get away somewhere tropical, unaware there's so much vibrant history here in the UK.

Of course, I know about lively London: famous Big Ben, the Houses of Parliament and St Paul's Cathedral. At school, I learnt all about the gruesome tales of Sweeny Todd and Jack the Ripper as well as the bubonic plague and the significance of Blackheath (where many Black Death victims were buried). I'm familiar with the Great Fire of London, Henry VIII and the imprisonment and execution of some of his many wives in the Tower of London, and the evacuation of the city's children to the countryside during the Second World War.

But although I could reel off facts about the London Underground (how sad am I?) and tell you about the capital's historical sights, I didn't know much about the rest of the UK. So, I made it my mission to change that. So far, Brandon and I have been to Devon and checked out Brixham, where my pap told us about the best fish and chip shop, and Clovelly, a beautiful sloping village by the sea complete with its own waterfall, tea rooms, pubs and restaurants. We've also been to Cornwall and visited St Ives, Padstow, Port Isaac and Falmouth. We've gone over to the Isle of Wight, and we've enjoyed breaks even closer to home, in Eastbourne and Pevensey Bay.

Even though I couldn't jump on a plane, I could still go places, meet different people and experience amazing things nearer to my own front door. Realising this fact really expanded my horizons. Also, I can't deny I still learnt valuable life lessons – in Glasgow especially. Specifically: don't hit the shots after a long day of travelling, and always check where you're booking a concert before you pay. Duh.

Cambodian sunset, south-east Asia

Andaman and Nicobar Islands, Bay of Bengal, India

Southern boundary, Koh Ta Kiev Island, south-east Asia

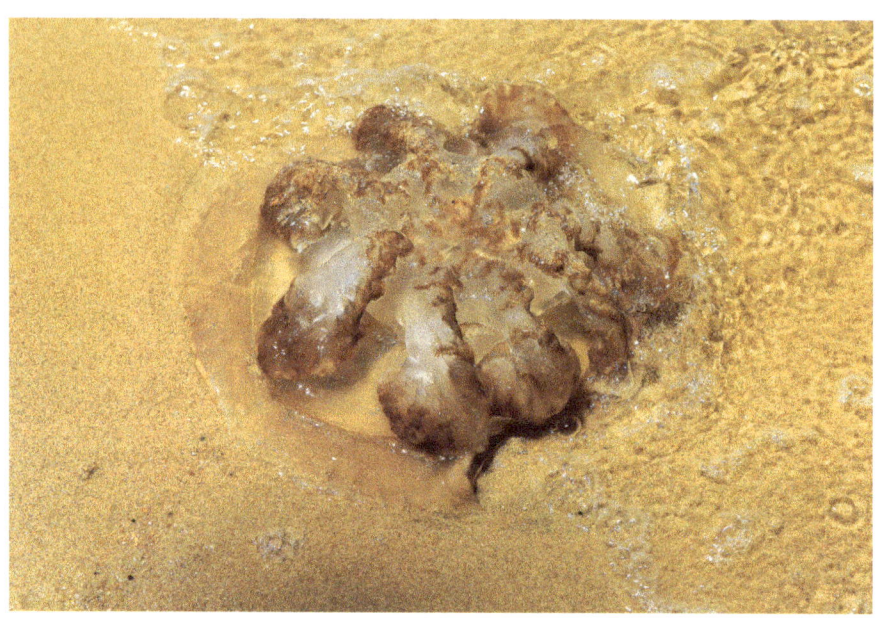

Jellyfish, Cambodia, south-east Asia

24

I'm Not Ending Up in That Guy's Basement

Rome

In an escape room, you have to work with your team to find your way out. Everyone's a little anxious because, well, you're trapped in a locked room – and where the hell is the fire escape? – but you're all hyped up because it's ultimately down to you to figure this puzzle out. Well, Rome was basically an impromptu escape room for me and my friend Lizzie. This trip was all about two of the most anxious people ever stepping into the big bad world on their own. And I think we handled it pretty well.

We'd booked our October getaway as a sunshine break for when it got a little chillier, and in the lead-up, we sat holed up in the Debenhams café (ah, Debenhams, such an underrated place; thanks, Covid, for snatching another of my favourite shops from me), poring over my laptop, checking different hotels, comparing distances to the city, weighing up the pros and cons of each package and researching sights as we counted down the days to our flight.

I'd never been to Italy before, but I'd always wanted to see the Colosseum. It looked magnificent in the photographs and I was eager to learn about the history of the city and see the magical architecture for myself. Also, I love pizza and pasta, so I knew Italy would be right up my street. Rome would be an exciting, welcome break for us, plus it wasn't too far to travel for a long weekend. However, if I'd been convinced that jetting off with a friend would mean no Bell travel dramas (I should totally trademark that), then I was to be proved monumentally mistaken.

We were due to fly on the Friday morning from Stansted, but rather than face the horror of rising early and trundling onto two different trains, lugging our suitcases as we went, we decided to book into an airport hotel the night before.

That way we would already be in the vicinity and could just hop onto the shuttle on Friday morning, no stress.

As it turned out, there *would* be stress indeed. Who am I kidding? I'm a magnet for anxiety-provoking situations. Of course, there was stress.

On the Wednesday before our departure, I woke feeling bunged-up, groggy and generally a bit crappy. I'd been to Cornwall the week before with Brandon, my cousin Harrison and his fiancée Siana. It had been lovely, but it had rained the entire time. We'd rented a little apartment, hoping to get out and about, see some Cornish beauty spots and bask in some late-season sunshine.

I'd been to Perranporth twice with Brandon and really enjoyed it. Thinking Cornwall would be a cool place to go back to with Harrison and Siana in tow, we booked to stay in Falmouth, but unfortunately, the weather wasn't on our side. Our rented accommodation was dim and damp, and I woke each morning with a wheeze. Everyone but me returned from Cornwall with coughs and colds. I thought I'd escaped that grisly fate, but sadly, I had not. A few days later, less than a week before Lizzie and I were due to fly to Rome, I felt like I'd swallowed razorblades. My nose was blocked and I developed a hacking cough. I really did feel like death warmed up.

Despite this, I soldiered on. I was now working for a start-up company as a content writer, so I logged on from home, dosed myself up with Lemsip and all was fine (ish). That was until I glanced at my reflection in the mirror on the Wednesday evening. A grotesque cyst-like spot had suddenly decided to rear its ugly head on my cheek; it was angry, painful and a mess to peer at.

No big deal, right? It was just a spot. Well, I have a complicated, gross relationship with pimples. So, if you don't want to be put off your breakfast/lunch/dinner, then skip this next part.

I'm a pimple popper and I can't, no matter how much I try, control my fingers. They itch to squeeze, and my willpower fails me every time. I enjoyed clear skin throughout my teens, and I thought I'd escaped major acne, but when I turned twenty-one, my complexion changed and my chin started to develop deep, cyst-like bumps. You couldn't always see them, but they hurt like crazy. I'd squeeze the cysts, even if there was no head. Which, by the way, is a really bad idea and you should never follow in my stupid footsteps.

The first time I popped a chin cyst, I damaged the surrounding skin so badly, it turned into impetigo, a skin infection caused by bacteria getting into an open wound. That spot became a gaping, disgusting, open wound. This first experience of the dreaded lurgy (also known as impetigo) was on New Year's Day 2017 (ah, perfect vibe for a new year: a bloody face infection). I'd aggressively worked on the spot the night before, with the help of a few Proseccos to dull the pain. Next morning, I shuffled over to my mirror, ran a brush through my curls and snapped open my moisturiser, ready to apply it. My eyes flickered sleepily to my reflection and zoned in on this yellow, oozing, crusty mess inhabiting the lower part of my face. I almost screamed. "Mum!" I shrieked as I hurtled down the stairs. "Something's happened to my face!" I whined, reverting to dramatic fourteen-year-old mode.

My mum peered at my chin. I'm amazed she didn't physically gag, it looked that revolting. We set off for the doctor's pronto when it started weeping, and they diagnosed impetigo and prescribed me antibiotics. It thankfully cleared up within the week, but I had to go to work armed with extra concealer and heavy-duty moisturiser, nipping off to the bathroom every hour to fix the crusty scab. Gross.

Since that fateful week, impetigo has returned whenever I've tried too hard to pop a spot not ready to be meddled with. You'd think I'd just stop squeezing them, right? But no. My caffeine addiction, being a worrywart and popping my pimples are my character flaws.

On that Wednesday evening before Rome, feeling like a *Walking Dead* extra anyway, due to my cold, I stumbled upstairs, all set with my Lemsip and my book (I know, I'm in my twenties, not nineties, but hey, I like my creature comforts). I was taking my make-up off when I spotted the unwelcome visitor lurking. I threw everything at it, which is also a tremendously bad idea, but my mind goes into manic mode when I spy a spot. Witch hazel, tea tree oil, Acnecide, toothpaste, Clearasil, Freederm, a Lush facemask...nothing worked. So, I gave in and popped it.

Next morning, I was in immense pain. The right side of my face had ballooned, and the spot, although not quite impetigo yet, was a disgusting bleeding scab. I lisped when I spoke. It looked and sounded like I had a gobstopper in my mouth.

Yeah, it was bad.

"Why does this always happen to me?" I grumbled, shrugging on my dressing gown, wearily checking my mirror to examine the damage. I answered my own question as I studied my obscene face. "Because you always mess with your spots." Exasperated, I slathered on some antiseptic cream, but it was too late. Far too late.

I'd also completely lost my voice and resembled the penguin from *Toy Story* whenever I tried to speak. My cough had got progressively worse and Lemsip wasn't cutting it.

My mum drove me to the doctor's, acting as interpreter because I couldn't get any words out. To cut a long story short, I was told I could fly and that the cold would sort itself out, and I was given antibiotics to bring down the swelling in my face.

"Have a good holiday! Try not to infect the whole of Europe!" my GP called cheerfully as we departed at the end of the consultation.

It's odd to think back on that comment, because less than a year later, not just the whole of Europe but the whole world was infected – with Covid-19. Maybe my doctor should go into fortune-telling.

So, off I went that evening. My dad and I picked up Lizzie and drove to our hotel in Stansted whilst I filled her in on my saga. But it was dark in the car, so I don't think she saw the worst of it until I jumped out to grab our bags. "I didn't know it was that bad!" she exclaimed, gazing at my puffy face.

Yes, it was that bad. Believe me.

On the plus side, my horrific-looking face meant I wasn't fussed about posting twenty million times a day on Instagram, my phone got a few days off and my Instagram-centred brain got a break. Thank God.

I waved to my dad as he drove away, and Lizzie and I hauled our suitcases into the hotel. I was thinking, I can totally do this. No problem. I can travel on my own, this is what I live for. Now, I don't know about Lizzie, but I never feel like a proper adult. I feel like one of those characters in a videogame where you've just completed the tutorial but weren't really paying attention. So now, you're just running around madly, with no idea what you're doing, wondering if everyone else feels the same. Me and Lizzie embarking on our own adventure was like that: thrilling but a bit surreal.

We checked in to the airport hotel and ordered room service, opting to binge a haunted house documentary on Netflix and have an early night. I was popping pills (antibiotic pills, that is) all over the shop and gulping down Lemsip every four hours like a junkie, but we were determined to have a good time. Infected face and flu or not.

198

Next morning, we caught the shuttle bus (which admittedly stopped right outside the hotel lobby and took you straight to departures), feeling pretty smug about this travelling lark so far. We were clear-headed and ready to go. Once through security, we had a browse around the shops, and soon enough, it was time to board. We were ecstatically excited, off on our trip away to see somewhere brand-new.

When we landed, we were raring to see the city as soon as possible. We hopped off the plane, located our luggage and exited the terminal into the dimming afternoon sun. I breathed in that deliciously familiar gust of exotic hot air. It hit me square in the face when I stepped out of the coolness of the arrivals lounge. That first inhalation of heat coupled with foreign scents and the chatter of different accents is special and I grinned up at the evening sky.

All wasn't straightforward though. We stood revelling in the sun for a few minutes before something inevitably went wrong. Our pre-arranged shuttle to the hotel was late, and when I say late, I mean it was delayed by an hour and a half. We sat on our cases, heads bobbing up whenever a vehicle halted in front of us, kicking dust into the hazy evening. It seemed like days before our shuttle rocked up; it had got darker and the sun had disappeared for the night, leaving a chillier air.

The man behind the wheel of the shuttle yelled Lizzie's name, and we dragged our luggage over, collapsing into the back seats, grateful to be embarking on the final step of our journey. A couple of around our age were waved over too; unbeknown to us, they were sharing our lift. As they ducked into the cramped back seats, they shot us that typical British half-smile. The universal sign of pure awkwardness. We returned the gesture and then all four of us turned to gaze out of our respective windows in weighted silence.

That sort of situation probably isn't as painful if you're not already terribly socially self-conscious, but I am, and so is Lizzie, so the silence in the taxi was deafening. Plus, the journey through the darkening Rome rush hour took close to two hours. That's two whole hours squished up with strangers in utter pin-drop silence. At one point, I went to take a swig of my water, and it went down the wrong way. I began to splutter and cough, tears streaming down my face, smudging my eyeliner. Everyone looked up in sympathy then went back to pondering the riveting blackness outside.

Ugh, it was a social nightmare, to say the least. We bumped into those two a few times during our trip, at a local restaurant and out and about in the streets.

We all gave each other half-nods and went on our way. Got to love English awkwardness, haven't you? Cringe or what.

After endless traffic jams and countless detours, we eventually arrived at the Kent Hotel in Porta Pia, a charming little place nestled down a tiny side road and surrounded by a fantastic array of authentic Italian restaurants. The rooms were rustic, like in an old-fashioned guesthouse, and I adored it.

We did a lot of walking on that trip, which my Fitbit loved me for. The weather was great, being warm but overcast, and perfectly comfortable for walking. The city centre took us about forty minutes to get to on foot, and we enjoyed immersing ourselves in the streets, discovering obscure places and things we might not have seen on the metro or the bus.

We frequented this little café for breakfast. Lizzie would grab a croissant, I'd order a latte and we'd set off for the city, chattering about what we wanted to see, armed with our enormous map. Lizzie used Google Maps when the original map failed us (yes, I know I mentioned I passed my bronze D of E award, but I am in no way an expert or even an amateur in map-reading; in fact, I'm hilariously terrible at it), so we reached everywhere we wanted to, it just took us a little longer, that's all.

We did get to see the Colosseum, the hotspot I'd been keen to set eyes on but only from the outside. Every time we tried to purchase tickets, the line was huge, even when we turned up early in the morning. From the outside, it was still magnificent. The sheer height of it against the sunny sky was mesmerising. I'd love to go back and explore inside one day.

We caught the metro to Vatican City, heading down deep beneath Rome's bustling streets to the trains. I'm an avid tube user back home; the London Underground is my happy place and I always feel so at ease down there. I know where I'm going, and I know where to get off for whatever destination I have in mind. This has been drummed into me since I was very little as my dad is like a walking tube map. If I ever need to know what the closest station is to anything, anything at all, I don't look at a map, I just ask him.

I do love the underground. I love zipping across the city, reaching my destination in mere minutes. I love sitting (or standing, in rush hour) side by side with my fellow commuters, all of us on our way to work. I even love the familiar colours of the upholstery and the different tube lines and how everyone hates the Bakerloo but likes the Circle, Central and Victoria lines. (I'm not a massive tube freak, I promise; it just feels familiar there.)

I'm at home on the underground, like a little scuttling mouse, I guess – a little scuttling mouse clutching a Costa vanilla latte in one hand and an iPod in the other. But the Rome metro system was different. It was grimy and dirty down there. There was admittedly a lot more space than I was used to on the London tube trains, but it was grey and depressingly dreary.

We slipped into the carriage, squinting up to decipher the Italian signage, and balanced ourselves, unable to reach the overhanging handles. There was no chance of us falling over though, even as the train abruptly ground to a halt at the first station. It was utterly crammed; no London Underground journey could have prepared me. Lizzie and I stood uncomfortably, my arm twisted behind me, and I stared upwards, feeling like I was slipping slowly to the ground, which was also questionable on the hygiene front. She caught my eye through the gap between one person's arm and another person's backpack and winced. Lucky we weren't claustrophobic. Eventually, our ride on the maddening metro came to an end, and we shuffled off at Vatican City and spent the afternoon there, grateful to be out in the open.

It was exceptionally hot, and although the puffiness in my face had reduced substantially, I'd woken that morning feeling awful. My head felt full of cotton wool, my eyes hurt, my throat was scratchy, and I just wanted to lie down in the middle of the street for a nap in the sun. Not even the rich aroma of a coffee in a quaint Vatican café could perk me up.

The Vatican was astounding though, the architecture tremendous, and I could see why it's such a holy place for so many. Home to the Pope and headquarters of the Roman Catholic Church, Vatican City has many a prestigious sight. It's famed for its museums and ancient Roman sculptures, and for the Sistine Chapel with its celebrated Michelangelo ceiling.

Crowds were massed outside St Peter's Basilica, the main church in Vatican City and said to be the final resting place of St Peter, with tourists taking pictures of its fine Renaissance facade or simply reflecting quietly. It's one of the largest churches in the world and hundreds were queuing to get inside. It was stunning, but in my fluey state, I probably didn't appreciate it as much as I could have.

When we visited the Trevi Fountain the next day, I felt a little better. I had dosed up on paracetamol and slathered my (gross as hell) face with concealer to hide the massive scab that always appears as the infection heals. We set off early, and I was determined to have a good time. Now I was feeling livelier, I was able to fully experience the fountain in all its extravagant beauty without feeling like I was going to pass out. I mean, that's always a plus, right?

The Trevi Fountain is one of the most famous fountains in the world and one of the oldest water sources in Rome, and it truly was inspiring. Just the sound and sight of it was enough to cool me down on that warm day, and I got some great pictures too. Designed by Italian architect Nicola Salvi, the fountain measures up at 26.3 metres high and 49.15 metres wide and attracts an immense number of tourists. It's estimated that around €3,000 is thrown into the fountain each day, because, you know, people love throwing coins into fountains. Wishes were being made as hands threw coins into the splashing water and selfies were being taken. The only dampener to the jaw-dropping view was the piercing whistle that was blown by the police guard at full volume every five seconds, warning people off touching the precious marble.

After lunch in a nearby café, we went on to see some old Roman ruins and stumbled across a street artist. I bought a fantastic painting of a typical Italian house; it's bright yellow and the walls are littered with winding climbing flowers. I have it framed on my wall at home, and when I gaze at it, I cast myself back, recalling the pleasant sun on my face as Lizzie and I wandered at leisure around the cobbled streets, chatting and poring over our massive folding map.

That afternoon, we got scammed by a local, who insisted he desperately needed money to buy shoes. We gave him our last notes, only to realise, after he'd scarpered, that… 'Oh my God, but he's wearing shoes.' We then watched him approach a friendly looking couple further down the street, presumably to spin them the same story.

Shaking our heads at the audacity, we set off again, eager to see as much as we could but now €30 down. We visited the Capuchin Crypt and catacombs, which was an eerie but strangely tranquil experience, and then, we dropped by the Hard Rock Café and enjoyed fajitas (chicken for me, veggie for Lizzie). We sipped cocktails at a local bar where we were the only customers, so the bartender proudly made us original offerings to try, serving them with fruit garnishes as we lounged in the open window. The warm breeze was pleasant as we watched the city lights and listened to people laughing, enjoying a typical night in Rome.

As we waited at a street crossing the next day, on our way to explore the park, an odd, older gentleman struck up a never-ending conversation with us. Then he followed us, insisting on trying to hug us every thirty seconds. He was omitting some seriously creepy vibes, and whenever we sped up our pace, so did he. The last straw was him asking if we wanted to come back to his house. We declined politely and got the hell out of there. Our picnic in the park turned abruptly into panic in the park as we hotfooted it back through the gates, sprinting away, glancing over our shoulders as he attempted to amble along behind. "What a weirdo," I muttered. We returned to the main road, where we felt safer, being among crowds of people. Although the catacombs had been hauntingly beautiful, I sure as hell didn't want to end up there myself, or you know, in that guy's basement.

We had fun developing pictures on my Polaroid camera, trying to take selfies like they used to do in pre-iPhone times. How on earth did anyone manage it? It's so difficult to get in frame.

I remember a story my mum and nan have told countless times of how my pap was essentially the creator of the 'selfie'. There's a snap of him back in the 70s, sitting in his car. Fiddling with his camera, he'd accidently taken a photo of himself gazing into the lens, cigarette hanging out of his mouth and a surprised look plastered on his face. So, I guess that's how they did it before iPhones. Completely by chance.

Back in Rome, giggling at our awful polaroid selfies, Lizzie and I gobbled amazing food, inhaling perfect pasta dishes and pizza favourites as a reward for all that exploring.

One evening, we'd chosen a rustic-looking place to eat; we'd ordered wine and Elizabeth opted for a penne dish.

Hers arrived in a great big bowl. I'd chosen meatballs, but when they came, it was just three meatballs on a plate drizzled in some fancy sauce. I'd assumed – wrongly – that you got spaghetti with a meatball order, as that was what I was used to at home. So, I learnt a lesson there: always know what you're ordering. As if I hadn't learnt from the zebra ordeal back in Kenya or the lobster ravioli episode in London. I was beyond disappointed and starving for the rest of the night. Lizzie offered me some of hers, but this was my own stupid fault, so I thanked her and ate my three meatballs grudgingly, leaving my stomach to rumble through the rest of the evening.

And if you're wondering, yes, the swelling did go down, slowly and steadily. By the time I returned home, my face was almost symmetrical. The lesson I learnt from that, the hard way (many times), was not to pop spots, but I can't say I follow that advice, even now.

25

Livin' for the Gram

Los Angeles

Less than a month later, face now fully healed but towing an arsenal of spot treatments in my suitcase as a precaution, I practically skipped onto the aircraft ready to depart to Los Angeles.

Settling down in my seat, I hit play on yet another California-themed song on my battered blue iPod touch. Yes, even my very limited musical palette boasts a great many songs dedicated to the Sunshine State, and, yes, at the time of this trip (late 2019), I still had my trusty iPod, before recent circumstances dragged me kicking and screaming into the world of Spotify. Oh, the horror.

My fingers were just itching to swipe something, anything, so my iPod had to do until I could log back onto Instagram when we landed.

I'd never been one for the world of social media. I half-heartedly signed up to Facebook when I was fourteen, just to keep up with the crowd. All my friends had accounts and we used to tag each other in silly memes or cartoons and take pictures of our Converse-clad feet in a circle (you know, those iconic yet cringey snaps from the 2000s).

I downloaded Twitter as part of a project we had to carry out at university, and I had Snapchat fleetingly, but I deleted those two after mere months, finding that they were clogging up my brain. I had no use for them in my life. But my social media obsession had been gnawing away at me ever since the Andaman Islands, and it was on this LA trip that it finally became apparent to me.

I bowed to peer pressure and downloaded the pesky Instagram app when I was twenty-two, and I then became low-key obsessed with it, posting incessantly and caring way too much about what other people thought about me. It became this weird toxic addition to my personality, clinging on for dear life like a bloodsucking leech. I was never without my phone. I never went anywhere without posting a picture. Ever.

Yeah. It was at the 'Hi, I'm Chloë and I'm an Instagram addict' level.

I didn't want to become that person, living my life through a screen, but that's how I ended up, and I regretted it. A lot. My anxiety tripled, and I felt inadequate all the goddamn time. Which, if you're already incredibly negative, is just horribly hard work. Think of it like being Eeyore on a downer.

I've since deleted my account and feel so much more present and less rattled. Ten out of ten people would totally recommend doing this. (I can actually take a walk in real-life nature now without snapping ninety-eight photos of a lonely-looking lavender sprig, oblivious to the picturesque views in front of me. Yes, that exact scenario has occurred before.)

Also, I'd started bingeing *Black Mirror* on Netflix and the whole 'technology will be the death of us' vibe was really making me think about just how much power we give to our bloody phones. And then there was that documentary *The Social Dilemma*, which I watched a few days after I broke up with the Gram. It reinforced my decision and I've never looked back.

I started to chart how this fake life we all strive to promote was actually heightening my anxiety, and I freaked out. The thought that in fifty years' time I wouldn't remember anything I'd done because all I'd recall would be snapping a photo for social media or living through filters began to stress me immensely. I felt like my life was passing me by.

I also missed being bored. I'd grown to hate that everything was there as soon as I wanted it. Information, an Uber, pizza.

But during our USA trip, I was still very much rooted in my Instagram-obsessed lifestyle. I simultaneously loved and hated uploading my life, but it was something I couldn't stop. It was like an itch I couldn't quite scratch. I was like a junkie, fingers eager to tap, swipe, post.

When I look back on that trip and the few holidays before (especially the Andaman Islands; I almost wish the demon baby had just mugged me for my phone, at least then I'd have been without it for more than two solid minutes), I regret missing things because I was too busy uploading photos. I mean, sure, I have countless digital memories to look back on, but I didn't experience anything properly; I wasn't immersed, there were too many stupid selfies. Plus no one needs fifty iPhone snaps of the same palm tree swaying delicately in the breeze, no matter how picture-perfect it seems. And then when I got home, I didn't feel like I had disconnected from my everyday life at all. It had been transported with me in my pocket, everywhere I went.

Damn kids, right? Living for the Gram. We don't know we're alive. I probably just sounded way older than my time, referring to it as the Gram, but you get my drift.

We were heading to California first, as a pit stop before flying on to Hawaii, and ironically (not to stereotype, just a general observation), Instagram use was pretty rife in Los Angeles, so I fitted in quite well in that respect. I saw it immediately, as if I was staring into a cracked mirror, and I didn't appreciate what was reflected back at me.

As soon as I hopped off that plane, there were phones everywhere as my fellow travellers snapped selfies of them at LAX picking up their luggage. I didn't indulge that time (for once). I was more interested in locating the nearest coffee spot. The brutal handover from my much-loved usual Costa Coffee to the USA's staple Starbucks was a struggle.

Starbucks breaks me out in a cold sweat; it's just not my cup of tea (or coffee – ha ha, see what I did there). I don't like how they need to know your name for marketing purposes, I don't like that it's always so bloody dark in there, and I especially don't like how (at home, at least) it's always crowded with pre-teen girls who look about twenty-five, judging your outfit as you stand in front of them in the queue. Starbucks is like that intimidating kid at school who makes your life a misery. Costa is the studious alternative, hanging out in the library with a good book and a more laid-back vibe.

As you can see, I have way too much time on my hands to be comparing Costa and Starbucks like they're characters in *Mean Girls*. But hey, it keeps me busy.

In LA, I adapted grudgingly and made a beeline for Starbucks, weaving through the chaos around me. Travellers were live-streaming, Snapchatting and recording videos of themselves, and I felt out of my depth, swamped by the selfie-taking. There were filters everywhere and, to be honest, it was a little unnerving.

I love airports as much as the next person, but what was happening? They were gushing to their phone cameras, tilting their heads this way and that, flicking their hair, speaking excitedly about 'being in LA' and whatever they were there for. Then: 'beep', stop recording, done. They gathered up their bags and headed off abruptly, their faces wiped of the excitement that had been plastered there mere seconds ago. As if all of that hadn't even happened. Like it had all been a performance, a show for the followers and the fans.

It was weird. I mean, I know Hollywood is the heart of the film industry, but I honestly felt like I'd landed in a movie of my own, only instead of a churned-out chick-flick, it was a gritty psychological thriller about the toxicity of social media pressures.

With my latte and my suitcase in tow, I joined my mum and dad and headed outside into the warm evening air to find a taxi. As we waited, my brain snapped back to less than an hour previously, when I'd been gazing out of the plane window with all these expectations whirling around my brain.

I'd been eager to land. I can do plane journeys – well, I can do half of most longer plane journeys. After around seven or eight hours, that's when my limits are tested. That, my friends, is when about three zits mysteriously pop up around my face, my skin gets cracked and dry, my hair feels greasy even if I've washed it that morning, my back aches, my legs need a stretch, and I feel like I've eaten my body weight in complimentary pretzels. But this plane journey, after I'd watched all the *Big Bang Theory* reruns, was spent reflecting on how travelling actually helps my anxiety, contrary to what I might have expected.

It is odd that I'm always eager to head off across the world at the drop of a hat. It's almost like, when I'm travelling, my brain is asked to do such a deep dive, with my routine being messed up so dramatically, that my anxiety doesn't know how to provide me with that good old hit of existential dread I've grown to expect on a daily basis at home. It's as if travel shocks it out of my system for a while.

Although I had a stronger leash on my anxiety by this point, I still had the stress, albeit on a much lower scale. I still had the worries; I'd just learnt how not to react to them. I'd come this far and had been enjoying my new and improved, less worrisome life. When I thought back to my holidays in Nerja and Java, it was like I was flipping through someone else's travel photos. The feeling of being grasped 24/7 by pure OCD panic was a faded snapshot, whereas the lessons I'd learnt in those same places were vivid in my mind's eye.

But even though I was less anxious, 2019 was an odd year, mismatched even, like one of those multi-coloured quilted blankets. It felt deflated even before it began, although there were a lot of important changes. When I look back, 2019 felt quiet, like it was gearing up for something horrific. We weren't to know that a global pandemic was right around the corner.

My mum and I had taken to jokingly hinting we wanted to go to Hawaii that year. My mum is a massive *Hawaii Five-O* fan and I just wanted to try surfing; it was one of those places my mum always had her eye on, so we'd intensified the hints back in January, not thinking in a million years my dad would cave.

When my birthday rolled around in August, my whole family threw my nan and me a wonderful joint Hawaiian-themed party in my nan and pap's garden, complete with tiki bar backdrops, Hawaiian garlands, cocktails, grass skirts and Hawaiian-themed photo booth props. It was a fantastic day, one of my all-time favourite memories, and I have framed snaps of me, my mum, dad, nan, pap, cousins and Brandon all clad in bright shirts and grinning, with cocktails in hand. They're up in my room, always there to make me smile.

Because of this party, I'm convinced my dad got so fed up with us rabbiting on about Hawaii that he gave in. A week later, he produced our flight itinerary with a flourish.

We were heading firstly to Los Angeles, then to Honolulu, and finally to San Francisco. Of course, we were ecstatic, feeling so lucky and excited, already packing our suitcases, ready to go months before our departure date. My mum bought a Lonely Planet travel guide on Hawaii and jotted down a list of everything we wanted to see and do. She earmarked pages – there were colour-coded sticky notes galore – and made a rough plan of the best places we needed to see.

We were thrilled to be going to Hawaii, but as the trip approached, I found myself even more excited to see LA. So, what was it about the golden city that I couldn't wait to immerse myself in? I don't know. Maybe it was the glitz and glamour, the pipedreams or the clichéd images of it. Many people groan at the very mention of LA, Hollywood, the City of Angels. The stereotype is that it's full of pretentious film stars, non-stop parties, drug overdoses, scandals, and vast amounts of corrupt money changing hands. Oh, and the avocados – don't forget about those. It's all juice bars by day, cocaine binges by night. It's cool, it's hip, it's the place to be, but I know there's a darker side too. Like anywhere, I suppose. Everyone has an opinion about LA; it's a place that causes debates. Maybe that's what sparked my curiosity.

I have one of my dad's photographs on my wall now. It's a snap of the Hollywood Sign and he's edited it to invert the colours so that it's an explosion of purple and green. It's arty and abstract, and I love it. But every time he sees it, he exclaims 'Hollywoooooood' in a pretentious, fake American accent and laughs.

Los Angeles was not a profound place by any stretch, and I wasn't expecting it to be. It wasn't even as glamorous as I'd thought. A good angle and a little bit of colour balance can do wonders to make a place look amazing in a picture when maybe the reality isn't so fabulous. You can Photoshop anything; that's the issue with today's society. Nothing online is how you see it in real life (ahem, sly dig at Instagram; I know, I know).

But, on a serious note, I wasn't aware of that app Facetune, or anything like, that until very recently. I didn't know that editing yourself to look unrecognisable was considered pretty normal on social media. You can make a photo look so much better than the genuine article with the tiniest bit of work, but then, aren't we losing the very flaws that make each of us unique?

A little further into the trip, when we were in San Francisco, the fog was way too heavy for us to get a clear photo of Alcatraz Island. My dad, being the talented photographer he is, later showed me some of the photos he got from there and, honestly, it looked like a different day. The power of editing, kids. The fog was still there, but he had worked on the photo so you could clearly see every single tiny window on the prison; you could make out the watchtower and the intricate detail. So, impressions from a picture sometimes don't count for much. Just like with the arty as hell Hollywood photograph, my dad's snaps look amazing but are different to how it was in real life. My photos? They came out pretty bad because I'm a writer, not a photographer, and although I love taking pictures, that – sadly – is not where my talent lies.

In Los Angeles, Hollywood Boulevard was in need of some serious reconstruction. The stars on the pavement (sorry, sidewalk) were chipped and cracked and some were fading. Others had been removed in the aftermath of recent scandalous news stories. There were also some questionable additions. I mean, I love Mickey Mouse as much as the next person, but does he really need his own star on the Hollywood Walk of Fame? Walt Disney (who is there too), yes, but Mickey Mouse? Maybe not. He isn't even real.

We got accosted by a man dressed as Spider-Man who purposefully sidestepped into our photos and then demanded $40 from us. He switched from laughing and joking to being pushy and downright weird in a matter of seconds. I wanted to scoff, 'Hey, yes, I am a tourist, but I've dealt with so many scammers like you back in London, I'm a pro at spotting one a mile off. Also, I was just trying to go about my day, taking pictures of the buildings and the Walk of Fame, I didn't ask you to photobomb us.' But I didn't, because, you know, awkward English politeness is maddening sometimes.

We ducked out and lost him in a sea of people milling around outside a McDonald's that was pretty normal-looking, considering it was on the Hollywood Boulevard. I don't know what I was expecting – gold-plated handles on the doors, maybe a red carpet outside. We stopped for breakfast, half because we were hungry and half to avoid the crazed Spider-Man storming around the streets outside looking for us. We filled up on my all-time favourite, sausage and egg McMuffins, oh, and an accompanying hash brown, don't forget that. Heaven.

Emerging with our takeaway coffees a little while later, sure that our suss Spider-Man had by now scuttled off to bother someone else, we continued our voyage down the boulevard. All that kept playing on a loop in my head was Green Day's *Boulevard of Broken Dreams*, because it seemed to be a bit…dark there. Something sinister seemed to lurk under the lights.

There was a lot of graffiti. Everywhere. And there were a few guys, around my own age, lounging around, lying down in the street, heads on their skateboards, holding signs up which read 'Money for drugs?'. Most of the 'friendly' locals we came across were either high, or trying to sell us extortionate, overpriced tours, or both.

I'm aware this account doesn't make LA sound like it would be a great place to holiday, or even spend any time, right? But I loved that it wasn't how I originally thought it would be. Plus, if you could look past the grime, you really did see the bling underneath. I was actually walking down the Hollywood Walk of Fame. There was an extravagant air about LA that even a few broken stars on the sidewalk couldn't quite dim. The sparkle was still there. Maybe it wasn't as shiny, but it was definitely still present. Scrub away the graffiti and you'd reveal evidence of its ritzy past. Plus, it was a bustling, busy city, and I'm always more than happy to get lost in one of those.

LA reminded me of a faded Polaroid, bleached-out but classic. Everywhere you looked, there was a haze, as if someone had put a filter on life there. And that's why I loved it, because although the sheen had worn off, it still felt recognisable. It was like London's self-assured, more chilled-out sibling. Yes, you had Hollywood Boulevard and the city, but we were also fifteen minutes from the beach, palm trees lined the roads everywhere, and the whole place had a slower pace. It knew it was cool. Whereas London, though I love it immensely, is more outwardly uptight. It's much more a representation of my own personality, to be honest. So, LA was refreshing in a way.

We only had time for a quick visit to LA, a few snaps and a brief photoshoot involving the Hollywood Sign, me in my massive sunglasses and our yellow taxi. The driver of our yellow taxi was the first Angelino we'd met (other than the lovely Sheraton Hotel staff) and he made a great impression on us. Surprisingly, those photos were not uploaded to Instagram, and I silently applauded my tiny win (Me: 1, Social Media: 0). However, my archenemy the Gram got me back, points-wise, at the Golden Gate Bridge later in the trip.

But that same City of Angels can be a hellhole for some. There is indeed a darker side. The missing stars on the Hollywood Walk of Fame brought home exactly how much corruption, racism, sexism, abuse, and crime there is, not just on the streets but within the film and music industries. I've since watched the popular documentary on Netflix all about the Hotel Cecil in downtown LA (Netflix bingeing during lockdown, gotta love it), and that offers a stark insight into LA's skid row, the massive drugs problem there and the sheer number of violent crimes happening on its streets each and every day. That glimpse into what goes on within the city made me rethink my initial impression of LA.

I was entranced by LA indeed, but there was something about it that was unnerving. Like no one was really themselves, everyone was wearing some sort of a mask (and this was before Covid, so, no, not that kind of mask!). I left LA feeling like I'd seen it on the surface. I would have loved to explore more, but it was only a stopover and we were travelling on to Hawaii that same evening.

If you're heading to California though and you have more time, I've been told that Santa Monica and Venice Beach are both well worth a visit. Also, a personal tip of mine, if you're a Harry Potter fan like I certainly am, Disneyland in LA is pretty central and has a whole Harry Potter World. I've heard nothing but great things about it. You can sip butterbeer, roam through magical sets and jump on some fantastically themed rides. It's like going to Hogwarts for real.

There's so much to do in LA even if none of the above are your style though. There are typical city excursions, of course; you can visit the Wax Museum, or jump on an open-topped bus to see where all the famous movie stars live; you can hit up the beach and learn to surf, or you can even try hot yoga (which apparently is a massive craze).

If we'd had more time there, I'd definitely have checked out some of the infamous Halloween events. I saw an advertisement for the Haunted Haystack event when we were exploring Hollywood Boulevard, as it was getting close to the creepiest day of the year. I've watched so many YouTube videos and I know that the USA really goes heavy at Halloween and loves all things horror. We do have our own counterpart here in the UK – Tulleys Shocktoberfest, hosted by a farm in Crawley – and, yes, we have various scare mazes all over, but America seems to do Halloween the very best. So, if you're a horror fan, I'd advise planning your trip in conjunction with the spooky holiday and trying out some of their spectacular mazes.

For us, though, it was time to move on. When the sun retreated into the candyfloss clouds, turning the sky a deep pink, and the cooler air settled around us, we grabbed our bags and headed to the taxi waiting to take us back to LAX. We departed the City of Lights and turned our thoughts towards its tropical paradise alter-ego a five-hour flight away.

26

Chainsaw-Wielding Clowns

Hawaii

From California, we flew to Honolulu. Home of *Hawaii Five-O*, Lilo and Stich, Elvis, hula skirts, pineapples and surfing. I was excited, but like many things, sometimes you have to go through some turbulence to get to something really worthwhile. In our case, literal turbulence.

The jetlag from the London to LA flight had kept me up the whole of the previous night. I was basically a hysterical mess because I'm one of those people who need sleep. Like really need sleep. I don't function very well on any less than a whopping great eight hours. I hate tossing and turning. I like to settle into bed and drop off more or less straight away. So, jetlag? It's my worst nightmare.

My eyes felt sore and gritty that day. I'd sat up awake all night in my LA hotel room, unable to drift off no matter what I did. I tried numerous cups of camomile tea, listened to sleep apps on my phone, read my book, gazed out the window, but nothing worked, so I just sat, slowly descending into my own sleep-deprived, maddened state, watching the day slowly get lighter and lighter. Eventually, at 5 am, I'd had enough, so I got up, had an angry shower and waited for the Starbucks down in the lobby to open its doors at 6 am.

I know, I'd become one of 'those people'. Someone who waits outside a Starbucks to get their caffeine fix. I mean, I'd probably consider waiting outside a Costa Coffee to open back at home, but Starbucks…nah. (I'm joking, I would not wait outside a coffee shop for it to open, I would google the opening times and then arrive bang on time. Research, my friends.)

Still on London time, fumbling through a mind fog and an otherwise quiet and sleeping hotel, I made it downstairs and mumbled a 'Hello, how are you?' to the happy-go-lucky barista who had arrived bright-eyed and bushy-tailed a few minutes before and seen me skulking about. I smiled at their drawn-out 'Oh my gaaawd, you're from England? That's so coooool!', sleepily stumbled through my order, secured two lattes with skimmed milk and a flat white, hauled myself back upstairs and presented the coffees to my surprised mum and dad with the air of someone who hadn't been awake all night like some sort of manic nocturnal human bush baby.

Waiting for them to get ready to go out, I sat by my window with my latte, sipping it and watching the pale orange haze spread across the sky like a watercolour bleeding its paint. Watching as the twinkling lights of the streets below slowly dimmed and the famous LA traffic built up ready for rush hour.

Jetlag has always affected me. One holiday, when I was much younger, it took hours and hours to reach our hotel in Bali, there'd been so many delays, and I was practically asleep on my feet. I had an afternoon nap as soon as we got there, despite my mum trying to keep me awake so I could adjust to our new time zone's night-time. Sure enough, they were woken at 4 am by me sprawled across their bed with all my colouring books and toys out, suitcase open and its contents in disarray, chattering to myself, oblivious to the fact that it was the middle of the night.

So now, back at LAX but this time with jetlag, I made my way through security like a zombie and instantly slumped down in my seat on the plane to Hawaii. I was asleep before we had even taken off. My eyelids fluttered closed, my head dipped, and I was out cold. The five-hour trip passed in a blur. I only woke twice, once when my head bounced off the plane window and then again when the aircraft dipped suddenly before swerving upwards, almost lifting me off my seat, my seatbelt yanking me back into place. Both times, I jolted awake for all of five seconds before dropping off again. "What's happened?" I murmured as my eyes closed. I didn't hear my mum's reply. I was already nestled back in my dreamlike state.

Afterwards, I was to hear that we had passed through an extremely bad storm, that the turbulence had lasted practically the whole flight, from take-off until landing, and that my mum and dad were honestly considering switching on their phones to text their goodbyes to my nan and the rest of our family in case we plummeted into the waves, never to be seen again. Ironic, really, given that we were flying to Hawaii and that was where (as we learnt on a tour of the island later) they had filmed the ABC series *Lost*, a popular drama about a group of plane-crash survivors washed up on a deserted beach.

I woke refreshed, oblivious to the worry of the other passengers, whose faces were still drained of colour, unaware of their relief at finally getting off the aircraft. All I had was a small bruise on my head where I'd smashed it against the side of the plane.

Whenever I think of our trip to Hawaii, I remember that flight, even though I was the only person that wasn't actually conscious during it. But I also remember the most jam-packed, most adventurous holiday we've ever been on. Hawaii, you say, is for lounging on the beach and drinking cocktails from a pineapple, no? Not our trip. Hawaii seemed like one of those once-in-a-lifetime holidays, so we were determined not to waste it, determined to make the most of an incredible experience. I mean, yes, I did drink a pina colada from a pineapple, and, yes, I did find myself wandering straight into the nearest giftshop on the first day and picking up a plumeria hairclip (you know, those beautiful white and yellow flowers that everyone has in their hair in Hawaii). Typical annoying English tourist girl. But that's not what I remember when I reflect on this part of our USA adventure.

Whereas LA was laid-back but still reminiscent of London city life, Hawaii was tropical and beautiful in a whole different way. Although I'd pictured deserted beaches, like the ones we'd been lucky enough to experience all over Asia, Hawaii was by no means lacking in crowds. There were people everywhere. All the time. So, this trip was packed full. Packed full of people but also filled to the very brim with everything we wanted to do. Because my mum had been wanting to visit Hawaii for years and years, and we didn't want to miss anything.

When she was younger, Mum's own nan used to tell her how she'd read about the famous movie stars visiting Hawaii, travelling there by boat. She told my mum that the first thing they would see would be the Aloha Tower, so my mum was determined to get to that specific spot herself, for her nan.

But we did so much more. We trekked up the Diamond Head State Monument – a volcanic crater which overlooks Honolulu and the Pacific – in the heat and humidity, and we were really proud of and amazed at my mum for doing that as she is terrified of heights and it was pretty damn high, to say the least. My dad and I had surfing lessons. I hired a surfboard twice more and went out on my own, surprising myself and finding a new obscure hobby. Granted, there is nowhere to surf in London – apart from the Thames – so I talked myself out of buying a custom surfboard. Although how cool would that have been?

We visited the historic Pearl Harbour and reflected on its history. We went on an island tour and took in the North Shore, where the professional, globally acclaimed surfing contests are held. We went to a macadamia nut farm (I hear the nut samples were delicious, but my allergy is a massive inconvenience when I want to try something new, so I missed out) and tried hot and spicy shrimp from a local shrimp van at the side of the road. We snorkelled in the turquoise paradise of Turtle Beach, alongside the tropical fish. We watched a fantastic fireworks display on the sand at night, beheld Iolani Palace and marvelled at the Ala Moana Centre, said to be the largest open-air shopping centre in the world, which honestly put Westfield to shame. And I love Westfield. Trust me.

The only thing we missed was seeing the *Hawaii Five-O* filming taking place in the next street to where we were staying, which, of course, would have made my mum's holiday, as it's one of her all-time favourite shows. We were walking down the road back to our hotel one afternoon when my mum stopped to read a notice saying there would be scheduled filming the next day, that there would be simulated gunfire and for the locals not to be alarmed. Me and my dad chuckled. "It might be *Hawaii Five-O*," my dad said.

My mum walked on and shook her head. She insisted it wouldn't be as they would have wrapped up for the next season by now. However, it turned out to be the long-awaited *Hawaii Five-O/Magnum PI* crossover episode and she was gutted. See, being nosy almost always pays off in some way or another, or maybe that's just the journalist in my dad and me.

Hawaii was full of beauty; it still had that movie-star feel, the same as Los Angeles. Filming was taking place everywhere and glitzy individuals live-streamed as they sipped their cocktails or sashayed off for a surfing lesson. A great deal of the pre-arranged island tour we embarked on centred around informing us which famous person lived here, who had a house over there, what films had been made on this beach and which jungle setting we'd see in that TV show. All of that was very interesting. Our guide was informative and genuinely fun to listen to. He reminded me of Kamekona from the *Hawaii Five-0* remake, the trusty informant who runs a beachside shrimp van and also acts as a bit of comic relief in the otherwise heavy show. Our tour guide was jolly just like him and made it his mission to make the fun facts he threw at us actually fun to listen to. He knew his stuff for sure, but he also enjoyed telling us his own personal experiences of Hawaii, which was the captivating part.

I found that the stories I enjoyed the most didn't involve learning about which Hollywood star lived in that ten-bedroom mansion with a view of the blissful beach below. No, it was seeing the real Hawaii and hearing all about the culture, the history and the role Hawaii has played in major global events, that's what I revelled in. We drank up the information as eagerly as the water I was downing every few minutes to counteract the extreme heat.

We also learnt why there aren't generally any snakes in Hawaii. Because it's so isolated, the only way for snakes to get there is to swim, which is, well, pretty unlikely. We also heard that it is a Class C felony to import or be in possession of a snake on the islands. Fun fact, guys.

As the bus sped along the coast, we gazed out of the window at the lapping waters, the sun dancing on the ripples. Avid surfers were tackling more monstrous waves much further out, catching the drift before flipping and tumbling into the arms of the salty ocean. It was calming to listen to our guide's gripping stories whilst watching these scenes from the cliffs above. It was like sitting around a cosy campfire and roasting marshmallows as folk tales and old legends were shared over the crackles and pops of the gently spitting flames.

I really loved to listen to the stories from the people around us the whole time we were in Hawaii. I loved getting ready for dinner in the evenings back at our hotel and thinking back on all the people we'd met that day, all the things we'd learnt and all the little details about the place and how diverse its culture was. I used to jot down my experiences in my travel journal, to remember them.

White Sands, the aptly named first hotel we stayed in, was beautiful, a great little base in Waikiki, although we were hardly there. It consisted of a group of small apartments with thatched roofs surrounding a swimming pool where you could chill out and just relax. There was a cosy patio corner behind the pool where I used to sit with my book some mornings, comprising a bench and a few tables and chairs, with palm trees that dangled lazily above, their lanky leaves tickling the top of my head. There was a quaint little bridge with a turquoise pond rippling under it, busy with multi-coloured fish zipping in between each other, crossing each other's paths momentarily and then forgetting in a flash; it reminded me of a Japanese garden. It was a tranquil place, a slice of calm away from the Honolulu rush that engulfed you once you stepped outside the front doors.

In Waikiki, I settled into an easy new routine. There was the flamboyant Tiki Grill and Bar around the corner, where we used to go for breakfast most mornings (eggs and bacon or tall stacks of pineapple pancakes) and for neon-coloured cocktails in the evenings. We could reach the bustle of Waikiki Beach in a leisurely ten-minute walk, and the other main sights, like the Ala Moana Centre, Pearl Harbour, Chinatown and Diamond Head Crater were at most an hour's bus ride away, so the hotel was pretty central. I liked the fact that we were in the midst of the action.

Waikiki was a city, but the beach was a stone's throw away. During the day, I would pop out of the hotel's entrance and saunter around the shops nearby. Flip-flops slapping against the burning hot concrete, I'd relish the scent of the salty sea air mixed with the soundtrack of the busy roads. But if I turned right instead of left out of the hotel entrance, my vision needed to adjust to take in the looming, lush green mountain, its top disappearing into the clouds as it watched over the ant-like people busying themselves below, going about their daily lives. Waikiki truly was the best of both worlds.

I felt safe enough strolling the streets during the day. As soon as it started to get dark though? Not so much. Honolulu as a whole was pretty and picturesque, a special place, but it wasn't somewhere I felt safe on my own at night and it definitely had a more sinister side. The quiet bar next door transformed into a noisy frat affair after the sun went down, and customers would stumble out into the street, getting into fist fights and doing drugs, passed out in the road.

There would be revellers as high as a kite queuing to get into the corner shop, counting up enough change for a packet of cigarettes and a bottle of cheap vodka, screaming at the shop assistant when they didn't have enough dollars to pay. It was crazy. Plus, when you just wanted a bottle of water and a packet of make-up wipes and you were waiting to pay, it was super annoying to be held up by a gaggle of abusive drunkards, speaking from first-hand experience.

I tapped my sandal-clad foot impatiently on the tiled floor as I waited and stepped back abruptly as the intoxicated guy in front of me threw his cents at the shop assistant and stumbled backwards, reeking of weed and tequila. He shuffled outside, yelling, and proceeded to throw up outside the doorway. "Every night," the cashier said sighing, rolling his eyes at me as I gave him a sympathetic smile and passed my water and wipes into his outstretched hands. My goods were likely the most ordinary night-time purchase the poor guy had dealt with since working there.

As a result of the noisy-neighbour nightmares who only came out after dark, we always decided to walk on a bit further whenever we went for dinner. But even elsewhere, there did seem to be a lot of fights and a lot of very wasted individuals around. Honestly, it was like heading out into the *Walking Dead* franchise. I guess it's a city, after all, and a rampant nightlife is a must-have for a lot of youngsters on holiday. Plus, hey, I'm not judging. Maybe these people were just enjoying themselves on a weeknight (or indeed every night). But I get cranky when I'm hungry, sort of like a massively overgrown baby who needs regular snacks, so when people are fighting in the street and I have to wait to get past them in order to slip into a restaurant, I get hangry.

The darker elements were also sometimes apparent before sundown. In broad daylight, my dad almost got arrested for taking a photo of the street outside our hotel. Seems innocent enough, right? Well, this simple snap caused a very intoxicated transvestite who was dancing in the middle of the traffic-jammed road to: 1) think my dad was taking a photo of them, and 2) go ballistic, grab a piece of wood from a nearby builder's van and start running around, hitting locals and tourists with it. They swept passers-by up in a frenzy, running at them in their stilettos, brandishing the piece of wood and screaming at them as cars slammed on their brakes and horns sounded everywhere. This went on for a good while, and it was complete mayhem. Tourists were screaming, locals were trying to calm the situation. My dad carried on snapping photos of the buildings, nothing getting in the way of his creative thought process, oblivious to the chaos around him.

The police arrived within a few minutes, six cop cars screeching to a halt outside our hotel. Officers jumped out in riot vests, yelling at the public to stay back. They stopped my dad and asked him what he was doing and if he had anything to do with the furore. He just looked at them blankly, suddenly registering the scene he was literally in the middle of. It was like a real episode from *Hawaii Five-0*. My dad eventually wandered back to the hotel, leaving a trail of destruction and flashing lights behind him, proudly presenting the great photo he'd got of the street as my mum and I watched from the balcony, aghast, while the police tackled the transvestite and attempted to break up the riot.

We witnessed some crazy fights at the beach too. On a visit to Chinatown, we got accosted by a Queen Mother fanatic who was firing questions at us about the royal family. He was eating a banana at the time and was so high that he couldn't stand without swaying. Bits of mushed-up banana kept flying out of his mouth as he was speaking, landing in my strands. I was too polite to say anything, so I just stood there like an idiot with chewed-up banana slime sticking to my hair until he eventually stopped yapping and disappeared. Speaking of hair, my natural curls quadrupled in size and frizz seemingly each day (but this does happen every single holiday, so I can't really attribute it to just Hawaii).

I fought the law myself, defying the bus's strict rules about not eating or drinking on board and smuggling in my Starbucks latte and drinking it inconspicuously from my bag every morning. But even my newfound badass status, swigging coffee illegally, didn't prepare me for the carnage of October 31st.

Halloween night was completely unreal. Ninety per cent of people were walking around dressed in odd costumes, and I don't just mean your usual run-of-the-mill Halloween get-ups. There was a man dressed as a giant baby, a clown with an actual chainsaw, and a guy in a blow-up dinosaur suit, to name but a few.

After much discussion, trying to find somewhere for dinner that Halloween evening that wasn't crammed full of drunk revellers, we decided on this nice-looking Chinese restaurant, which you had to go down some steps and under the street to access. It was lovely: great food, nice place – until I stupidly ordered the kung pao chicken.

Now, back at home, we have a takeaway one night a week and we always go to the same place. We've been going every Saturday since I was about six years old and the staff know us in there. I used to trot in after my dad to 'help' him order our dinner, and there used to be a whole family running the place, with children close to my own age. I remember once, a few years back, I went in with my dad and my auntie to order and the lady behind the counter said, "I remember you! When you were little." Their kids have grown up and now work in the restaurant. But I digress. I rotate the same five or so dishes and kung pao chicken is one of them. I always ask for it without peanuts (I have a moderate peanut allergy), and it's delicious.

So, I chose the same dish in Hawaii and asked for it without peanuts, thinking it would be the same sort of thing. It wasn't. I should have just ordered something I knew wouldn't ever have peanuts in it, like sweet and sour, another of my favourites. But I didn't, and within a few minutes, I was wheezing, gasping for my inhaler, and my throat was painful and incredibly itchy. So, our trip out to dinner got cut short. My bad.

As we were paying and heading out, the restaurant owner was making conversation, asking us how we liked the area. He told us that Halloween was a massive thing in Hawaii and that 'the really weird ones come out after 9 pm'. I glanced down at the time on my phone – 8.50 pm – and we all laughed at his comment but swiftly departed to the safety of our nearby tiki cocktail bar. From there, we watched the madness unfold.

It was like all bets were off. It reminded me of that horror film *The Purge*, where all crime is legal for twelve whole hours. Swarms and swarms of people jostled down the road, screaming and pushing each other, laughing and shouting. It was hard to tell if they were threatening or not. Everywhere was saturated in noise and colour.

Next morning, we woke up to the news that someone had been stabbed on one of the other islands during the Halloween festivities, which brought home to us that, yes, the beach was a stone's throw away, but we were still in a city. There was still danger out there.

Hawaii is great though as long as you're vigilant, and that's like anywhere. Once the sun rose the next morning, it would be completely different. Back to normal. Kind of.

*

We enjoyed our sun-soaked afternoons on the beach and even learnt to surf. Well, I did. My dad almost got swept out to sea multiple times whilst on our first lesson. The waves were carrying him further and further out, to the soundtrack of 'Mr Steve! Mr Steve, come back! You're going the wrong way!' from our two desperate instructors. They had to paddle out hurriedly and grab his board and flip it around for him. He'd been praised for his perfect positioning on the board when it was laid out in front of him on the sand, but when he tried it in the sea, he turned out not to have the knack. Maybe he got a bit too cocky.

Me though? I performed much better than I ever expected. I had an anxiously rocky start though, where my mind went blank and I couldn't work out where to put my feet. I couldn't grasp how to pull myself up that quickly and just balance, focussing on the momentum of the wave beneath me. But after that, I seemed to thrive in the saltwater. I was enjoying the sun beating down on my freckle-splattered face as I stood up on my board, caught my first wave and was propelled at speed back to the beach.

Momentum gathering, arms out straight to balance, I was grinning from ear to ear before I jumped back into the salty current and swam back for another go. And another, and another. Dad gave up after the first hurdle, deciding that surfing just wasn't his forte. He paddled around on his board and just concentrated on not being pulled too far from the shore.

My mum was watching from the beach, eager to snap some photos of us out there. She was squinting into the sun, trying to make out which silhouetted figures were me and my dad. Eventually, she caught sight of someone she thought was me, but when they stood up quickly on the board and got the hang of riding the waves pretty quickly, she decided it couldn't possibly be me. When we emerged later on to greet her on the beach, she was dumbfounded. "I thought that was you," she exclaimed, "but when you stood up, you looked like you'd done it before, I thought it couldn't be." So there are no action shots of us as savvy surfers. But I found a hobby that I'd happily have another go at, again and again.

However, I may have got a little over-confident, for when I rented my own board the next day, I discovered that it was hard work without the guidance of an instructor. I almost got knocked out by my own surfboard, twice, whilst trying to haul it out of the water – those things are really heavy! I was at the water's edge, trying to grip the board and pull it onto the sand, finished for the day. My dad was a few feet away, taking pictures of a faraway boat sailing into shore, and I yelled at him for help as a wave suddenly engulfed me, dragging my board under and back into the deep water, with me still attached to it by my ankle.

"Dad, help!" I spluttered, grabbing fistfuls of sand and coughing up saltwater. But he was oblivious, studying the frames he'd just captured on his camera. My voice was drowned out by another wave enveloping me. I managed to crawl up and stand, scooping up my board, but yet another wave crashed over my head and I lost control and the board spun around, almost knocking out two kids playing in the shallows. Luckily, my dad then noticed and sprang into action to help.

"Sorry!" I apologised to the kids I'd almost knocked out, then traipsed across the sand, my dad helping me drag the board.

"Nice surf?" my mum asked as I un-velcroed myself from the ankle tag, sand sticking to my wet feet.

"I almost bloody drowned and knocked out two kids." I huffed, sitting down to wring out my hair, giving her an exasperated look.

We got to watch the locals surfing up on the North Shore as well, during our island tour. It was inspiring. They were incredibly talented and were practising for an upcoming contest. The waves were something else, nothing like the ones

I'd learnt on at Waikiki Beach. No, these waves were reserved for the best of the best surfers, reaching heights of fifty feet. They were not for the faint-hearted.

Our guide told us the true tale of 31-year-old Eddie Aikau, a well-known Hawaiian lifeguard and surfer who braved these waves on a daily basis. He went out to ride the waves one evening, was swamped and caught off guard by a sudden surge of water, and was never seen again. This story alone was enough to have me put my short-lived pipedream of finding overnight success as a famous Hawaii-based surfer to bed. Also, it was only towards the end of the trip that I learnt there'd been multiple shark attacks recently, all relatively close to Waikiki's shore. So, the fact that I'd got into the water at all astounded me.

"Actual shark attacks? Like actual sharks?" I whispered to my mum, who was seated next to me on the bus. Our tour guide had already moved on to telling us about the celebrated shrimps and how they were cooked, kind of glossing over the shark thing.

"Yeah, haven't you seen *50 First Dates*?" She laughed, referring to the Drew Barrymore and Adam Sandler flick where one of the supporting characters gets attacked by a shark.

Funnily enough, I had seen *50 First Dates*, many times. We'd all re-watched it on the flight from London to LA, in preparation for Hawaii, and we'd already visited some of the places where it was filmed, including the beach scene, as well as the café Drew Barrymore's character goes to every morning for waffles.

"Yeah, I think I'm done with the surfing," I muttered, sipping my water and gazing out at the choppy waters as we speeded around a mountain bend.

Those waves suddenly looked threatening, like you didn't know what the hell was under there. To think I'd been swimming out (pretty far out, actually) with my board, catching the waves and jumping back into the water with ease, not even thinking about the damn sharks. That wasn't like my anxious little brain at all. Usually, I'd have point-blank refused to go into the water, my mind flitting to and fro, trying to recall the exact figures on how many shark deaths there were per year all over the world. Maybe it was best I didn't know, after all.

There was a reason our tour guide was now telling us about the shrimps. We'd just pulled up at a shrimp shack, which proved to be an absolutely excellent experience. I'd never tried shrimps before; I'd only ever had the smaller prawns, so I opted to share some hot and spicy shrimp with my dad.

Fumi's Shrimp is essentially a pitstop along the Kamehameha Highway and somewhere you could easily miss. It's the equivalent of those burger vans you get in B&Q car parks in the UK, but the food was so much better, as was the location and the decor. Imagine trading grey and dreary English weather for glistening sunshine and 31-degree heat. Then swap burgers for delicious, freshly caught and freshly cooked shrimps, drizzled with every possible sauce topping you can think of – coconut, garlic, spicy, lemon pepper, the works. Finally, transport yourself from a B&Q car park to a little hut at the side of a Hawaiian highway. You get the contrast. It was like getting back to nature, enjoying the sun on our faces as we devoured our lunch. Perfect.

Another place you should definitely visit if you want to glimpse the real Hawaii, grab some great food and snap some cool photos is the Dole Pineapple Plantation in Oahu, which was our last stop on the island tour. The plantation is spectacular and deemed to be one of Oahu's best attractions for good reason.

Admission is free and there are lots of things to do if you have children or like family-friendly activities. It's home to the world's largest maze (which turns into a spooky-sounding live horror maze at Halloween, though my dad and I were too chicken to try it out), the pineapple express train, and an extremely extensive giftshop which sells pineapple…well, everything: keychains, T-shirts, pancake mix, tote bags, body lotion, cuddly toys, the lot. Seriously, who on earth wants a cuddly pineapple toy? But do make sure you try the Dole pineapple whip, which was, in all honesty, the nicest ice cream I had ever tasted.

It was compelling to learn about Hawaii's pineapple industry, but even that wasn't the most impressive part. I was even more taken by the Eucalyptus deglupta trees on the Dole plantation. Originally found in the rainforests of the Philippines, these trees grow in a few places around Hawaii and are simply magical to behold. Their eye-catching bark comes in shades of bright blue, green, orange, and purple as it sheds throughout the seasons, so it looks like someone has taken a paintbrush to the trees and used the bark as their easel. My dad and I marvelled at this bark, and he got some truly inspiring photos of the trees proudly showing off their splashes of colour. It was like looking into a pastel firework, a cornucopia of colour engaging our eyes, pulling us into its mysterious nature.

Simple things like that may not impress everyone, but it's amazing to witness something totally nature-made, not meddled with, completely organic and arguably more beautiful than anything manmade. The reminder of the extraordinary things nature can produce just made me appreciate Hawaii and its beauty even more.

*

Speaking of extraordinary things, we accidentally got checked in to someone else's rooms at our second hotel in Waikiki. The lovely White Sands apartments we'd been staying in for the first half of our trip had to close due to planned refurbishments, so we had to find somewhere else, which we did, right around the corner. It happened to be right next door to the tiki bar we frequented most days, so win-win – or so we thought.

The second hotel was still nice, but it was a high-rise building, so instead of carefree, calm beach vibes it felt more city-orientated. Or much more like LA's infamous Cecil Hotel, as we came to discover.

As soon as we arrived to check in to our rooms, heaving our suitcases down the street in the blistering heat, it was evident the lady behind the reception desk was stressed. And not just a little. Massively. She barked at guests, motioning to them aggressively, and when my dad stepped forward, she snapped some more. She snatched our passports out of our hands and busied herself tapping away for what felt like hours. Eventually, she practically threw our keys at us.

"Sixteenth floor. Elevator is over there." She waved absently towards a cubbyhole, the lift being hidden behind a massive crowd of people waiting to get in it. Her snootiness was palpable, and she came across as quite an unpleasant character. "The elevator is having issues, so you'll have to wait," she snapped, not looking up. "Next!"

"Oh my God," I huffed, dragging my suitcase over and joining the queue.

I glanced back, catching my mum's eye. The receptionist had been right about the lift. Because it was on the blink, it took ages for it to even reach the ground floor. We waited a good ten minutes before it pinged and the doors finally opened to allow the waiting crowd to swarm into the ridiculously tiny space.

After the longest lift ride up, squashed in like sardines with about twenty other guests (it seems odd now to recall a time when you could actually be within two metres of a stranger without being armed with a mask and hand sanitiser), we eventually squeezed out with our luggage on the sixteenth floor to choruses of 'Sorry', 'Excuse me', 'So sorry' as we awkwardly edged past.

We located our rooms, and I heaved a big sigh as I dumped my case at the side of the bed and walked immediately to the balcony to check out the sights. The view was amazing. You could see the maze of sky-scraping high-rise city buildings all around us. They were almost close enough to touch, sunlight bouncing off the glass windows, a contrast with the sparkling sea visible behind. It was truly beautiful and although this hotel was a lot different to our previous one, it was stunning in an alternative way.

I stepped further out of the doors and my feet met the concrete with a soft patter. I was eager for a better look, but that's when I instantly grabbed hold of the door in shock. "Crap," I squealed, my eyes darting around. The balcony sloped downwards at a very sharp angle, and the plastic chair that had been placed there to brighten up the surroundings had slid towards the railings. I pulled it back towards me, let go, and it slipped right back to its original spot.

I gawped down and felt my stomach lurch. The balcony by no means felt sturdy enough to have me even put a foot on it. A gentle gust of wind rippled through my hair and I gripped the door tightly. "Jesus Christ," I muttered, hitching my bag up onto my shoulder and retreating into the safety of the room to unpack. Well, there went any hopes of the balcony being my new reading spot.

So, I thought, the balcony maybe needed some altering, but the room seemed nice enough. I started going about my business, unloading my folded clothes and placing them in a pile on the bed. I took out my washbag and wandered into the bathroom to lay out my stuff, hoping to take a shower.

"Oh, wow." I grinned, noticing that there was some of that luxurious Hawaiian Tropic shampoo, conditioner and sun cream by the sink. That's good of them, I thought to myself. I loved Hawaiian Tropic. I picked up a body lotion, unscrewed the top and sniffed. It smelt like the beach.

As I started lining up my toothbrush and toothpaste next to the other commodities, I noticed there was already a tube of toothpaste there. I frowned when I saw it was rolled up at the bottom.

It hadn't clicked yet, but as I re-entered the bedroom, I caught sight of the snacks piled high on the bedside table – Lay's, Pringles, Taffy, the lot – oh, and the clothes hanging in the open wardrobe. Clothes that definitely weren't complimentary.

There was a dog-eared novel on the bedside table with a pair of glasses perched on top. And as I stepped forwards, I tripped over a pair of slippers and clocked the folded pyjamas poking out from behind each pillow.

"Oh crap, oh crap, oh crap," I muttered, gathering up my stuff, eager to get the hell out of there. I felt like Goldilocks, snooping in the three bears' house, tasting their porridge (or their Hawaiian Tropic body lotion). This was very clearly someone else's hotel room, and I didn't think they'd take too kindly to me rummaging around in their stuff. Obviously.

I threw my clothes and washbag back into my case, grabbed my bags and exited pretty swiftly.

We all ended up back downstairs, patiently queuing up yet again to talk to the Miss Trunchbull character who'd thrown our keys at us earlier. She'd obviously got the floor wrong or the digits incorrect by a hundred or something. What worried me was how on earth she had given us someone else's keys without checking thoroughly first.

My dad explained the situation, but she was shaking her head before he'd finished speaking. "No, we don't make mistakes here, sir," she said sarcastically. "You obviously used the key in the wrong door," she added, eyeing me with a raised eyebrow like I'd made the whole thing up.

"How would I have done that? Or, more to the point, if that's even possible, why do your keys work in multiple doors? Bit weird," I wanted to retort. But I didn't. I just shrugged, my anxiety flaring at this awkward social situation.

This conversation went on and on, around in circles, until she eventually harrumphed angrily, shuffled through some papers, abruptly rose from her seat and stormed upstairs to check. Well, she returned bashfully, mumbling to herself. With no apology whatsoever, she pushed us some new keys and started tapping away at her computer again, dismissing us with her silence.

We dragged ourselves back up to find our new rooms. Thankfully, this time they seemed to be empty, which is just how I like my hotel suites.

Over the next few days, my dad and I got stuck in that bloody lift for half an hour on two separate occasions when it just ground to a shuddering halt between floors.

Guessing we needed some comic relief, my dad thought it was hilarious to go into Starbucks every morning and tell the barista 'Danno' when they asked what name to put on the cup. You know Daniel 'Danno' Williams, aka Steve McGarrett's trusty partner in *Hawaii-Five-0*? Dad would grin and laugh at his own joke as it flew over their heads. Or maybe it didn't, and they were just sick of tourists making that same quip. Who knows?

*

I had several creepy encounters with unwanted new 'friends' on our Hawaii trip, beginning with an old man who started asking me in-depth questions about someone else's dog while we were in the bank.

My dad had been queuing at the bank to change some money and my mum and I had gone in too, eager to enjoy the air con rather than swelter outside. I'd slumped down on one of the empty chairs and glanced up when the doors opened and this older gentleman came in. He was wearing a massive hat and sunglasses and sporting a very jazzy Hawaiian shirt.

He queued behind my dad for a bit, wandered away, returned and re-joined the line for a while, then shuffled over to sit down next to me. I smiled briefly and went back to swiping through the photos I'd just taken outside, pulling my feet back under my chair to let a woman and her little French bulldog past.

"What kind of dog is that?" I suddenly heard.

"Oh…Sorry?" I looked up apologetically, not having heard exactly what he'd said.

The man was now looking at me expectantly.

"What kind of dog is that?" He pointed at the dog, which had sat down heavily and was gazing up at its owner, little ears twitching.

"Uh…" I glanced over. "A French bulldog, I think."

"A what?"

"A French bulldog."

"Oh. Where do you get those from then?"

"I'm…not too sure actually," I answered as we both watched the dog.

My dad walked over and my mum and I shifted, ready to leave. I smiled a goodbye at the man, surprised that he was now standing too.

"What's its name, do you think?"

"Oh, I…don't know." I smiled again, slipping my bag onto my shoulder and nodding before I edged out the door.

Outside, the sunlight and stifling heat hit me square in the face, and I jammed on my sunglasses. My mum and dad were already ahead, walking to the bus stop for the centre.

"Do you want this Filipino change?" the man asked, catching up with me.

I spun around, startled. "Oh, uh, no, I'm okay, but thanks." I looked down, smiling awkwardly as he happily brandished a fistful of coins, holding them out to me.

"Why?"

"Because…I don't think I'll be going to the Philippines anytime soon, but thank you." I started to scuttle away, alarmed that he was keeping up with me.

"Why?"

He was starting to sound like a child playing the 'why' game – you know, the incredibly annoying skit where they just answer 'why' to every single thing you say to them.

"Take it anyway," he insisted. "Are you getting the bus?"

"Uh, no, I don't think so," I mumbled as I picked up my pace.

My mum and dad had turned around to wait for me and were shooting me quizzical looks as I approached them, my new friend trailing behind me.

We saw him every single day after that, skulking outside McDonald's or the same bank, waiting at the bus stop or just loitering. My mum and I took to referring to him as Jeremy Corbyn because he sure looked a lot like the then leader of the Labour Party.

There was another local (and very intoxicated) man who liked to hang around the place where you could get free leaflets about the area. He was extremely protective of the leaflet rack. When we tried to pick up a leaflet one morning, he lost it and chased us down the road, yelling gibberish and trying to grab hold of my arm aggressively but in extreme slow motion. I don't know what he was on, but whenever someone passed the rack, he popped up like a troll under a bridge and tried to snatch at them, shouting about his stack of cents on the sidewalk.

I also had a weird encounter with two Japanese tourists at the top of Diamond Hill Crater. We set off on the hike early one afternoon, keen to see the views from the summit. At the first viewpoint, my mum was admiring the scenery, pointing out different sights, and I was snapping a few photos. Suddenly, I noticed that this Japanese guy, probably about my age, was standing abnormally close to me, his backpack nudging my arm. His friend had been taking his photo, so I moved away to avoid photobombing them. But this guy inched closer still, until he was practically standing on my foot. I sidestepped again, getting annoyed now. Every time I moved away, he'd be back in my space again, his friend grinning irritatingly and motioning for him to get closer as he held up his iPhone. Was he trying to take a picture with me?

I eventually just exited the viewpoint and went to find my mum and dad. But then, I got a tap on my shoulder. The Japanese guy was standing there, grinning, pointing at my leg.

"Sorry?" I said as he began to speak in Japanese. "Oh, sorry, I don't understand." I turned to leave. He was being super creepy, waving his hands in my face. But he tapped my arm again, shoving his phone under my nose; I glanced down and Google Translate was up on the screen.

"Your leg is injured," it read.

"What?" I replied bluntly. This guy was starting to seriously annoy me. I didn't take too kindly to being photographed and followed around at the top of a bloody volcanic crater. He motioned to my leg again and pointed to his phone screen. I looked down at my shin to see a miniscule red dot on it. An old mosquito bite from days and days ago, now healed and all but disappeared. It was so damn tiny, I had no clue how he had even spotted it.

"Oh. Thanks," I muttered, turning to leave again, a bit weirded-out, to be honest.

I ducked through the growing crowd, but when I glanced back, they were still following me, so I stopped near the railings and gazed across the heads of the milling masses, trying to locate my mum. She was waving from a few metres away. Spinning around to get back to her, I tut-tutted. There this bloody guy was again, right next to me, as if he were my shadow. He drew a pair of binoculars from his anorak pocket and began to stare into the distance with them. Every few seconds, though, he'd look over to see if I was watching him. He would then grin and pretend to peer through the lenses again.

Managing to get away from Creepy-Mc-Creeperson and his super cool binoculars, I found my way back to my mum and complained to her. "These weird people keep stalking me." I sighed dramatically.

She glanced over at where the two weirdos were giggling like school kids, still trying to follow me, and she gave them the glare. Her glare is not just any glare, though; it's a special kind of expression. We can both do it. It's a look that tells people we're ten-out-of-ten mad and not to mess with us. My mum uses it sparingly, but over the last few years, I've deployed it quite frequently.

We eventually lost the Japanese guys, but we also lost my dad a few times up there too. We kept wandering around, looking for him in the sea of tourists, then spying him happily snapping away while leaning over the edge or something.

Later that night, my mum checked items off her Hawaii bucket list as we sat on the hotel balcony and watched the lights of the traffic down below. I checked off mine too: surfing, drinking out of a pineapple, trying an acai bowl (I've tried so many times since to re-create an acai bowl and failed; I just can't muster up the same flavour as the ones back in Hawaii, but my mum does a pretty good imitation), and going to Hot Topic (we don't have one at home) to get a Waterparks T-shirt.

The Hot Topic saga was something else. Because I'm a rocker at heart, I was always envious of American teens being able to head to Hot Topic and complete their emo wardrobe with band tees galore. I've always felt it's an alternative kid's rite of passage, and I missed out on that. The equivalent in the UK is Camden Market, which, to be fair, did provide me with a pretty sweet jacket inspired by My Chemical Romance and endless band badges during my grunge years.

For my fifteenth birthday, I'd asked for an Escape the Fate T-shirt and my mum had found the one I wanted online at Hot Topic. Ordered and paid for, it was delivered after two weeks, which was fine, but the import tax made the £12 T-shirt cost £55, so, after that, it was no more Hot Topic for me. I mean, it was a nice T-shirt, but it wasn't worth £55. Being in Hawaii meant that I could finally hunt down this Waterparks T-shirt I'd been eyeing online. I was going to see them live in a few months with Brandon and I really wanted some merch to wear.

So, I dragged my dad around all the Hot Topics on the island, but we still came up short. The last resort was the store at the Ala Moana Centre, a beautifully designed semi-outdoor shopping centre which basically housed every shop you could think of. Feeling defeated as I scoured the stacks of folded merch, I plucked up enough courage to approach the guy at the counter. He looked up, sufficiently goth, with his cool dark eye make-up and ear stretchers.

I stood there, pale English girl with curls for days, swinging my All Time Low tote bag over my shoulder and suddenly felt like I didn't even belong in there. Hot Topic, my dream home. Without my normal winged eyeliner (the muggy heat made it way too hot for that; I'd ditched my make-up on day one, back in LA), I felt like I'd lost my 'rock' edge.

"Do you have any Waterparks T-shirts?" I asked, but my question was met with a quizzical stare.

He looked for one anyway, sifting through all the displays before returning to the computer behind the desk and tapping away to check the stock. All around, individuals looking way cooler than me were browsing band tees. I wished I could swipe some eyeliner on asap or scream, 'Hey, I'm one of you guys, I promise.'

"Waterparks, right?" the guy asked, frowning. "I've never heard of them, but it looks like we have one out back."

"What? Never heard of Waterparks?" I wanted to exclaim "But...they're amazing. They're like All Time Low, Fall Out Boy and Green Day combined. What?"

He returned within moments, clutching my prized T-shirt. I thanked him and grinned as he scanned it, elated that I had now accomplished my bucket-list bullet points in Hawaii. Purchase Waterparks tee. Check. Go to a Hot Topic. Check.

I put it on straightaway and wore it all day over my summery playsuit. There's a photo of me on the beach later on, sitting in the dark as I watch the fireworks exploding overhead, smiling from ear to ear. Hair wild and curly, freckles on full display. That damn T-shirt demanding full attention.

27

Creepy Is My Thing Now

San Francisco

The very first thing I noticed when I stepped out of the sliding doors at San Francisco International Airport was the temperature drop. Oh, and the thick sheet of fog obscuring my view.

I'd heard of Fog City, I knew San Francisco was famous for its mist, but I wasn't expecting to be dropped right into a scene from *Silent Hill*. I thought people were exaggerating about the weather there, but as it turned out, they really weren't. It was eerie, but, despite my anxious nature, I love anything to do ghosts and ghouls. I wasn't always like that though. I used to hate horror flicks; I'd refuse to watch them when I was younger.

When I was fourteen, I hosted a sleepover with my friends and we watched a slew of scary films including the recently released first *Paranormal Activity*. I couldn't sleep properly for two weeks after that – not helped by my (usually quite secure) clock on the wall randomly crashing to the floor at 3 am the following night. The witching hour. Coincidence? I think not. I didn't sleep a wink, convinced it was a sign that demons were setting up residence in my house. I stayed up reading with the lights on and stumbled into school the next morning bleary-eyed, dead on my feet.

But in the years that followed, I developed a passion for suspenseful, scary films, the sheer thrill of them. I binged all the classics – *Scream, Nightmare on Elm Street, Friday the 13th* and *Halloween* – and I'd happily rock up to Tulleys Scream Farm or hit up the most frightening escape rooms with live actors prowling around in them. I loved all of that. Now my favourite films (alongside *Harry Potter*, obviously) are Stephen King's *It, The Conjuring*, and *The Woman in Black*. Creepy is my thing now. So, San Francisco, no matter how outwardly chilly, was warming to me. I found the vibe enchanting.

The people were less friendly than in LA and Hawaii, as if the cooler weather had a direct effect on their personalities. People tended to leave us alone in San Francisco and, to be honest, that was just what we wanted. We didn't want to be constantly told where to go and what to do, sometimes we wanted to just turn up to places on a whim and discover for ourselves. Out of our three US destinations on that trip, San Francisco was the place I felt most at ease in. I think I'd be able to live there, if I had to choose somewhere other than London.

We'd also been to other parts of the US – New York and Florida – when I was quite young. In New York, everything had towered over me, everything had seemed so tall. I remembered the bagels, 'coffee' being pronounced 'cwoffee', and everyone calling my dad 'buddy'. We saw so many sights – Ground Zero, the Empire State Building, the Stature of Liberty from the Staten Island Ferry – but at six years old, I didn't appreciate the culture or the feel of the city properly. I moaned, dragged my feet and wanted to get an ice cream. I was desperate to check out the famous toy shop (you know, the one from that Tom Hanks' film *Big*), but we couldn't for the life of us figure out where it was.

Florida was very Disneyland-orientated, so we didn't see much of the state as a whole. My mum and dad were too busy chasing around after Stitch and a host of other Disney characters for signatures so I could fill up my autograph book. I was too shy to speak to them myself, so my adult parents had to excitedly queue to see each character.

What stuck in my mind about Florida – apart from how unbeatably magic Disneyland was for an eight-year-old – were the thunderstorms. Lightning all the colours of an electric rainbow zigzagged across the inky night sky in flashes of pink, blue, green, and purple. I'd watch from our hotel room, mesmerised; it was truly magnificent to behold. That was another example of nature really showcasing its beauty and it was the kind of beauty that you appreciated all the more because it hadn't been manufactured.

That's what I search for when I'm travelling. I love to see things that amaze me, that will stick with me forever, things that create a memory and make me think, wow, I can't believe I saw something as extraordinary as that. I mean, obviously, meeting a life-sized Stitch falls into that category too.

But San Francisco delivered indeed. Also situated in California, San Francisco – nicknamed Fog City, San Fran, Frisco…the list goes on – at first appears to be Los Angeles' darker and moodier twin. Things are less extravagant in San Fran. There's less glitz, less glamour, fewer people demanding money for dressing up as Spider-Man and launching themselves into your personal photographs.

We were staying in a hotel near to the airport so we could explore the city the next day and then return to pick up our stuff ready for our flight home. We arrived at 10 pm local time, and the next major difference to LA or even Hawaii was that pretty much everything was closed. The hotel we were staying at had a bar and a restaurant, but these had shut at 8 pm. So, my dad and I had to hunt around for somewhere, anywhere, to get dinner. Meanwhile, my mum retired to bed. In Hawaii, she'd developed several painful, angry red rashes on the backs of her legs and she could still barely walk, despite having used up the two tubes of cream we'd got from a pharmacist. She was just looking forward to getting home and being able to book an appointment with our GP.

Dad and I planned to get pizza or something and bring it back to the room, but things weren't as simple as that. Not by a long shot. It was like someone had closed San Francisco. Yeah, it was 10 pm, but we were near a major airport, and I assumed it would be like London and everything would be open. But there wasn't a McDonald's in sight, no restaurants, the petrol stations were in darkness and there were zero taxis.

In LA, we'd had no problem finding multiple places to eat and grab a cocktail near our LAX hotel. Plus, the Starbucks and the giftshop in our hotel had been open until midnight, in case someone was really craving a latte in the middle of the night or had the urge to do a bout of compulsive shopping. (Yes, the latter was me, I admit it.) San Francisco Airport was smaller, admittedly, but when we ventured out into the chilly air, it was a ghost town, a scene from a zombie movie. Someone had switched all the lights out and told us to go to sleep already.

We walked around for twenty minutes, bearing in mind it was now around 11 pm and getting quite chilly. I shivered, still wearing my bright yellow playsuit I'd left Hawaii in, and my sandals, with a thick hoodie draped around my shoulders. I'd grown accustomed to 32-degree heat in the two weeks we'd been in Waikiki, so the 16-degree Frisco weather, although not particularly cold compared to the UK, was giving me chills.

"What about here, Dad?" I stopped, pointing at some lights, glaringly bright in the darkness.

It looked to be an odd sort of diner, in a hotel across the road from ours, and everything about it screamed *Bates Motel*. But we could smell food (well, I sure as hell hoped it was food), so my dad nodded and we went over to check it out.

It was pretty much deserted inside, and the barmaid abruptly stated that she was clocking off soon. "You can still order food if you're quick about it, and we'll lock you in." She shoved two menus at us as she ran a damp cloth over the bar and checked her watch.

I snuck a sideways glance at my dad, who looked alarmed. Lock us in?

There were two other groups of people in the room, just to note, in case you're thinking this sounds like a set-up for a murder/hostage situation or the start of a horror movie. But we still felt uneasy. The walls were painted black, and the air was freezing. Icy cold by now, we sat at the bar and flicked through the very limited menu, both deciding on paninis. I texted Mum to ask if she fancied anything and snapped a photo of the creepy surroundings, but she said she was fine, she'd found some Reese's Peanut Butter Cups and was happy enough.

We hurriedly ordered and spent dinner dodging the guy cleaning the surfaces and floor around our tables and feeling uncomfortable as the two other groups grew louder and louder the more alcohol they consumed. Needless to say, we ate and got the hell out of there. Major creepy vibes are what I think of when I recall our night in San Francisco. It was very reminiscent of those eighties' American movies when the characters go to a diner in the middle of nowhere to find some clue or meet someone who has some information. I felt like an undercover police officer (or cop, I should say).

The next day was less mismatched. We got to see the city and eat something more substantial. We were up early, dressed and packed. I shrugged on my denim jacket and wrapped the winter scarf I'd left London in around my neck, determined not to fall into the same trap as the night before, where I'd been shivering, unprepared for the drop in temperature. Leaving our suitcases at the hotel reception, we jumped in a taxi for the 40-minute journey to the Golden Gate Bridge, where we stopped off to refuel with a coffee in the café overlooking it.

It was immensely foggy at the bridge, which gave the whole place a sinister feel, cementing my first impressions. Alcatraz Prison was looming ominously, just about in sight, like a ghost, watching. It appeared bit by bit as the fog gradually lifted. It didn't surprise me that people assume it's haunted.

Everything looked like a set for a spine-tingling thriller. *Silent Hill* sprang to mind again, and I began to wonder if I was in an alternative universe, but then, I took a sip of my coffee and my rambling thoughts melted away. (The café was making speciality hot chocolates with whipped cream, waffle pieces and marshmallows; I wished I'd tried one, but I was craving the caffeine hit of my usual latte.) In actual fact, the horror film-esque atmosphere made me more intrigued to learn more about a place I knew little as yet.

It was around 10 am, so it was still on the cooler side, but already the viewing platforms were flooded with tourists. Everyone was jostling to get the perfect picture of the enormous bridge, the now visible Alcatraz and the ultimate selfie with the best background. I dodged past a couple taking part in a full-on photoshoot and ducked down to read the boards which gave you the lowdown on the history of the Golden Gate Bridge.

The bridge was built in 1933, the longest and largest suspension bridge in the world at that time. Declared a modern marvel and voted the most photographed bridge ever, it really was magnificent to look at. It's a staggering 4,200 feet long (to put this in perspective, Tower Bridge in London only spans 800 feet) and is painted orange, not because construction workers forgot to order enough gold paint but to fit with its coastal setting, allow it to stand out, and so that it can be easily seen by incoming boats. The bridge gets its name from the Golden Gate Strait, which is the narrow entrance between the Pacific Ocean and San Francisco Bay.

I turned from my reading to focus on it fully and take it all in: the fog curling around it, contrasting with the bright orange of the metal; the sheer height of it. It was awesome. My mum was less enthusiastic, however. She'd been envisioning a different bridge (the Brooklyn Bridge in New York) and had got them mixed up, so this was not the 'wonder' she was expecting to see. She and my dad joined me and we clutched our coffees in awed silence until my mum said loudly, "Is that it?"

Yeah. So that was probably the worst reaction to the Golden Gate Bridge ever. To be fair to my mum, she was still in pain from the rash and wasn't feeling like wandering around that much. So, I suppose staring at a bridge wasn't her idea of fun.

"Mum!" I exclaimed. "Don't you think it's cool? Did you read all the stuff about how they built it?" I asked incredulously, ready to reel off how it got its name and how long it took to walk over it and back (seventy minutes, if anyone's interested, because my mum sure wasn't). I got a look shot at me that said, 'Yes, I read it. And no, I'm not impressed.'

But my dad and I really enjoyed snapping photos of it. I forced them both to be in a selfie with me (my mum giving my phone camera a death stare), then my dad went on the hunt for a 'better angle'. He has the eye, and he's always looking for alternative viewpoints, always aiming to get a photo from somewhere other than where everyone else is taking theirs. He ended up getting some really impressive shots of Alcatraz through the fog, once it had lifted enough for us to see it more clearly, some fantastic ones of the bridge, and a few hilarious ones of me halfway across the 227-metre-high span, gripping the central post for dear life. See, I stupidly thought it would be a piece of cake walking across the bridge itself. My mum, being scared of heights, settled down on a bench and refused to even step foot on it. But me? I'm not scared of heights at all.

One Father's Day, my dad and I climbed over the O2 Arena in London and I didn't feel scared once. (Just to confirm, this is a genuine booked excursion you can do; it wasn't just me and my dad deciding to hike up there one day – we're not that badass.) The scariest part of that experience was watching Dad learn to take his first ever selfie up there whilst attached to the side by a flimsy-looking harness.

I can walk over London's Tower Bridge with no issues, and even the Millennium Bridge, which I swear moves in the wind and is anything but secure. But the Golden Gate Bridge? As soon as the ground disappeared from under us and all I could see was water when I glanced over the sides, my legs turned to jelly. I had to link arms with my dad and inch forwards. When he wanted to take some photos off the edge, he had to escort me to the handrail, where I stayed, eyes rooted to the floor, wincing every time a lorry sped past and shook the whole suspension, which, by the way, was way too often.

We only made it halfway across, but hey, at least my dad got some classically funny photos of me clinging onto the rails. It really didn't help that there were nets up or that I'd just read how many suicides had occurred on the bridge since it was built. Feeling uneasy, I waited patiently, and then, we shuffled all the way back, reuniting with my mum, who was now waiting back near the coffee shop on safe, solid ground.

Union Square was up next, so, after taking a detour via the giftshop – I know, very authentic – we jumped onto one of the local buses speeding to the city and made our way into the heart of San Francisco. The pace in San Francisco seemed faster than in LA or Honolulu; it was similar to New York in that way. The buses were crowded, and the people were pretty abrupt. Everything was hurried.

"Are you getting on or are you not getting on?" the driver yelled at the group in front of us. His San Francisco drawl was evident, his tone sharp. We were all herded on, and before the doors even closed behind us, he'd stamped on the accelerator and the bus was careering around the roundabout and roaring up the hill.

We all grabbed for a railing as we fell against the other passengers, apologising in our typically irritating English manner. My dad always has a massive backpack of camera equipment with him, filled with spare batteries and chargers and usually a bigger camera looped around his neck as well, so he does take up quite a lot of space on public transport. We joke that if he was to fall over backwards, he'd be like a tortoise, unable to get up again due to the sheer weight of his bag. Luckily, though, he caught himself and we all clung on for dear life for the entirety of the journey.

The bus eventually came to an abrupt halt at the terminus, sending bags scattering. It was like that scene in *Harry Potter and the Prisoner of Azkaban* where the Knight Bus suddenly slams on its brakes and Harry goes flying into the window, his face smushed up against the glass.

We stepped out of the doors and as our eyes adjusted to the streaks of sunlight, it seemed like we'd been dropped at the wrong place. It was basically an alleyway. Bodies lay sleeping on the pavement, others were huddled together sniffing substances or lighting roll-up cigarettes, there was sick on the floor and one shoe had been tossed aside.

Everyone else on the bus hurried off, dodging left and right, heading across the road to their various destinations. I gazed around, wondering if this was Union Square, whilst my mum spiralled into proper tourist mode, whipping out the massive map we'd picked up from the giftshop. "Up here." She pointed up the hill, and we made our way to (the actual) Union Square.

As we rounded the corner, I caught sight of a tram speeding up the hill and guessed this was the main hub of the city. And yes, it was stunning, nothing like the alleyway we'd just come through. The trees had twinkling fairy lights wrapped around their trunks, the trams loaded up with people and shot off, and busy workers in suits hurried this way and that. As we reached Union Square itself, we gazed up at the massive Christmas tree standing proud in the middle, as high as the buildings that surrounded it. It was expertly decorated with baubles and tinsel.

We climbed further up the hill in search of somewhere to eat and eventually came across an old-school American eatery called Mason's Diner. We were intrigued. As soon as you entered, you were transported back to the 1950s. There were red booths galore, jukeboxes belted out music, and masses of Elvis memorabilia adorned the walls and corners. There were even black and white checked floors like in the movies. The staff wore the kinds of uniforms you see in old American TV shows, all pink shirts and pinnies.

The menu offered so many delights too. I was originally leaning towards 'the Golden Gate Bridge', which consisted of waffles arranged in the shape of the bridge and whipped cream to serve as the fog, but I was hankering for something savoury so opted for the tuna panini, which did not disappoint. The cheese melted perfectly into the tuna and I felt sufficiently full up afterwards, ready for some more exploring before our flight.

We jumped on another bus, which at first seemed to be less manic than the last one. But as we passed through a particularly busy intersection, a very intoxicated woman ran headfirst into the closed doors at the red light, banging loudly on the glass. Unfazed, the bus driver swung open the front doors for her and she stumbled in, shouting, made her way through the throng of standing passengers and plonked herself down in front of me and my dad. She then proceeded to yell into the ear of the woman sitting next to her, who literally didn't even bat an eyelid.

It was truly bizarre to watch, but it made me smile (internally, because I didn't want the drunk woman to turn on me) because that's exactly what it's like back home on the tube. A zombie with two heads, oozing green slime from its mouth, could crash onto a District Line carriage in rush hour and no one would even look up. Not one single person. We're a nation of awkward individuals who want nothing more than to be left to our own devices on our commute. I thought that was just our polite British behaviour, but it seems this is a universal thing. People hate awkwardness.

I remember travelling into work one morning a few years prior. I'd caught the earlier commuter train, so it was packed, full to the brim with business people tapping away on iPhones, sipping coffee, ignoring everyone around them. It was uncomfortably stuffy in the carriage because it was the middle of November and everyone was bundled up, clad in their winter wear. I'd secured myself a spot by the door and was chugging my latte when the train suddenly jolted sideways. My coffee slipped down my throat the wrong way and I started choking, and every single person ignored me.

Someone turned the other way, another actually tut-tutted, like I had any control over my choking habits. The only person who asked me if I was all right after two straight minutes spluttering into my gloved hands was a young French woman. "Are you okay?" she whispered over the sound of Twitter notifications and phones ringing.

I nodded, tears streaming down my face as my eyes watered and my make-up ran. "Yep, all good," I croaked. I hurriedly got off at the next stop, way before my destination of London Victoria, and waited for the next train, completely embarrassed, face like a beetroot (if a beetroot can sport raccoon eyes where its eyeliner has run).

But clearly this prim, 'oh I'll just ignore any awkward confrontations in public' attitude exists overseas too. On the San Francisco bus, the drunk woman's eyes had now swivelled towards my dad and me and she started shouting at us too. I stared out the window and tried not to notice and my dad busied himself with his camera. Getting no attention from us, the woman then proceeded to rummage through the bag of the lady next to her – until the lady noticed, whipped her belongings away and moved down the bus, without saying a word.

So, all in all, San Francisco buses were basically like London buses. You took your chances on them. In London, you don't tend to go upstairs or to the back of the bus if you can help it, that's guaranteed weirdo territory. On San Francisco buses, everywhere was weirdo territory, it seemed.

The three of us slipped off the bus at the next stop, but unfortunately so did the drunk woman. She jumped out of the front doors and began smacking the side of the bus with her hands, running alongside it as it drove off. Traffic swerved and cars blared their horns around her, but she appeared oblivious. Shaking her fist in the air, she stumbled up onto the pavement and began to rant at the innocent people waiting at the bus stop.

Eyebrows raised but feeling like we'd dealt with enough oddities that trip, we set off to cram in some last sights before it was time to leave. I located a Westfield – believe me, I'm like a homing pigeon when it comes to Westfield; the centre at Shepherd's Bush is like my staycation home, so I have a sixth sense for whenever there's one nearby. We wandered around it and grabbed yet another coffee. Then my mum and I headed to the toilets before our trip back to the airport.

Because the toilets at Westfield in London are incredibly nice, we possibly set our standards too high. There was a massive queue, wet tissue and rubbish was strewn all over the floor, and a girl who looked around fifteen was being sick into a corner bin whilst her friends took selfies and snapped each other laughing. They were all clutching cans of White Claw. (Apparently that's all the rage now. When I first started going to pubs, it was all about the blindingly neon WKDs or whatever sugary, watered-down cocktail pitcher was new in Wetherspoons.)

To the soundtrack of this girl retching into the bin, I briefly cast my mind back to when I was fifteen. My friends and I used to flick through science textbooks, pick a random unflattering picture and declare 'That's you'. We'd draw in each other's planners and sneak Lucozade and crisps into the library, and the baddest thing we ever did was bunk off double-PE lessons on a Wednesday to go to Costa. We weren't being sick into bins at Westfield though, that's for sure.

Feeling impatient, Mum and I left, not needing to pee so urgently anymore. It had already taken me a good week to get used to American toilets anyway. I found them mind-bending. They were always alarmingly close to the floor, plus what was with the massive gaps either side of the doors, and why didn't the doors reach the ground? Luckily, over the two weeks we were in the US, I managed to get used to these unusual features, but I was glad to spy a proper toilet when we touched down at Heathrow.

The flight back was uneventful, we were knackered, and my mum just wanted to get home so she could go to our GP about her legs. The plane was reasonably empty, and, believe me, if I'd known that was to be the last time I'd set foot on a flight for the foreseeable future while Covid-19 ravaged the planet, I would have made the most of it. I would have revelled in that recycled air, enjoyed the familiar popping in my ears as the plane steadied itself thousands of feet above the earth. I would have gazed down at the glimmering lights of San Francisco in the dark and been all the more amazed by them.

There's something inspiring about being up in the air. It's like you're not anywhere. Not in any specific country. You're unreachable by phone, email or any other notification. You're hovering above any worries or stresses you may have down on the ground. I miss that feeling. But, like I said, I didn't know that would be the last for a while, so I didn't really make the most of it.

Instead, I huddled down in my seat, exhausted, my feet aching, my mind on my life back home, upcoming meetings and articles I needed to finish. I plugged in my earphones and cranked up the volume to drown out the girl behind who was on the phone, very loudly, to someone in the UK right until we were airborne. I knew her life story within ten minutes, and I'd had enough, I was tired. I'd had a fantastic trip and was sad to be going back to normality. But I was ready for our typical chilly English weather, proper toilets and my own bed. Trying to ignore the incessant chatter of the girl, I fell asleep, dreaming of surfing, hiking up craters and attracting mischief everywhere we went.

Hollywood Hills, Los Angeles, California, USA

Oahu, east shore, Hawaii

Golden Gate Bridge, San Francisco, California, USA

28

I'm Not a Terrorist! Gatwick Is My Favourite Airport!

Dublin

I visited a lot of new cities in 2019 – Glasgow, Rome, Los Angeles, Honolulu and San Francisco – and finally came to understand that cities are not all basically the same, regardless of where they are in the world. Until then, I'd always focussed on the similarities between other cities and London rather than the contrasts. I think my preconception that urban life was the same wherever you went clouded my ability to really see a city for its unique nature. Because, of course, they're in no way the same. What surprised me was how different they all are under the surface.

My mum and I decided to plan a special trip for my dad's birthday in the December of 2019, and as he loves Guinness, Mum suggested Dublin. It was somewhere we'd never been, and we thought he'd like an extended weekend break. It was originally meant to be a complete surprise, but we ended up lasting about a month before we told him. I know, no prizes here for secret-keeping, but we were excited.

As the months preceding the Dublin trip had been filled with a lot of travelling, boarding the flight to Ireland and realising it would only take a measly hour and a half was a welcome relief. I'd not been home for more than a week at a time in between all our trips, and although I quite liked this jet-setting lifestyle, I needed a break as I was feeling a little rundown.

I hadn't recovered from the USA-induced jetlag. I was wide awake until 5 am most nights and then would sleep until 10 am, hauling myself up, feeling exhausted, unable to get my body-clock back on London time. This continued for months. Plus, my skin was begging for a breather as it never agrees with the recycled air on planes. I'd been breaking out like no one's business, and I'd only just got over that awful skin infection.

We arrived, bright-eyed and bushy-tailed at Gatwick on the morning we were flying to Dublin, freezing cold, hefting our hand luggage through the checks, no issues. We'd done it a million times before, so I was unfazed. I skipped through the body scanner with confidence and stood waiting for my bag, expecting to pick it straight up as usual, shrug on my jacket, grab my laptop, and slip my boots back on with minimal effort. Ready to go.

Not this time.

My dad is usually the one holding up the line as the security team take apart his bag and look intensely at his cameras. As they're professional ones, they're not your run-of-the-mill handheld devices, so a lot of airport staff seem to get suspicious. They ask him what they are, why he needs them all, and he has to explain his whole job to them. Well, this time, my mum and dad scooped up their bags and glanced around for me, confused.

I was in trouble.

A member of the security team very suddenly slammed my carry-on down in front of me on the counter, making me jump out of my skin.

"Is this your bag, miss?"

My gaze flickered up to meet her narrowed eyes. Oh my God, I thought anxiously, what have I done? Did someone slip something into my bag? Do I have actual drugs in there? Am I going to jail? How did this happen?

Jail? My stream of thought jittered as I zoned out. Not jail, prison – oh my God, I've picked up American slang as well now; people are going to hate me behind bars; I'll be bullied; they'll think I'm trying to look cool.

My worry levels spiked. I'll become one of those snitches like Homer. You know, in that episode of *The Simpsons* when he goes to prison and gets luxury items for telling tales on his fellow inmates. Could that be a plausible way to survive in prison? Would I have to wear one of those little snitch hats?

"Miss?"

Guilt crept over me, and my hands went clammy. You know, that weird sort of guilt you get when you're browsing in a shop and decide not to buy anything. So you leave, but this strange anxiety infects your brain as soon as you reach the threshold. You start to think people are going to assume you've stolen something. It's as though it's suspicious to go into a shop and not buy anything. Does anyone else get this? No? Just me. Okay then.

"Um, yes," I replied, glancing back at my mum and dad, who were looking over quizzically. I shrugged and mouthed 'I don't know' at them.

"It's tested positive for explosives, miss," the woman said abruptly, eyeing me, an eyebrow raised.

If I'd had a mouth full of coffee – I use this as an example, because I have a coffee in my hand 99.9 percent of the time – I would have spat it out in shock. You know, how they do in films. My eyes widened and I stared at my bag in shock, as if it had deliberately betrayed me. What did she just say?

That damn bag. I knew it would cause me nothing but trouble. It was from Jack Wills and I'd been lusting after it for months. It was a good-quality pink and navy striped weekend bag, boasting loads of inside pockets. Each time I ambled past a Jack Wills store, I'd sidle in, trying to justify spending £50 on a bag I'd rarely use.

And then, I went to Bluewater with Brandon and our friend Matt. I'd been hauling them around, eager to pick out some new lipstick for a work do, and they'd been dragging their feet, getting bored. Well, Bluewater's Jack Wills store was having a closing-down sale and was trying to get rid of stock. My beloved bag had been reduced to £35 and there was one left. It was a sign, surely. So, convinced I'd nabbed a bargain, I impulsively bought it and emerged grinning from ear to ear as Brandon and Matt rolled their eyes at me happily spending £35 on a ridiculous-looking bag.

Now this very same bag had forsaken me.

I watched, eyes like saucers, as another member of airport staff was motioned over. The original lady emptied the contents, wiping down the inside with a special cloth. Other passengers were starting to look over, ears pricking up. Hearing the word 'explosives' created a strange atmosphere around me. I felt eyes on the back of my head and heard whispers as they craned their necks to see what was going on. I actually felt like a terrorist.

I'd turned beetroot and was silently willing the rubberneckers to just take a hike already whilst the staff looked at me accusingly. 'I love Gatwick!' I wanted to yell at them indignantly. 'It's my all-time favourite airport! Stop looking at me like that, I'm not a bloody terrorist!' But I didn't. I shuffled my feet and bit the inside of my cheek as I waited for them to finish messing with my bag and tell me what the hell was happening. The two women kept glancing at me every few seconds, as if to make sure I hadn't scarpered. I avoided eye contact.

By this time, I was utterly convinced I was going to prison. For what, you ask? I have no idea. I'd completely accepted my fate and assumed I just looked generally shifty. I mean, I must do. On the way to LA, I'd been pulled out of the queue before boarding and whisked off into a little side room, where the staff had sternly proceeded to scan all my electronics. I later discovered that random passengers get selected for scanning, but they could have explained this instead of just ominously gesturing to me and saying, "Could you come with us this way, miss." Talk about triggering a panic attack for no apparent reason.

As I stood there, tapping my foot, trying not to look shifty, my bag got snatched away again and another member of staff suddenly appeared. He started firing questions at me, demanding to know where I was going and when I'd be back in the country. "You're back on Monday?" he asked, glowering. I nodded, and he scribbled something on a clipboard, looking reluctant. Eventually, my bag was thrown through the scanner twice more and returned to me.

"Sometimes make-up or perfume can test positive for explosives," the original lady explained, her expression softer now.

I sighed with relief, though maybe she could have mentioned that before. I'd assumed some unscrupulous person had slipped an actual bomb into my bag and I had unwittingly become part of some awful terror plot. That's exactly the sort of mad crap I'd accidentally get involved in. My family and friends would catch me on BBC News at Ten, sigh and exclaim, 'Typical Chloë'.

Fast-forward past a mini lecture about the toxic chemicals we put on our faces from the same security lady as she eyed my winged eyeliner and dark lipstick, and we were now rushing to the gate, just making our flight. It was then I remembered that I'd sprayed my bag the day before (quite generously) with my Coconut Body Spritz, to freshen it up after having used the bag for Cornwall, Rome, and Hawaii. Bloody hell, I better not stand near any open flames, I thought to myself.

If I'd concluded that after my immensely stressful saga I'd be rewarded with a relaxing flight complete with mini pretzels and a cheeky binge-watch of *The Vampire Diaries* (why is that always featured on planes?), I was gravely mistaken.

This was a short-haul flight and, although that meant we'd be there in no time, it also meant no need for mini TVs or pretzels. Instead, I settled down to peek out of the window as we got ready to take off. The family behind us chattered loudly and the surly teenager sitting directly behind me kept kicking my seat, chewing his way through a packet of Haribo with (what sounded like) his mouth wide open. I plugged myself into my headphones, but I could still hear every snaffle and feel every thump as he swung his legs. In many ways, this short flight was emotionally longer than London to LA. I tut-tutted and huffed, annoyed as I checked my watch and willed for our landing time to magically shoot forward.

Eventually, we did land, and we exited Dublin airport into the bitingly cold Irish weather, something we'd become accustomed to in the coming days. Our city-centre hotel, Stauntons on the Green, was a welcome sight. From the outside, it looked like a posh townhouse, radiant with its beautiful cream exterior. Christmas wreaths hung on the gates and adorned the front door; it was truly spectacular. As we entered, the warmth enveloped us like an old friend, and it was huge inside.

As I lifted my suitcase over the threshold, I glanced up, catching sight of a massive Christmas tree, beautifully decorated and perfectly placed by the winding stairs up to the rooms. The receptionist checked us in and recommended the best places to see during our stay. She fished out a map, circling points of interest and the best transport links to get there. The rooms were exquisite – like the rest of the hotel – and overlooked the spanning, frost-covered gardens. Although the courtyard was stunning, it was too cold to venture out with our coffees, but it must be absolutely fantastic to lounge out there in the summer.

After I'd got changed and reapplied my eyeliner (priorities; the talk on the importance of natural, skin-friendly products had been truly wasted on me), we were back out, huddled up in our winter warmers, raring to explore. The heart of the city was a brisk ten-minute walk away and the infamous Temple Bar was easily reachable.

Temple Bar, for those who don't know (I was confused at first), is a district in Dublin. It's a collection of restaurants, bars and cafés and is essentially like Leicester Square in London. I was expecting to rock up and for it to be, well, a bar. Although, saying that, there is the iconic drinking spot also named Temple Bar there, just to confuse the hell out of you. A distinctive red building with green plants snaking up the walls, it shares its name with the bustling area. I love looking at the magnet we bought of that very pub; it's stuck to our fridge and brings back some great memories of walking around, having nowhere in particular to be, enjoying being out and about as the chilly winds nipped at our noses.

It was my dad's birthday the next day, so we surprised him with a flurry of cards and presents before whisking him downstairs to enjoy a nice breakfast. I'd spent ages picking out his gift, an anniversary book with vintage clippings from all different newspapers about the Beatles. He likes cool music, so does my mum. I think that's why I've always veered towards the alternative scene, which I'm grateful for. I wouldn't be me without my love of rock, punk, and metal.

My dad loves the Beatles, the Jam, and the Sex Pistols – the original punks; my mum is a fan of the Damned, the Stone Roses and the Ramones. Back in his early photojournalism days, my dad started a music column for the local paper. He'd go and cover gigs and get so many great action shots. At one point, he even managed a band, although they were atrociously flaky and never turned up to the recording studio.

When he first started working for the Daily Express, he rented a London flat in Golden Square, a stone's throw from the infectious atmosphere of Piccadilly Circus, and whenever we're in the area, he always points it out. It's right next to Bauer radio studios, home to Absolute, Heart and Kiss (oh, and Kerrang! I noted instantly, a specialist rock station I used to be obsessed with when I was growing up). So, I get my passion for music from both of them, and since I've started getting into older bands (thanks, Spotify recommended), I've been able to see how the artists I love so much have been influenced musically.

My dad was thrilled with his Beatles book, and after we'd devoured our breakfast, we bundled up and braved the cold wind as we went off in search of the Guinness Factory. I'd never tasted Guinness before and wasn't sure what to expect, but my dad loves the stuff and I thought it would be interesting to learn about how it's made.

Entering the factory was like a big, cosy Guinness hug, a welcome temperature change after the chill outside. There was a deliciously aromatic smell wafting around, which reminded me of *Charlie and the Chocolate Factory* but with alcohol. We learnt that Guinness is the most popular alcoholic beverage in Ireland, where it's brewed, and that it's been around since 1759. We heard about previous Guinness marketing strategies and took photos with the famous characters from the adverts. I felt like a genuine Oompa-Loompa and was half expecting Willy Wonka to sweep in with offerings of sweets and treats. We snapped many a selfie and had a laugh wandering about. But when we reached the highlight – the tasting room – it turned out I didn't like Guinness. At all. Plot twist.

It was way too bitter for my liking. My face scrunched up involuntarily as the liquid hit my tongue. My dad was well in his element and even my mum finished her sample. Me though? I passed my miniature cup to my dad in disgust, scrabbling for my water to whisk the taste away. The Guinness crisps and Guinness caramel chocolate were much more up my street. The flavouring was subtle, more of an aftertaste than an assault on the palate.

We spent some fun time checking out everything Guinness-related in the giftshop before heading up for a drink in the bar. The photos of me tasting Guinness the second time are priceless. I don't know why I decided to have another go – if I hadn't liked my first sip, my tastebuds were hardly going to magically start craving it within the hour. My mum carried on snapping, so you get to witness my expression turn sour very quickly. The pictures go from me grinning, holding up the glass, to me raising it to my mouth, to my lips curling up and my brow furrowing, a faint Guinness moustache evident on my top lip. Then the glass leaves my lips, my tongue shoots out and my eyes are watering. It's safe to say I've not tried another mouthful since. My dad always laughs about that, and every time he pours himself a Guinness back home, he jokingly offers me some, knowing the disgusted expression he'll receive back.

Heading to the Hard Rock Café for dinner, I was reminded of why it's always so devastatingly cool in there. Guitars were strung up on every wall, there was music memorabilia everywhere you peered, and rock tracks blared from the overhead speakers. I always love the vibe in a Hard Rock Café. I can't believe it took me so long to discover them as one of my prime hangouts, though I'm not sure I'd have appreciated them when I was younger.

Having said that, when I was small, I was a Beatles fanatic myself. I had this obsession with watching my dad's *Yellow Submarine* videotape over and over, and I'd randomly shout Beatles lyrics when being pushed in my pram. I'd sing at the top of my little lungs as I was wheeled about in public. So maybe the Hard Rock Café wouldn't have been lost on me after all.

The next morning, my mum and dad went down for breakfast while I busied myself with my make-up. So, I missed out on the commotion.

My mum ordered eggs and my dad opted for a full Irish with side splatter of spinach. He will always pick the oddest thing on the menu, taking it as a challenge. One time in Bali, he ate a few mouthfuls of his breakfast curry and decided he didn't like it. However, he then ordered the exact same dish for the next three mornings, just in case he actually did like it. Spoiler alert, he enjoyed it zero of those times. I'm not sure why on earth he kept choosing it.

This time, they'd been eating, discussing what sights to see, when suddenly my dad started choking and spluttering. My mum thumped him on the back and everyone turned around to stare. In a panic, unable to breathe, he reached into his mouth and pulled out this never-ending string of spinach that had got lodged in his throat. My mum detailed – in between heaving – that it was like the scene in *The Ring* when the girl pulls that long, winding piece of hair from her mouth and it just keeps coming. Calmly, my dad then wrapped the offending spinach in his napkin and continued to eat, as if nothing had happened and no one was looking at him in amazement.

After this eventful breakfast, which I sadly missed (not), we headed to The Vaults, which was pretty much like The Dungeons in London but all about Irish folklore. We all really loved it and learnt a lot about Dublin's grisly history in the process. My mum and I were praying that the actors wouldn't pick on us, but my dad was happy enough to join in – better him than us. He got hauled into the dock and sent to jail for supposedly 'wearing ladies' underwear in public' and, you know what, that just sums him up really. It was a fun afternoon, and we all had a giggle.

The journey home was less eventful although still immensely stressful. We'd arrived at the airport in enough time to grab some dinner and then settled down to wait for our flight to flash up on the departure board. We sat at a high, round table on massive stools, my legs dangling as I finished my burrito. I was tired; it was freezing; the temperature had dropped considerably. We wanted this last, tedious part of our trip to be done and were keen to get home.

"Gate 3," my dad said suddenly, grabbing our bags and shooting off.

My mum and I followed. Walking quickly, we zigzagged through the crowds of passengers. I yawned, knocked off balance briefly by a man barging past me, his laptop bag hitting my shoulder. "Oh crap!" I stopped abruptly. "Mum, I've left my bag at the table – it's got my laptop in it!"

My mum halted, looking exasperated, as I sprinted back to the food court, hoping to God that my bag, phone, MacBook and purse were still exactly where I'd left them. Luckily, by some mad chance, my abandoned bag was still there on the table. I rushed forwards, snatched it up and turned on my heel. No one glanced up. No one had even noticed the unaccompanied bag. Dublin was no Gatwick when it came to security policies, it seemed.

Finally aboard the plane, I collapsed into my seat, feeling a bittersweet wash of emotion engulf me as I stared out of the window at the passing wisps of cotton-candy clouds. I mentally bid farewell to the tiny outline of Dublin as we rose higher in the sky, and I grinned. I'd enjoyed a busy couple of months but hadn't had a chance to catch up with my thoughts. Up in the atmosphere, I realised something had changed again that year.

I'd returned from Nerja, back in 2013, knowing I had an anxiety problem that needed sorting, and I'd flown back from Java the following year with the determination to finally claw my way out of it. I spent the new few years working on myself, working out who I wanted to be, trying out different jobs, securing my own path in life. But even so, I was still unsure of where I was going. I had all these wonderful lessons learnt from exciting experiences in faraway places stored in my mind, but processing them was overwhelming. It was like starting on a huge jigsaw puzzle. I had all the pieces but didn't know how to fit the advice together yet.

Nonetheless, I returned from Dublin feeling that maybe I was doing okay, after all. I was living my life how I wanted. I was writing for a living, had a great family, wonderful friends, and I was happy. I was unequivocally me and proud of that, finally.

I'd achieved a lot over the past few years, conquered a lot of fears, dealt with a lot of anxieties, tackled change and handled it well (for me, anyway). I felt mentally stronger and more aware. I owed that largely to having got out into the big, wide world.

I need to write about this, I thought; my brain's cogs turning as I began to see much more clearly the connections between the active pushing of boundaries necessitated by my travels and the reduction in my anxiety levels. My hands fidgeted eagerly in my lap. I couldn't wait to get home and start tapping away on my laptop, recording my memories, curating this book, finally slotting the pieces of the jigsaw together.

But as I sat there, recalling my travels and the extreme jet-setting lifestyle I'd adopted over the last month, living out of my suitcase, always off to the next place, I had a single thought: I could never be a rockstar on a world tour. I'd need a few months to recuperate after every bloody show. It seemed that pipedream was out the window, along with becoming a world-class surfer.

29

I Get This

So that, ladies and gentlemen, is when I experienced that magical movie turning point where the protagonist gasps in awe and is all, like, 'I get this!' That was the moment my travels had been leading to. My epiphany.

In the movies, the protagonist will be staring out at a glorious sunrise at 5 am, writing in their battered journal (seriously, why doesn't anyone in these films look after their books?); they're on a deserted beach, watching clouds materialise out of the darkness like ink blots, as the rising sun grows ever brighter and more beautiful. The perfectly timed metaphor for their big realisation.

They make a life-changing decision and it's so easy for them; they return home a completely different person. But I didn't want to be a different person – well, maybe a slightly less anxious one – I just wanted to know what to do with the rest of my life.

Although the flash of initial clarity occurred on that Dublin flight, the deeper understanding didn't come while I was abroad. It struck at home, in my room, while I was reflecting on things. It was a few months after my return from Ireland, the world was in the clasp of coronavirus and life was looking bleak. I lit my lavender-scented candles in my bedroom and allowed my worries about my lack of a job, the pandemic and when we'd all be able to see our family and friends again to be sent to the backburner for a few minutes. My anxiety melted like the deep purple wax and I watched the tiny flames dance.

Niggles about how on earth I was going to finish this damn book when I could barely muster the creativity to draw, blog or conjure up something more adventurous for lockdown dinner than meatballs (*with* the spaghetti, of course) were cast aside. My anxious mind calmed itself for a moment and I flung myself onto my bed and sipped at my tea, not really thinking, just being.

I let my eyes wander the way I wished my feet could wander right then: around a cramped market in India, the stalls a riot of colour and chaos, wading through warm waves, gazing up at the sun and clear skies on a tropical island, palm trees and coconuts everywhere (but not being thrown at me by a baby in jewelled pants). As I absentmindedly stared around my walls, taking in the photographs, a mix from everywhere on the planet all on one heart-shaped noticeboard, something clicked.

I looked, really looked, and saw the smiles on our faces: on mine and on those of my family and friends. I saw backdrops of sun, sea, beaches and exotic destinations and I really felt as if I was back in each location. I envied my younger self. She'd been able to experience all these fantastic places, while current me was unable to travel half an hour down the bloody road and wouldn't be able to go anywhere much for the foreseeable future. I was shut inside my home as a pandemic raged outside, threatening our lives, our freedom and everything we hadn't realised we took for granted. It was a health-anxiety sufferer's nightmare. Well, it was everyone's worst nightmare.

I narrowed my eyes at the Chloë from six months earlier, grinning as she sipped out of a massive pineapple in Hawaii, freckles galore, make-up free, wild curls taking up the frame. Current me couldn't even go to my local Sainsbury's because I'd already been out for my hour's exercise and Boris said no. But something flipped in my brain like a switch, suddenly, in my familiar surroundings. I got life. Or I got some of it, at least, and that was a start.

I realised that life isn't meant to be clear, concise, orderly or predictable like I'd thought. I'd been thinking about it all wrong. Anything can happen at any time: you can be going about your day-to-day business, content in your job, and then, boom, Covid hits and you're unemployed. You're unable to hug your grandparents, see your friends, go to concerts, get on a plane, go to the gym or hit up the shops without being armed with a facemask and gallons of hand sanitiser.

The point of us being here, on this odd as hell planet, is to broaden our minds, have adventures and laugh. The point is to make memories with the people closest to us. And I had so many of those already, so many crazy memories with my family, things we could all share and look back on together. Life is about taking photographs, re-watching videos from ten years ago with a smile on your face and recalling the sights, smells and feelings experienced in a special place and with special people.

Sometimes everything has to be cruelly whipped away from you for you to realise what you do have. For you to see how lucky you are to have a fantastic family and memories that are more valuable than any amount of money. Bleached-out photographs and faded diary entries from a trip taken fifteen years ago are worth more than millions of pounds.

Finally, it clicked that the point in life is to be able to accept that we don't know things; that we should embrace life with its messiness and imperfections. And I think that messiness and imperfection are what authentic travelling is all about. No matter how much you plan, things will always go wrong and turn out differently from how you expected.

Accepting things is vital. I have anxiety, and for years, I've struggled with OCD and the gnawing sense that imminent doom is hovering over my head. I've generally found life difficult to navigate so far. I worry about everything and will probably have to deal with anxiety in some form for the rest of my life. But that's all right too. My mind is imperfect, like everyone else's.

Travel taught me – and I hope will continue to teach me – that anxiety doesn't define any of us. None of our struggles do. We make our own choices, and if there's something you want to do, something you want to achieve, then do it. Don't let anything hold you back, especially not anxiety. It's just a feeling, it's not worth more than you. It's incredibly annoying, but you don't want to look back and regret it having taken over your whole life. Been there, done that. Yawn.

Travel has been that saviour for me. I should have felt so stressed on every trip, having to deal with the absence of my all-important routines. My worry levels should have been in overdrive, and sometimes, they were. But then, something magnificent happened. I learnt to adapt. I relaxed. The chaos actually had a calming effect on my mind, and I feel so grateful to have been helped like that. I got used to the mishaps. They became endearing rather than the end of the world. They became things I look back on with a laugh, things that made our travels more colourful, more authentic, more us.

Maybe I haven't been backpacking like my mum and dad, maybe my trips haven't been solely self-sufficient. I haven't globetrotted the planet by myself, that's not how I've tried to figure out life. But my travels have all been special. They're unique to me, and they've shown me a great deal. They've helped me cope with my annoying brain and taught me to be okay (ish) with uncertainty.

With travel, things don't go to plan. You'll always have to wake up the whole hotel – and city – in hysterics, searching for your dad in the Philippines; you'll unknowingly break some laws taking photographs and almost get arrested practically every holiday (ahem, Dad); you'll almost get knocked out by your own surfboard; you'll get heatstroke because you're too stubborn to put sun cream on; you'll get stuck on a rock pretending to be Simba and have to be rescued by your pap as your mum and nan giggle from the side-lines; you'll get lost and maps won't make sense; you'll run into your dad's camera, break your Harry Potter glasses, get them bandaged up by your nana and then receive disapproving glares from locals; you'll scream the place down when a baby monkey grabs you by the ankle and attempts to drag you into the shrubbery.

Missing flights, changing plans, getting bitten by mosquitos, temporarily losing your suitcase, bickering, laughing, enduring terrifying turbulence, watching amazing sights and capturing them not just with your camera or your writing but with your mind and the people you value most, the people you want to spend your life with, family – that is what it's all about. And that's what I want to continue to experience.

I also learnt a lot about the value of life as we were plunged into lockdown after lockdown while coronavirus spread across the world. Travel became something I yearned for but couldn't participate in. I spent more time at home, writing, searching for inspiration, and I felt stuck for a while, as if my creativity had been zapped away from me. I couldn't recapture that spark, that wonderful feeling, until suddenly it came to me, as the winter weather started to ease.

I woke up one morning, early, in London, with sunlight streaming into my room, warming my face and casting beautiful patterns across the walls, the birds chirping outside, and a soft breeze rustling the leaves on the trees, imitating the sound of lapping waves. The windchimes outside were gently jangling and I felt like I was somewhere, on one of our many trips. That was enough to push my creative buttons, get me up, ready to write again. I thought about the moment I had grasped the point of all of that, and my fingers began tapping away at my keyboard once more.

I also had a lot of time to ponder my relationship with social media, and I came to the realisation that I was wasting my life on it. I missed travelling so much, and I knew that when it became possible to go overseas again, I'd want to be completely immersed in my new environment. I thought about the three latest holidays and how much I'd not seen, my eyes cast down at my phone rather than absorbing things around me.

I wanted to make my family proud; I wanted to write something that would show them how grateful I am to them for having made these pivotal experiences of my life so special. I wanted to write until I felt proud, like I'd accomplished something. So, I did. Without any distractions from things that no longer mattered: likes, comments, false lives. I deleted my Instagram account for the sake of my (hopefully) upcoming travels, for productivity's sake, so I could finish this book and because I knew deep down it would help ease my anxiety, even just a tiny bit.

And for the first time in years, I felt my mind completely unclog itself. Suddenly, I was able to start writing this book again. It's not a magic fix, I'm not anti-social media as such, but it worked for me, and I've not looked back.

I started to enjoy real life. I spent more time with my family, unconcerned that my phone was out of battery in my bag. I went for coffee with my mum, played tennis with my dad, had wonderful times catching up with my nan and pap, getting their recommendations for places to go, near and far. I heard which books my nan was enjoying and how well my pap was getting on with his paintings, matchstick models and puzzles.

After months of disheartening interviews, I secured a fantastic new role as a content journalist, which I absolutely love. I revived old friendships and formed new ones, immersing myself in actual events rather than flicking back through my phone thinking, oh, that's a cool photo, though I don't remember that day.

I can't wait to start exploring the world again, and this time, it won't be seen through my phone screen. I'll be fully engaged in the magical moments, sharing them with my family and friends, the people who make the trip. I want to experience the world as I did when I was younger, with awe and fresh eyes, not skewed by filters. I was so amazed at life, at everything. That's something I want to recapture and enjoy again.

I won't be missing out on amazing sights that pass me by as I try to get that perfect Instagram selfie. It's a darker aspect of our world, this need for technology to be present in everything we do, the obsession with being perfect, comparing ourselves to people we don't even know. No, when I travel again, I'll be seeing this planet in every weird and wonderful way I can, with every weird and wonderful person who matters to me. Five-year-old carefree Chloë would approve indeed.

African sunset

African tribesman elder